AF470681

THE
JUBILEE TESTS

THE
JUBILEE TESTS
ENGLAND v AUSTRALIA 1977
and the Packer Revolution

CHRISTOPHER MARTIN-JENKINS

With Photographs by Patrick Eagar

MACDONALD AND JANE'S · LONDON

Copyright as to photographs © 1977 Patrick Eagar
Copyright © 1977 Christopher Martin-Jenkins
First published in Great Britain in 1977 by
Macdonald and Jane's Publishers Ltd
Paulton House
8 Shepherdess Walk   London N1 7LW
ISBN 0 354 04230 0

Printed and bound in Great Britain by
Redwood Burn Limited, Trowbridge and Esher

CONTENTS

FOREWORD

Cricket is supposed to be a game but Test Matches between England and Australia have never been anything less than campaigns. Fortunately, I suppose, I have no difficulty in feeling neutral but if I do want to feel biased I find myself supporting the underdog. This has its problems when the home side is doing well, as it did in Australia during the Centenary Test and later in England during the regular Test Series. I only regret I did not see more of the matches in the Jubilee Year.

It may be just a game but few games can produce such sustained drama and even fewer can have inspired such volumes of brilliant commentary. Cricket writing is almost as subtle as the game itself.

HRH THE DUKE OF EDINBURGH

THE PACKER REVOLUTION

Chapter One
COURAGEOUS COUP OR SHABBY SABOTAGE?

Money may, in the words of the song, make the world go round, but it almost swung the cricket world off its axis early in 1977. The trouble began when the Australian TV magnate Kerry Packer saw a way of cashing in on the current boom in the game while at the same time giving the players who were so effectively pulling in the crowds a greater share of the rewards than the cricket authorities were prepared, or were able, to give them. The origin of the affair was very much Australian, but Packer's master-stroke was to engage Tony Greig, the one man with the charisma to persuade the leading players of other countries to risk their Test careers not only in order to earn big money themselves but also, according to Greig's persuasive argument, to raise the overall lot of the average professional cricketer. His theory was that in any business, if the salary of the directors rises, so in time will the salaries of all the employees. There was a strong counter-argument that if the rival series of matches which the signatories were planning to play were to have the effect (unintended, they said) of devaluing traditional Test cricket, the income of the average player, in England at least, would be lowered, since two main sources of his salary were Test match receipts and the receipts from television companies paying for the right to cover the Tests. But very few apart from Greig, a special case in that he was already a wealthy man, saw themselves in such an altruistic light. They were frankly prepared to admit that they were about to earn money of a magnitude they had hardly dreamt of before. The actual amount stipulated in each man's contract varied, and was not officially revealed. It was reputed to be around £20,000 a man, but in a BBC interview Barry Richards mentioned the sum of £14,000 for each of the three seasons that he was contracted to Packer plus a share of the £60,000 prize money on offer for each of the five-day matches. (The money given to Richards and other early signings was later increased to bring them into line with subsequent signings.) Again, a man like Alan Knott, who places his family life and loyalties above even his allegiance to his country, naturally preferred the prospect of a winter in Australia with his family to the strain of a tour of Pakistan without them. For a cricketer like him, nonetheless, the decision must have been desperately difficult: less so for the West Indians, Pakistanis and above all the South Africans, who were already, at certain times of the year, cricket mercenaries.

Whatever the motives of the players, they found the advantages of the terms they were offered irresistible. The negotiations were handled largely by John Cornell, a leading sports promoter in Australia, and his associate Austin Robertson. They claimed that only one man, Geoff Boycott, refused to join the circus. According to Cornell, this was because Boycott wanted to choose his captain – either himself or Ray Illingworth; according to himself, Boycott initially agreed to join when he thought that only one winter's cricket in Australia was involved but withdrew when he heard mention of the circus coming to England and of possible conflict with his county committee and the TCCB. At any rate, the refusal by Boycott to join the circus started a lobby for his return to the England team as captain. Not surprisingly, after his long absence from the England side, it was unsuccessful. Boycott anyway had himself been making money in Australia whilst MCC were battling it out in India.

One by one, nineteen of the leading Australian cricketers – some, like Ian Chappell, Ross Edwards and Ian Redpath, recently retired – received offers they could not refuse. Godfather Packer, backed by the power of his highly enterprising multi-million dollar business, gradually widened the circle. With Ian Chappell at his side from the start it was not hard to persuade brother Greg and the two great drawing cards, Lillee and Thomson, to join the fold too and so to defy the Australian cricket establishment. For young, less established players in the early days of their Test careers the decision whether or not to join must have been harder, but for all of them, apparently, the choice was to go with the tide. Of the seventeen players picked to tour England, only four, Cosier, Hughes, Serjeant and Dymock, were not secretly signed on when the tour began. So whilst the great players of the past were gathering in Melbourne, whilst all the grand words were being spoken and written in praise of the incomparable history of Anglo/Australian Tests, whilst the organisers and sponsors were receiving acclamations from all concerned, including the players, the Australian team had already planned a coup which was both daring and treacherous.

The approach to Greig was made after the Centenary Test had finished. After thinking the matter over for a few days – if he had fully appreciated what he was about to do he might have deliberated a little longer – he accepted. In the next month, without any reference to the authorities at Lord's, he signed his Sussex colleague John Snow and the two players of undisputed world class in the England side, Alan Knott and Derek Underwood. Both were essential members of a developing England side; now they were, with open eyes, rebelling. All of them hoped that a direct conflict with planned Test matches would somehow be avoided by a compromise between Packer and the authorities; in other words all wished to have their cake and eat it, but all of them must have known that such a compromise was unlikely.

Next, Greig went to the West Indies, where Pakistan were on tour. Telling his friends that he and his wife were taking a short holiday in Trinidad, Greig in fact was on a crucial business mission. Again, his persuasive charm combined with Packer's attractive terms seduced all who were approached. From the West Indian galaxy Clive Lloyd, Gordon Greenidge, Viv Richards, Andy Roberts and Michael Holding all joined, though Holding, unlike all the others, signed on for one year only. He said that he felt a loyalty to the Jamaican government which employed him as a computer analyst. Three-year agreements were also signed by Mushtaq Mohammad, Asif Iqbal, Majid Khan, Zaheer Abbas and Imran Khan from Pakistan. All involved received handsome signing-on fees.

The simplest part of Greig's job was to sign on his native South Africans. Barry Richards, Eddie Barlow, Graeme Pollock and Mike Procter were ageing but still effective cricketers of world class, members of one of the most talented sides in history which was outlawed from Test cricket as a result of a worldwide movement of revulsion against South Africa's apartheid policies. South Africa had not played a Test match since 1969 when they had overwhelmed Australia. For these men, and the young leg-spinner Denys Hobson, the only little-known cricketer originally selected by Greig for his world team, there was no great moral conflict. They all wanted South Africa to play Test cricket again, but for all except Hobson time was getting shorter. Procter, Richards and Barlow were already used to the life of a cricket mercenary, and although even these men received condemnation from cricket officials at home they could hardly have been expected to look their gift horse in the mouth.

By early May, all were safely gathered in. Now it was just a question of the timing of an announcement that would shatter the harmony of cricket lovers the world over. Cricket by its nature and its tradition is a game where the highest standards are demanded. It is held by many to be almost sacred; that is why the challenge to Test cricket was a heresy as hard to bear as a challenge to papal authority in the Catholic Church.

The announcement of Packer's televised series between Australia and the Rest of the World was planned for 23 June, but on the night of Saturday 7 May, during the match between Sussex and the Australians, Tony and Donna Greig gave a party at their expensively modernised house in Hove. A marquee covered the lawn in the shadow of the Sussex Downs, and as 150 guests danced and drank one of them said something to an Australian journalist. Very soon the cat was out of the bag and on Monday morning the news was on every front page. During one of his early interviews Kerry Packer uttered these words of dark foreboding: 'This thing has happened; it will not go away.' For better or for worse, and it seemed at once that it would be better for the few and worse for cricket, the game would never be the same. I personally had heard rumours and hints before that Monday, without until then grasping the full substance and significance of what had happened. Many people, after reading Ian Wooldridge's comprehensive exposé in the *Daily Mail*, must have felt at once a sick apprehension. For those of us who admittedly take the game (which is, or was, *just* a game) too seriously, it was like learning that a wife whom one loved and trusted had been secretly, and for some time, making love to another man.

For all one's gut disapproval of an underhand threat to the traditional, time-proven format of Test cricket, familiarity with which bred contentment, it was perfectly possible to feel sympathetic towards those players involved in the coup. The motives of the Englishmen and Australians concerned bear closest examination, not just because they are the *dramatis personae* of this book but because, as already explained, the idea of becoming a cricket mercenary was less strange to most of those South Africans, West Indians and Pakistanis involved. The great majority of them were already playing for money away from home in English county cricket, although not of course at a time when they might instead have been playing Test cricket in their home country since the English season falls at a different time of the year.

There were those who believed that in Australia the rebellion had to come. For a start, the Australian is by nature a commercial animal. Although Australia, like every other capitalist country, has been burdened by inflation, the standard of living in the 'land of opportunity' is uniformly high. In that fast-moving, acquisitive society, the sportsman, hugely publicised by press, radio and television and generally placed on a pinnacle by a society whose life is based on the great outdoors, expects recognition and fame. He also expects big rewards. The Australian cricketers, encouraged by men like Ian Chappell and Dennis Lillee, both members of a generation who had little respect for administrators who would not see their point of view, began to compare their own earnings with those of other leading sportsmen. They claimed that cricket on television in Australia had higher ratings than 'Starsky and Hutch', the most popular American serial of the day. They pointed to the huge crowds which had flocked to see them in action when Lillee and Thomson were 'blasting the Poms' and in subsequent series. And they asked, with good reason, whether they were getting a fair share of the large profits which were being made. Of course the Australian cricketer had until recently been considered an amateur, but that position had by now changed completely. Wooldridge told the story of some members of the 1972 touring team to England, whose basic tour salary exclusive of prize money was about £16 a day, chatting to Barry Sheene, the world motor-cycling champion. Sheene's reply, when asked what he earned, was apparently: 'About a hundred.' 'Would that be £100 a week or £100 a ride?' his inquisitors persisted. Sheene enlightened them that it was £100,000 a year. Closer to home, Graham Marsh, the golfing brother of Rodney, was in an average year earning six times as much as one of the major personalities in world cricket. The official takings from the Centenary Test match were 262,086 Australian dollars, of which the Australian team and the twelfth man were allowed to share out 3,000 dollars, or 250 each. For four months in England the 1977 Australian touring team were earning a basic £3,570 each, which would be substantially increased by a share in the prize money (£20,000 for the five Tests and £2,000 for the winners of each of the three Prudential Internationals plus £200 each to the Man of the Match) but which would not approach the £15,000 minimum offered by Packer for 54 days' cricket.

This was the case for the impatient, determined and bluntly selfish Australian cricketers, who believed that they were not being paid what they were worth. But there was another side to the story. The truth was that players had already been making much more in recent seasons than ever before. Prize money had been rising fast as sponsors all over the world saw cricket as a worthy and profitable method of getting publicity. Benson and Hedges of Australia, for instance, invested 200,000 Australian dollars in the 1976–77 season and in February 1977 announced that their investment in the next three years would be $350,000, of which the Australian Board were to distribute 70 percent to the players, keeping the remaining 30 percent for administrative expenses and for ploughing back into youth cricket. This was in itself a recent shift of emphasis towards the players in response to the growing feeling by all parties that they deserved a greater share of the receipts.

In England events had been moving in the same direction, even though the Test match fee in 1977 was only £210 a match, boosting the salary of around £3,000 which a Test player would be getting from his county to a little over £4,000 for the six-month season. In addition for the Test players there was prize money, again getting bigger each year. It was money well earned because, though Test cricket may be glamorous, it is also an intense strain for the competitor, played as it is under the scrutiny of millions of critical eyes watching from the armchair or on the ground itself, not to mention from the press or commentary box.

But the Test player was now more and more able to exploit his place in the public eye. With another salary possible from a winter tour (albeit an arduous one away from home and family) plus endorsements for equipment and fees for broadcast interviews or for ghosted books or articles, a Test 'star' might raise that basic £4,000 to nearer £10,000. In the case of a popular cricketer like Alan Knott this was boosted by a tax-free £27,000 from his benefit year, and all the poorly paid county cricketers who lasted long enough could take consolation from a considerable nest egg towards the end of their playing days. Most of them could also expect a good job when their playing days were over because the county cricketer as a breed is a respected and responsible man and there are so many cricket-lovers in so many businesses that alternative or additional employment is on the whole not hard to find.

Tony Greig himself was an exception to these generalities: in one winter alone in 1975–76 he earned some £50,000 – it was believed by some to be as much as £100,000 – and it was then, one feels, that his grandiose ideas for the future were formulated. For all his protestations that he had found his true home in Sussex by the sea there were those who believed he would always end up in Australia. 'I tell you, man, that's the place to live in,' he would remark to his friends ambiguously from time to time. If this single trip to Australia was exceptional, Greig was certainly expecting at least a minimum of £20,000 a year at the time he signed up with Packer – from advertising, endorsements, income from books, articles, interviews, his connections with the expanding firm of cricket equipment, 'St Peter' (the joke went that although Greig had been called the Messiah of English cricket when he became captain, he would prefer to be known as St Peter), and from his direct earnings with Sussex and England. Greig did not deny that, as he put it, he was 'alright, Jack'. He claimed to be taking a stand on behalf of others, simply because he could afford to make sacrifices – which included the ultimate one of the captaincy of England, a post, he said, which was the greatest honour in cricket, an honour which 'money just can't ever buy.'

Greig, then, was an exception, but the general picture was nonetheless clear before Packer exploded his bombshell. Partly as a result of a new aggression on the part of the players, inspired by men like Ian Chappell, Dennis Lillee and Tony Greig as they strove to be recognised as the big-time entertainers they were, and partly as a result of a growing enlightenment on the part of administrators – even in reactionary Pakistan a player revolution had succeeded in forcing better terms for the players for the long tour of Australia and the West Indies – things were looking up for Test cricketers the world over. Few of them were rich or even in the same league as the Peles and Beckenbauers of football or the stars of the individual sports – Connors, Nastase, Sheene, Hunt, Piggott and the like – but they were certainly comfortably off by comparison with Mr Average, and the same man in the street would give his right arm for the privilege of being paid for playing a game. (Of course, once you start playing a game for money it becomes a job, with all the ups and downs and worries and frustrations of any job – but the man in the street does not necessarily reason this out: he would much rather travel the world playing cricket for better money than screw nuts on an assembly line.)

But we come now to the crux of the matter. Test cricketers do not float to the top of their tree by magic. They have had to climb up, and without the tree to support them they would fall. Test cricket, and the various levels of the game beneath it, are interdependent. A player rises to the top by virtue of performances at lower levels, and when he gets there it is the fruits of his labours whilst at the top which enable all the other levels to be financed. Without Test cricket, to take the position in England alone, county cricket would die overnight. The county game runs at a huge loss and is only kept going by the annual hand-out from the governing body, the Test and County Cricket Board. Again, by an increasingly aggressive policy, the Board's income has been going up in a healthy fashion during the game's recent boom years. Sponsors have been both plentiful and prepared to pay large sums for the publicity they derive from the game. The BBC, after protracted negotiations, was squeezed tight for the right to televise the Tests and to broadcast them on radio. (The TV and radio contracts are separately negotiated.) In 1976 most of the Counties made modest profits after the broiling weather and the glamorous cricket played by the West Indies touring team had enabled a record hand-out from the Board to the Counties, Minor Counties and Universities of more than one million pounds. But such was the enormous expense of keeping up large cricket grounds and employing playing and other staff that the profits *were* only modest. They would have been huge losses but for the £500,000 which came to the Board directly from Test receipts. These were boosted by the BBC's contribution of £150,000, and by some £20,000 from the Post Office, whose 'UMP' latest-score service attracted a staggering 23 million calls, yet another example of the boom in the game. (In 1977 Kerry Packer's company itself paid a further £150,000, outbidding the Australian Broadcasting Commission for the television rights to the series.) The rest of the Board's income came mainly from the sponsors of the various county competitions – Gillette, John Player, Benson and Hedges and, in 1977 for the first time, Schweppes.

So the overall position was simple. Test cricket kept all cricket going. Without other cricket there would in time be no Test players: they had to develop their skills somewhere. Yet even with all these sources of income the game in England was doing no more than keeping its head above water. The money was certainly not lining the pockets of the administrators, themselves poorly paid and almost to a man honest toilers for the good of a game and a way of life they loved and believed in. Without a general collapse of the established system, therefore, the Test players could not take much more of the spoils. It was not just Test cricket which was threatened by the Packer revolution but county cricket as well.

Ironically, before county cricket established itself after 1864, the main players of first-class cricket in England had been a wandering circus of professionals – the All-England XI of William Clarke. This original cricket 'circus' was formed in 1846. Like the United XI of Wisden and Dean it went around England playing fifteens, eighteens and twenty-twos, and whilst its members may have felt some missionary spirit – they certainly raised the level of cricket generally by their example – they were also, to put it crudely, in it for the cash. County cricket developed partly from the widespread competitive urge which they helped to foster and so too did the foreign tours, beginning with George Parr's team to the United States and Canada in 1859 and leading on to the visits to Australia and eventually to the establishment of regular Test cricket. How ironic if the Packer circus were to destroy County and Test cricket by the same process!

The vulnerability of county cricket has long been apparent. Any business must always be liable to collapse if the outside sources which sustain it begin to dry up. In times of economic uncertainty this is something which could happen at any time. A ban on tobacco sponsorship could of itself be a near-mortal blow. But the danger to Test cricket had not been foreseen until Packer, Cornell, Robertson, Chappell and Greig threw down the gauntlet. The power struggle between these men who had chosen to take the law into their own hands and the international administrators who had hitherto held tight control was only just beginning.

Packer is recognised by all to be a shrewd and determined man backed by a large multi-million-pound business. In the early weeks of the crisis it was customary for the players he had signed on to warn people that Packer was a habitual winner. He was certainly born to win. His father, Sir Frank Packer, a boxing champion in his youth, carved out a newspaper, magazine and television empire. At school Packer junior (he was Sir Frank's second son) used to have his work typed for him. When a schoolmaster tried to force him to write it out himself Packer minor successfully pleaded that there was no point if he was always going to get things typed for him anyway. Ironically he was educated in the company of the establishment he would later challenge in sporting circles – at the famous Geelong Grammar School, attended by prime ministers and princes. Sir Frank Packer spent millions on his dream of building an Australian yacht to win the America's Cup. His sports-minded younger son put £100,000 a year into the Australian Open Golf tournament, partly to put it on the world map, partly because it made good television for his company, and he successfully outbid the Australian Broadcasting Commission for the coverage of the 1977 series of Tests in England. But he failed to beat the ABC to coverage of the 1980 Moscow Olympics (when he reputedly bid £150 million) or to coverage of Test matches in his own country. This, apparently, is what rankled most with him. The TCCB had preferred the extra cash that Packer offered (the game, they reasoned, needed it) to any loyalty they might have felt to the ABC. The Australian Board, on the other hand, put loyalty first and refused to negotiate further when, it is reported, Packer told them that everyone is a harlot and that every harlot has a price. Getting no response, Packer decided to challenge the Board, some of whose members were golfing friends of his, head on.

In fact, Packer did not accept that this was what he was doing. Having made his plans and through agents signed on his players, he claimed that it was now time to start negotiating and compromising. Tony Greig took the same line, on Packer's behalf, in England. It was as if squatters had moved in on a country gentleman's mansion with its three hundred productive acres, which had always been conscientiously and for the most part efficiently run for the benefit of as many people as possible, and asked him to start negotiating for a part of the house and a part of the land – not to mention the farm workers as well.

At first the administrators reacted with extreme caution. The Australian Board refused to be harried into precipitate action. After a 'phone-call to the Chairman Bob Parish in Sydney, Len Maddocks, himself one of the fourteen members of the Board, called a players' meeting at their hotel in Hove and warned them that if they went ahead with their plans to play in matches not authorised by the Board they would be putting their careers in jeopardy. He added that as they were already contracted for the current tour of England there would be no question of anyone being sent home. 'We are in England to play a Test series,' he told the media; 'I want them to forget the excitement now.' But how could they? They were forced to play as if in a vacuum, with no idea what fate awaited them when they got home. Nor were the Board giving any secrets away. They refused suggestions that some compromise might be possible if they were to talk to Packer, and awaited discussions with other members of the International Cricket Conference. Yet it seemed that their only alternatives were either to attempt to get Packer to modify his programme of 54 days' cricket (to be televised and played at prearranged grounds on the assumption that the Board would not allow them to use the traditional cricket venues under their jurisdiction) or to have no dealings at all with him and to outlaw those players who had signed, even though this would mean meeting India with a second eleven, taking a second eleven to the West Indies, if that scheduled tour came about, and even facing the prospect of effectively handing the Ashes to England in 1978–79 when MCC were due to tour. Their calculations were that spectators in Australia were as conservative as anywhere else. They would prefer the traditional Test combat – nation versus nation at the historic Test centres – to a sham series drummed up for television and played on strange grounds. It didn't matter, the Board may have reasoned, if Packer had most of the best cricketers in the world and the best groundsman in Australia signed up as well (John Maley from Brisbane): it was still artificial and its initial impact would quickly lose its force.

The complete refusal of the Australian Board to issue any public statement contrasted with the approach of the authorities in England, who quickly made their attitude plain. On the day after the announcement Donald Carr, the TCCB secretary, said that all the ramifications would be fully discussed, that he would be very sorry if four of England's best cricketers were to be unavailable to tour, and that he found it saddening that after all the TCCB's attempts to consult the cricketers on matters affecting them, these four should have gone ahead and signed up with Mr Packer without discussing matters first with Lord's. With typical fairness he insisted on speaking to the three current members of the England side, Greig, Knott and Underwood, to hear their side of the story, before an emergency committee of the Cricket Council was called to discuss whether the England selectors should be allowed to pick them for the coming series.

Underwood and Knott kept quiet once they were outside Carr's office, but Greig was only too pleased to describe *his* motives to an eager world. On the Wednesday after the news had been leaked he held a press conference at Hove at which he told how he had acted as Packer's agent and how he realised he was risking his England captaincy, even his whole cricket future in England. He claimed that he was acting in the interests of those 'who give their life to the game', and he countered those who could not understand how a few top players earning big money would ever be able to help the average county professional by asserting that Packer had *already* helped them by paying £150,000 to televise the 1977 series and that he (Packer) would in future make donations to organisations like the Cricketers' Association.

Whereas players like Clive Lloyd and Barry Richards were frankly admitting that they were taking part in the venture be-cause it would pay them far more than they had ever received before, and Alan Knott was privately explaining that he would much rather spend his winter in Australia with his wife Jan and son James than in Pakistan without them, Greig was posing as something of a martyr for cricketers everywhere. He had clearly convinced himself that this was the case, and his persuasive tongue convinced others too, notably at Hove where his contribution to Sussex cricket was genuinely revered by the majority. Yet he was also extremely naïve – or disingenuous – in his approach to the whole matter. 'I did not consult Lord's before signing,' he said, 'because there was no way they could have kept the matter quiet.' Yet he now said that he expected Lord's – and their Australian counterparts – to go sheepishly to Packer and seek a compromise which would enable Greig and the other play-ers to take part in both official and unofficial Tests. He wanted to remain captain of England, he said; it was the greatest honour which had befallen him. He wanted to go on playing for England against Australia. He and his associates were not holding world cricket to ransom. But, of course, they were, and after the way he had behaved he must have known that he had not measured up to the 'honour' he had been granted, and that it was inevitable that it should be taken away from him.

The special committee of the Cricket Council, the governing body of British cricket, met on the Friday after the leak, and at four o'clock that day a 'phone-call from Donald Carr told Greig at his home in Hove that he had lost the captaincy. He had done so because he had impaired the trust which existed between the cricket authorities and the captain of the England team by recruiting players for 'an organisation which had been set up in conflict with scheduled series of Test matches'. Freddie Brown, chairman of the Council, summed up the views of the emergency committee which sacked Greig when he pointed out that the captain has to be in close liaison with the selectors in management and selection of the England team and in the development of players for the future. 'Clearly,' said Brown, 'Greig is unlikely to be able to do this as his stated intention is to be contracted elsewhere during the next three winters.'

Greig was due to captain England for the fifteenth time in a Test at Lord's in the Jubilee match in June. It was to have been the start, we had hoped, of another untroubled summer for cricket. When Greig took over as captain at Lord's in 1975 English fortunes were at a low ebb, and although there was an immediate revival of spirit England were as soundly thrashed as they had ever been by the West Indies in 1976. But in the winter it was clear the tide was turning as England defeated India on their home soil three-one and narrowly lost the Centenary Test at Melbourne. They were a developing side under an inspiring captain who was gradually improving his tactical know-how and still able to play his part as the side's leading all-rounder. His Test record belied those who still maintained he was a player of average ability: in his 53 Tests Greig had scored 3373 runs at an average of 41 and taken 152 wickets, not to mention many brilliant catches. Off the field he had been a popular leader with the media, always willing to talk openly both of success and failure. He had always been as headstrong as he was charming. One inevitably remembers the cheap opportunism of his running out of Alvin Kallicharran in the West Indies and his unfortunate remark in 1976 that he would like to see the West Indies grovel if England got on top. He was never allowed to forget it, but as a resilient if sensitive character he soon hit back and his stock had never been higher than it was when he was approached by Packer after the Centenary Test. Greig still says that he thought carefully about the consequences of what he was doing. Yet he miscalculated if he truly believed that massive payments to super-stars would aid the cause of the run-of-the-mill county cricketer and if he seriously thought that the cricket administrators of the world would be prepared to change long-term plans to suit a television entrepreneur. In a nutshell, the latest mistake by this most likeable man was to overestimate the power of money.

Greig's dismissal as captain was not, of course, the end of the affair. The Council's Emergency Committee decided that he, Knott and Underwood should all be available for selection against Australia pending the special meeting of the International Cricket Conference which had been called to discuss the world-wide implications in advance of its regular meeting at Lord's at the end of July. The full members of the ICC met together at head-quarters on a rainy day on 14 June. There was just one item on the agenda but it was eight hours before they broke up and issued the following statement:

At a special meeting of the ICC at Lord's, representatives of the Test-match-playing countries – England, Australia, India, New Zealand, Pakistan and West Indies – were unanimous in their view that the structure of cricket for which their governing bodies, member associations and clubs are responsible, could be severely damaged by the attempted entry of private promoters into international cricket.

The governing bodies, their member associations and clubs undertake the promotion of, and the responsibility for, the game at all levels, through schools, youth cricket and club, first class cricket and finally Test level.

These activities are costly and, to a large extent, are financed by profits from Test matches and sponsorship. Private promotion may, because of the involvement of 'name' players, have an effect on attendances at, and possibly sponsorship of, Test and other first class cricket.

This can only be detrimental to the game at all levels.

Whilst it is agreed that top class players should be adequately rewarded for their skills, such rewards must be commensurate with the overall welfare of the game and the interest of all players. Major public interest is in Test cricket and the game depends on international competition at this level.

Test matches can only be between teams representing their countries. The ambition of every cricketer should be to play for his country, both at home and abroad.

Anything that detracts from this ambition and risks lowering the status of Test cricket is against the interest of the game.

Bearing in mind the foregoing, Mr Kerry Packer is being advised that should he wish to discuss his plans with representatives of the Test match playing countries, a meeting will be arranged at the earliest convenient opportunity.

The most important part of the statement, of course, was the final paragraph. It was not exactly a welcoming invitation, but the important thing was that the gesture had been made. Mr Packer could no longer claim that no one was prepared to discuss matters with him. However, in an apparent attempt to retain the initiative he left London exactly an hour before the statement was issued, bound for his native Australia via America. A cable from Jack Bailey, the ICC Secretary, awaited his return.

Packer had not been idle during his time in England. The day before the ICC's meeting, it was announced that he had further extended his circus by signing on Dennis Amiss, whose only comment was: 'I could not refuse Mr Packer's offer – it was as simple as that,' and two more West Indians, Alvin Kallicharran and Collis King. A few days later Gordon Greenidge, the highly gifted Hampshire and Barbados opener, revealed that he too had signed, and it soon emerged that the original plan for Australia to play the Rest of the World was escalating into something still more grandiose. The new plan was to have a Rest of the World team, an Australian squad and an equally large West Indian contingent. It was not long before Packer was able to announce that sixteen of the leading West Indian players were safely in his net.

Packer now accepted the invitation from the ICC, and for a few days the cricket world lived in hope of a compromise. The news that he would be returning to England came during the Lord's Test match, and for fourteen of the players involved, ten of the Australian team and four of the English, hopes were raised that the longed-for compromise would be achieved and that they might yet have their cake and eat it at the same time. The Packer signatories were undoubtedly, to a greater or lesser degree, feeling uneasy. It was more than just a feeling of anxiety caused by the uncertain future which lay ahead of them. Would they be banned from Test cricket? Had they hitched their wagons to the right star? Did Packer have their interests or his own as his main concern? Might he, as many believed, discard them like so many useless pieces of paper once he had fulfilled his desire to win the Australian television cricket contract for himself or once they had lost their power to attract large crowds, big television audiences and therefore big advertising income for Mr Packer's company? Over and above this feeling of anxiety there was, unless they were very insensitive to public opinion, a certain guilt that they might possibly have let down the game which had made them famous, as well as the administrators and coaches, who had worked hard for the good of the game for far less financial reward, and the public who, in the case of most of the English players anyway, had contributed generously to huge tax-free benefits. (The sums declared by the players were, it is widely believed, considerably less than the actual amounts collected.) By souring the public over the Packer contracts these already wealthy players were inevitably reducing the amounts which might be made by other county cricketers in the future.

On the other hand, in defence of those who signed one must also ask what person would not, in any profession, accept a larger recompense for doing the same job. Who could blame the likes of Tony Greig, Alan Knott, Derek Underwood and Dennis Amiss, all married men with young families, for choosing to go to Australia, where there would be nothing to prevent them bringing their families too and money a-plenty to pay for them, rather than going to Pakistan, which would have meant yet another painful break between husband on the one hand and wife and children on the other? By succumbing to what Colin Cowdrey called this 'sickening temptation', these men were also expressing a growing unhappiness with this regular winter separation. It was the same with some of the Australians. Lillee's decision not to tour England was made in part because he wanted to see more of his wife, and Greg Chappell had stated privately that he had no intention anyway of going to the West Indies for a full tour so shortly after the long tour of England. Chappell's first child was born during the 1975 tour of England. His second arrived shortly before he left for the Jubilee tour. These men are not soldiers, forced to leave their wives to cope on their own, and both they and more particularly their wives were asking, in the era of the liberated woman, why cricketers had accepted these regular separations for so many years.

The Packer circus was therefore a reflection of changing social attitudes as well as of the new commercialism in the game of cricket. Knowing Amiss, Knott and Underwood well I believe that this family aspect weighed more strongly than any other in their decision to risk their futures by signing for Packer.

On 23 June, a perfect summer's day, Packer arrived at Lord's for his momentous meeting with the Sub-Committee of the ICC comprising most of those who had met there in emergency session nine days before. He was accompanied by two business associates and Richie Benaud, who was acting as a consultant and adviser to Packer in the whole affair. They were all smiles as they arrived at the Grace Gates and entered the pavilion, and there were smiles all round again as the two parties greeted one another in the committee room in the early afternoon. Outside, photographers and journalists gathered and waited. At first all went well in the talks. Mr Packer reiterated his desire for a compromise. The ICC delegates said that they had no wish to be unnecessarily obstructive so long as his plans did not seriously interfere with their own, which followed the traditional pattern and had long been formulated. The five conditions for which the ICC asked were set out in the statement they issued after the meeting (printed at the end of this chapter) and seem to be eminently reasonable. It must be remembered that the authority of the various national Boards of Control had not, since their formation around the time that cricket developed into an international sport at the end of the last century, been seriously challenged. It was accepted that they did their best, honourably if not always efficiently or with great foresight, for the good of the game at all levels. The delegates recognised, in the last five words of the fourth of their conditions, that there might have to be a clash of interests between some of the matches played under the auspices of the Australian Board and those organised by Mr Packer. Moreover, beyond the official statement, the Australian delegates said that they were even prepared to lend their active blessing to Mr Packer's matches, which presumably meant releasing the best grounds and giving him the benefit of their experience in organising major matches. This latter gesture might well have been declined, but there was nevertheless a clear willingness to give Packer elbow room so long as he did things according to the ICC's terms.

Packer and his colleagues studied the conditions and they too found them reasonable. They were prepared to cut their plans to fit them into a six-week period. They asked in return that the players who had signed should not be 'victimised'. The ICC delegates were glad to agree that, so long as there was no clash with Test cricket, players would not have to be suspended. Indeed they would be welcomed back into the fold, as it were.

So far, so good. It was agreed that working committees could be set up to examine plans in more detail. Then Packer produced his one major condition, and at this point the whole talks broke down. What he wanted, all indeed, as it transpired, that he had ever wanted, was a monopoly of television coverage of cricket in Australia. He did not make the demand immediately. He was content to allow the Australian Cricket Board's current agreement with the Australian Broadcasting Commission to run its course. Once the contract expired with the start of the 1979–80 season in Australia, Packer wanted an exclusive contract to televise cricket in Australia. Without it, he said, there could be no deal and he would go ahead with his plans, give no help to anyone and the 'Devil take the hindmost'. Perhaps the Australian delegates to the meeting, Bob Parish and Ray Steele, had known all along that this would be the crux of the matter. To the others, Packer's demand came as a complete surprise. They had seen Packer as a man who wanted to promote cricket in a big way. They now saw him as a ruthless businessman who only wanted to promote cricket because by so doing he hoped to corner a particular market. The friendly talk ceased. Mr Packer, his deep-set but striking blue eyes shifting, suggested, reasonably enough, that the delegates might like to discuss this point amongst themselves. He had always wanted to see Lord's. Might he take a look whilst they debated? This was agreed. Richie Benaud showed the business tycoon round the ground whose famous history he now threatened to alter. Inside the Committee Room the Australian delegates briefly told how the Australian Broadcasting Commission had loyally covered Test and Sheffield Shield cricket over the years through times of boom and slump. They explained that the ABC had never, however, had exclusive rights to television although they were the only organisation capable of beaming cricket to all places in Australia. They did not see how they could agree to let Packer have an exclusive contract three years hence for an indefinite period. They were happy to let Packer's Channel Nine Company negotiate when the time came, but for him to demand a monopoly for an undefined period was unacceptable.

The issue now was seen in all its ironic simplicity. Kerry Packer was holding the cricket establishment to ransom in order to secure a business deal. Though he had no *desire* to do so, he was determined to disrupt Test cricket by buying the best players in the world at a minimum cost of five million Australian dollars (about three million pounds) and televising their artificial matches in direct competition with traditional Test cricket. Asked later why he should expect to get the contract as of right rather than competing for it with other companies, he said that he had bought the players, and if he gave them up he was entitled to something in return. The players whose standard of living he and his associates professed to being so concerned with were, in effect, mere pawns in his high-powered business game.

There was to be, however, no deal. The other delegates were unanimous in agreeing with the Australians that it was unreasonable to accept Packer's demand. As a matter of principle, they felt, if they agreed to give him his way with a loaded pistol at their heads, other businessmen in the future might find other equally effective bargaining points and in the words of the ICC secretary, Jack Bailey, cricket would not be in control of its own destiny.

So Packer, with a humourless smile, emerged to answer the questions of a horde of journalists. Now it was open war. He had, at this point, signed on 51 players and, stung by one question about Test cricket's future, he was unguarded enough to say that he couldn't care less about it and nor could the players. He may have been speaking his own mind, but surely not those of the puppets who had now to make a success of their breakaway circus – or bust. A suitably impressive large black limousine swept him out again through the Grace Gates and on that soft summer evening at Lord's it seemed that international cricket had changed course irrevocably.

The Statement issued by the ICC after the meeting on 23 June read as follows:

The Sub-Committee of representatives of Test Match playing countries met today with Mr Packer and his associates: Messrs. Taylor, McNicoll and Benaud. The Sub-Committee advised Mr Packer that they would be prepared to recommend to their respective Boards that the Boards approve his privately promoted professional series, subject to the following conditions:

1. The programme and venues are acceptable to the home authority and the length of programme be six weeks, unless otherwise agreed. The matches would be under the control of the home authority and played in accordance with the Laws of Cricket.
2. No player to participate in these games without the permission of his home authority; this permission would not be withheld unreasonably.
3. No teams taking part in these matches could be represented as national teams [i.e. not Australia; possibly an Australian XI].
4. Players contracted to Mr Packer to be available for Test Matches, first-class fixtures and other home authority sponsored matches where there was no clash.
5. The home authority must be able to honour all contractual commitments to existing sponsors and advertisers.

It was put to Mr Packer that if he could agree to negotiate within the broad framework of these basic points a Sub-Committee would be appointed to endeavour to reach agreement on a mutually acceptable programme of matches.

Mr Packer was adamant, however, that he was not prepared to consider entering into any negotiations unless he was given an absolute guarantee now that his company would be granted exclusive television rights to cover Australian cricket at the conclusion of the Australian Board's current contract in 1978/79. Representatives of all countries present were unanimous that no Member Country should be asked to submit to such a demand, either now or in the future.

The Australian representatives indicated that they were prepared to recommend to their Board that they give consideration to the principle of exclusive television rights, not previously granted in Australia, and if approved then Mr Packer's company would be given an equal opportunity with others to submit an offer. This proposal unfortunately proved unacceptable.

A report will be circulated to all Members of the International Cricket Conference for consideration by the Conference in July.

The man in the middle! Kerry Packer, the central figure in the most contentious issue in cricket's history, striving to improve his public relations in a match between the English and Australian journalists at Harrogate in August.

The Jubilee Test at Lord's. *Above* Australia, for once, hold the initiative as Chappell late-cuts Underwood. Woolmer is at short-leg. *Below* Greig on the way to his 91: aggressive, ungainly, but effective.

Chapter Two
THE CRISIS DEEPENS

In the month which intervened between the breakdown of the talks at Lord's and the annual meeting of the International Cricket Conference there on 26 and 27 July, the battle lines on both sides were drawn up. Packer undoubtedly faced the greater problems, if only because the weight of public opinion in both England and Australia, and no doubt all the cricketing countries, was firmly against his breakaway movement, now so clearly exposed as a personal vendetta against the Australian Cricket Board rather than a crusade on behalf of the poor downtrodden cricketer as it had at first been presented by Greig.

Packer returned to Australia 48 hours after the meeting, leaving a philosophical but perhaps somewhat sheepish Richie Benaud behind to commentate on Test cricketers whose future was shrouded in doubt and who had been drawn into a conflict of far bigger proportions than most of them can have imagined. On the one side there was Packer, his business aspirations foiled, fighting for power and his own pride as well as for the finances of his empire; on the other side were the cricket authorities battling to regain control of the game in their various countries. In this mortal strife the players, their professional lives at stake too, were the premier weapons.

Packer may have had 51 leading cricketers contracted or on the point of being so. But apart from pursuing the immediate object of wooing viewers to watch the circus play on television he needed to acquire certain essentials to make his exercise credible. A cricket match fit for public consumption needs umpires and scorers. If it is going to be given major television coverage, it needs major names to commentate. But above all it needs suitable cricket grounds.

The more grandiose his plans became, the more Packer and his associates needed these essentials. Vain offers went out to England's leading umpire Dicky Bird, to England's respected physiotherapist Bernard Thomas, and to certain established commentators. But the tide of optimism on which the project had first been launched and which had persuaded every player approached except Geoff Boycott to sign for bigger sums than they had dreamt of had dissolved, and with the press firmly falling in behind the ranks of authority Packer and his players soon found themselves to be virtual outlaws.

Despite receiving huge offers for renting their grounds, the Australian state cricket authorities resisted temptation. The Sydney Cricket Ground is run by a Trust and was therefore vulnerable, but the Trust resisted a big offer for the hire of the ground because, in the words of the Trust chairman, Pat Hills, 'the Trust considered it had a responsibility to support the New South Wales Cricket Association'. The so called 'Super-Tests' therefore looked like being played on grounds normally used for football, or at least not on grounds normally associated with major cricket occasions. This seemed bound to give the matches an air of artificiality, which indeed they had anyway from their very conception. The impression was strengthened when it was announced that John Maley, the Brisbane groundsman whom Packer had lured away to prepare pitches for his games, was planning to transport special strips of turf around in concrete containers and to lower these into the middle of grounds where cricket is not normally played. The basis of a good cricket wicket is its solid foundations, and batsmen like Dennis Amiss who were apprehensive enough about facing the likes of Lillee and Thomson on even the most perfect pitches must have heard of this plan for a mobile wicket with a certain horror

Meanwhile, the cricket officials in England were meeting almost weekly to prepare for the International Cricket Conference. The Chairman's Advisory Committee of the Test and County Cricket Board, consisting of the chairmen of the Board's various sub-committees, met first and took advice on the legal implications of any bans they might impose on the Packer signatories, some twenty of whom were employed by English counties. They made three recommendations to the Board, which were then transmitted to the full TCCB meeting on 15 July, from where they were passed on to the supreme domestic authority, the Cricket Council, which met on 19 July, and so, finally, they appeared before the ICC.

Opinion was hardening all the time against the so-called superstars who had dared to challenge the existing order of things (which were healthier, anyway, than they had been for many years) and the belief was growing that they must be totally out-lawed. The TCCB proposals were that England players with Packer contracts should be banned from Tests at the end of the Jubilee series with Australia; and that the ban should be extended to all first-class cricket, possibly from a later date in order to give those who had signed contracts a chance to change their minds. County clubs who did not abide by a majority decision on this would be fined or even banned from the Championship.

In Australia the tough line was also seen to be the only possible one. Players would be banned from state and even club cricket if the laws of the land permitted. Both England and Australia were hoping for support from the other members of the ICC, and it seemed likely that the challenge from Packer would make an organisation which had not in the past been noted for either its unity or its decisiveness close ranks in a remarkable way. Another incidental effect of the affair was to force the various employers of professional cricketers to tighten contracts. It was now suggested that lawyers would have to be consulted in the drawing-up of con-tracts which would bar Test cricketers from playing for Packer or similar rival organisations if they conflicted with Tests. County cricketers needed to be given a clearer definition of their duties, their privileges and their pay, and in return for a more binding contract they could reasonably expect the highest remuneration their employers could afford to give them. It would need to be reasserted, also, that benefits were granted to cricketers for loyalty and long service, and there was a move to grant these only at the end of a player's career so as to stop men like Knott, Amiss, Underwood and Snow offering their services elsewhere soon after receiving huge tax-free sums.

The Australian system of giving substantial pensions to Test cricketers at the end of their careers was, in any case, in the control of the Australian Board, and it was believed that Doug Walters, by signing for Packer, risked depriving himself of some £15,000 which would have been due to him at the Board's discretion.

The open war started to get hotter in the days before the crucial ICC meeting. On 23 July Greg Chappell released a statement via the J.P. Sports organisation (which, through John Cornell and Austin Robertson, had with Ian Chappell's assistance set the circus in motion) denying the increasing number of reports that some of the players signed on by Packer were having second thoughts. This statement was eagerly confirmed by Mr Packer himself, who said in an interview in one of his papers, the *Sydney Sun Herald*, that his colleagues had been in touch with all the 51 players and that none of them 'wanted out'. 'They are most upset by the reports,' he said. He announced that he had secured grounds – though not of course the famous cricket grounds – in Melbourne and Adelaide, and was still hoping to hire the Sydney Cricket Ground. These hopes were dashed, however, within 24 hours when the SCG Trust met and decided to be loyal to the New South Wales Cricket Association. With characteristic reserve Mr Packer described this as a 'vindictive' decision made 'by a group of crusty old men sitting behind closed doors'. (The crusty old men included two extremely fit and youthful-looking ex-cricketers in Arthur Morris and Ian Craig!)

Packer revealed that he was sinking four million Australian dollars (£2.6 million) into the series – which was to last a mere twelve weeks, estimated that some players would earn $40,000 in that time and repeated that $100,000 would be the winner-take-all purse for the successful side in each of the various series planned between the Australian, West Indian and Rest of the World sides. He also repeated that he had offered half a million dollars a year for three years for the exclusive right to cover Test cricket in Australia once the ABC's contract had expired and confirmed that he would not have been interested in starting the circus if he had got the exclusive rights in the first place.

Before the ICC meeting he declared that he would take legal action against any bans imposed, claiming restraint of trade. He also accused the cricket authorities of double standards in that they were planning to ban the players only when the current series between England and Australia was over. However, it was only right and proper for the ICC to act in concert with the Australian Board, which had made contracts for the tour of England before the circus was announced, and there was no logical reason for banning any players until the rival matches began.

The months of anxious waiting for those who had tied themselves to their pugnacious new master ended on 26 July when, at the end of a six-hour meeting, Jack Bailey read out to a crowd of journalists in the Writing Room at Lord's the historic statement which confirmed that from 1 October Test cricket would be closed to them – probably for ever.

The full realisation of what had happened took time to sink in.

It was as if a patient had died after a long illness. The expected outcome came as no surprise but the impact of it was delayed. Slowly, players and public alike began to realise that for so many great names of the past few years the glamour and glory of Test cricket were over, and the prospect of a complete disappearance from first-class cricket of so much talent was sad indeed. For young players, men like Viv Richards, Imran Khan and possibly David Hookes, who were only in the early years of careers which might have earned them comparison with the great players of the past, the price of their clandestine commitment to the pirate cricketers was especially high.

The ICC, never in the past noted for its unity or decisiveness, had acted in the crisis with ruthless unanimity. In an attempt to pre-empt any legal moves they began by officially disapproving any match 'arranged or to be arranged by J. P. Sports Ltd, Kerry Packer, Richie Benaud or associated companies or persons, to take place in Australia or elsewhere between 1 October (1977) and 31 March 1979'. They then stated that any player who made himself available to play in these matches would be, from October, ineligible for Test cricket. They strongly recommended that the individual countries should extend the ban to all cricket under their jurisdiction. In addition they made it clear that the series of matches to be played in Australia would not rank as first-class or qualify for a place in the official records. Individuals who had signed for Mr Packer were given the chance to retract before October, but thereafter it would be tough for them to get back into the fold. They would have to apply to the Board of Control for permission to play in official cricket in their country, and their case would then be referred to the ICC.

The Conference took their firm line because, as they had said before, they believed that promotions like Mr Packer's could severely damage the whole structure of cricket. It now remained to be seen whether the circus would do exactly that or whether it would collapse, sooner or later, in the face of public indifference. Now it was neither the players, who had gambled with their futures, nor the establishment, who sought to outlaw them for disobeying the rules and abusing the traditions in which they had learned the game, but the public and the media who would decide the success of the Packer revolution. If the promotions in Australia in 1977–78 were to be successful their interest and compliance were essential. If this was forthcoming there was a clear possibility that Test cricket might in future be the final step for emerging young players before they took the springboard to greater riches in Mr Packer's world of 'super' cricketers. If, as seemed far more likely, the public preferred traditional matches with a history and a partisan flavour to add spice to them, rather than a show-biz razzmatazz, the biggest bubble in the history of cricket would burst, and many good players, some super, some not so super, would disappear.

The officials who passed the ICC resolutions of 26 July 1977 were: Chairman: W.H. Webster (President of MCC); Delegates: *UK*: Freddie Brown, chairman of the Cricket Council, and Doug Insole, chairman of TCCB. *Australia*: Tim Caldwell, former chairman of the Australian Cricket Board, and John Warr, former England and Middlesex bowler. *West Indies*: Jeff Stollmeyer and Alan Rae, both former Test players. *India*: R.P. Mehra, president of the Indian Board of Control, and secretary Ghulam Ahmed, former Test bowler. *Pakistan*: Col. Zafir Ahmed, secretary of the Pakistan Board of Control. *New Zealand*: Walter Hadlee, former Test captain, and Colin Cowdrey, England and Kent.

Their decisions had an immediate effect because on the eve of the Trent Bridge Test Jeff Thomson announced that he would not, after all, be joining the circus. The reasons given were that he had a contract already with the Brisbane radio company 4IP which bound him to play for Queensland, and that he had been misled by Packer's agents into believing that a contract with Packer would not interfere with his radio contract or his first-class cricket career. Presumably, therefore, Thomson had no right in the first place to sign a contract with Mr Packer, whose organisation anyway was a media rival to Thomson's radio station. But any concern on this count was forgotten as the majority who were hoping the circus would fail because of its challenge to the traditional format of the game rejoiced at the news of this first important prodigal son returning from the wilderness.

Thomson was soon followed by another 'defector' in Alvin Kallicharran, who shared the same financial adviser in David Lord, an Australian journalist who strongly believed that to join the circus would be wrong for young players with a future in Test cricket. Viv Richards was another with an association with Radio 4IP, and it was because he saw signs of a movement away from his circus spreading fast that Mr Packer made yet another visit to

England to do any necessary persuading at first hand and to seek legal aid for his cause. Indeed there was much talk of legal action in the air now, Radio 4IP apparently claiming that they had prior demands on the players and would sue to defend them, and Packer warning that he would sue if any players tried to wriggle out of their contracts and return their signing-on fees. In Kallicharran's case this came to £400, and Lord said that 'Kalli' had been so worried about the whole affair that he had not dared to pay the money into his bank.

The situation continued to change whilst England and Australia were locked in classic Test combat at Trent Bridge, and on the fourth day of that match, the hot and sultry 1st of August, there was a dramatic double development, first with the arrival of Mr Packer in London and then with the news of a scheme by a London businessman to woo the English players back into the fold and to keep any others from being tempted by the circus.

The scheme was initially misrepresented, as a result of a misunderstanding between Mike Brearley and the businessman, David Evans, the boss of a North London office-cleaning firm. At first it was reported that Mr Evans' company was prepared to put up half a million pounds to carry out three main proposals: firstly, that the contracts between Mr Packer and his five English signatories would be bought off; secondly, that his company would sponsor every England Test player for £1,000 for every home Test for three years; and thirdly, that a £1,000 retainer would be paid each season for three years to each member of a pool of fifty English players, chosen by the selectors, so long as they guaranteed to be available for England. On this basis each player who took part in five Tests a summer would get £6,000 on top of his fees from the TCCB, which were about to be substantially increased in any case. However it transpired that Mr Evans was putting his company's business first and his love of cricket's status quo second. He stressed that his main proposals would only be carried out if his office-cleaning firm could gain a million pounds-worth of new business per annum. If it could, the profits would be put towards this sponsorship scheme for English Test cricketers. Time would tell whether or not this was just a large red herring in a stormy sea.

In any case, the reason for Mr Packer's arrival in London soon became clear. On 2 August, a few hours after the third Test had ended in a second successive victory for England, he held a press conference at the Dorchester Hotel in Park Lane to announce that he was to start legal proceedings before a High Court vacation judge against the ICC, the TCCB, and David Lord. He did not have to wait long for an answer. After listening to lawyers appearing for Mr Packer on one side and the cricket authorities on the other, Mr Justice Slynn made three judicial orders. These were: (1) A seven-day injunction to J.P. Sports Ltd, restraining Mr David Lord, the Australian manager of Jeff Thomson, Alvin Kallicharan and Vivian Richards, from 'wrongfully inducing them or attempting to induce' them or other players to break their contracts with the company. (2) In lieu of injunctions which were refused against the International Cricket Conference and the Test and County Cricket Board the judge accepted undertakings from the TCCB that any decision made at their next meeting would be subject to the court's ruling and that no ban would be implemented before next April. The ICC, having made their recommendation, were not present or represented and thus could give no undertaking. (3) An order for a speedy trial of the main issues involved, the judge saying that he was quite satisfied that there were serious legal issues involved and that Mr Packer was not bringing a frivolous or vexatious action.

The TCCB met on 5 August, the day after this judgment, and a few days later, after taking advice from leading Counsel, announced that, subject to the result of the trial, they would extend the ban, as recommended by the ICC, to cover all county cricket from 1978. All players who were ineligible for Test cricket because of playing, or making themselves available to play in, matches disapproved of by the ICC would be barred from all county games for two years from the date of last being involved with a disapproved match, subject to the decision of the 'speedy trial' ordered by Mr Justice Slynn.

The trial would no doubt take into effect not only the prohibitive nature of these moves by the ICC and the TCCB but the equally tough wording of the contacts drawn up for the players by J. P. Sports which 'bound them hand and foot' to Mr Packer and in particular tied them, according to one contract published in the *Daily Mail*, to play anywhere in the world for him at any time.

Meanwhile the plans of the Kerry Packer organisation continued to be released. In Sydney, on 12 August, Mr Brian Treasure, entitled the 'administrative controller of world series cricket', confirmed the dates of six of the games to be released by Channel

Nine. Three matches between Australia and West Indian elevens would take place on 2–6 December; 16–20 December; and 31 December to 4 January; and three between Australian and World Elevens would follow on 13–17 January; 27–31 January and 9–13 February. Forty-six names were published as being contracted to Mr Packer. They were: Ian Chappell, Ray Bright, Greg Chappell, Ian Davis, Ross Edwards, Gary Gilmour, David Hookes, Martin Kent, Dennis Lillee, Rodney Marsh, Rick McCosker, Mick Malone, Kerry O'Keeffe, Len Pascoe, Ian Redpath, Richie Robinson, Max Walker and Doug Walters, all of Australia; Clive Lloyd, Wayne Daniel, Roy Fredericks, Joel Garner, Gordon Greenidge, Michael Holding, David Holford, Bernard Julien, Alvin Kallicharran, Collis King, Deryck Murray, Albert Padmore, Vivian Richards, Andy Roberts and Lawrence Rowe, all of West Indies; Tony Greig, Dennis Amiss, Alan Knott, John Snow and Derek Underwood, all of England; Zaheer Abbas, Asif Iqbal, Imran Khan, Majid Khan, Mushtaq Mohammad, all of Pakistan; and Eddie Barlow, Mike Procter and Barry Richards, of South Africa. Twenty-two of these 46 were currently employed in English County cricket.

All these 46 had presumably signed contracts similar to or identical with the one published in the *Daily Mail*, which bound the player to 'the promoter' (the title given in the contract to Mr Packer's agents, J. P. Sports Pty Ltd) in a relationship which looked less like one between employer and employee than one between master and slave. In return for a minimum of £15,000 per series, plus reasonable expenses and economy-class fares, the player agreed to:

1. Play for no one else anywhere in the world without the promoter's permission.

2. Play in a maximum of 65 days' cricket in Australia in a season (defined as starting on 1 September and ending the following 30 March) and also in any 'series of matches outside Australia'.

3. Abide by strict rules laid down by the promoter governing where he should play, where he should stay, when and how he should travel and how he should dress and behave.

4. Give no interviews to press or broadcasting organisations, make no personal appearances, and endorse no sports goods, without the promoter's written permission.

The player risked termination of his contract if he disobeyed any 'direction, decision or requirement of the promoter' or involved himself in 'any misconduct which in the decision of the promoter is contrary to the well-being of the tour'. The promoter retained the right to withhold wages as well as terminating a contract (subject to appeal to the 'Tour Principal', appointed by the promoter). He also had the right to sell the contract to anyone prepared to buy it.

Whether they were moved by need or by greed, it was remarkable indeed that so many of the world's best cricketers were prepared to tie themselves so completely to an organisation about which most of them knew little or nothing, and to follow a trend set by a few strong characters like Ian Chappell and Tony Greig, against their better judgment or not. Whatever their private doubts the players continued to express publicly their faith in the viability of the revolutionary Packer venture. They avoided the basic objection of the vast majority of committed cricket followers (as opposed to fringe fans likely to be attracted by the novelty of it all) that what they were doing was a potential threat to the whole structure of international cricket and Test cricket in particular.

Everyone was aware that if on the one hand the High Court ruling went against Mr Packer he still had every intention of promoting his matches simultaneously with Test matches, as well as taking legal action in Australia too, and that if it went against the ICC and the TCCB selectors could still not be forced to pick cricketers for national, or even for county, sides if they did not wish to do so. By making themselves unavailable for some Tests, Packer players were in any case unlikely to be chosen in preference to others who were always available to play for their country. The county position was quite different, until such time as Mr Packer carried out threats to bring his matches to England. He seemed unlikely to be welcomed by enough people to make this a worthwhile gamble. Assuming he avoided the English season, bans on his players in county cricket were vulnerable and questionable because they were restrictive and retaliatory in nature rather than defensive. His matches were not (yet) a direct threat to county cricket as they were to Tests. But if the county sides were to be half-filled with Packer players, all ineligible or unavailable for Tests, England's selectors would be at an unfair disadvantage. County cricket, in fact, would be helping to sustain the Packer circus as well as Test cricket.

Now, however, it was the people's decision. The judgment of

the courts could not alter the fact that the Packer revolution would succeed or fail according to the choice of cricket spectators. Would they prefer traditional Tests or 'super Tests'? It did not help the cause of the rebels that most of the Australian players concerned in the Packer matches against West Indian and Rest of the World teams had just received at the hands of England a hiding of unexpected proportions which made them look anything but super. Yet the cricket played for the cherished prize of the Ashes in the summer of 1977 was full of skill, character and supercharged excitement which was only accentuated by the unyielding atmosphere of tension which the Packer crisis engendered. It is time now to turn to the dramatic story of those matches, starting with the Centenary Test at Melbourne where, behind the scenes, the first moves in the Packer affair were being made.

PART TWO

ENGLAND V. AUSTRALIA 1977

Chapter One
THE CENTENARY TEST

The story of the 1977 battle for the Ashes began not at Lord's in June but exactly three months before at an equally historic cricket ground on the other side of the world. On 12 March the Melbourne Cricket Club – scene of the 1956 Olympic Games and of the annual final of the Australian Football Cup, venue for a Billy Graham crusade in 1959 which attracted 130,000 people and for a Eucharistic Congress which was attended by almost the same number in 1973, centre for international sporting events which have included lacrosse, bowls, baseball, tennis and hockey – staged the most remarkable of its many spectacular productions: the Centenary Test match. It was a unique occasion, which, almost incidentally, gave the two teams who would be playing for the Ashes later in the year a chance to evaluate each other. The real purpose of the match was to celebrate one hundred years of passionate sporting rivalry. The love-hate relationship between English and Australian cricketers was reaffirmed in an almost mystic ceremony, and the players of the present, through television more than ever the focus of public attention and through sponsorship more than ever tempted to use any means to win, were given a timely reminder of their own comparatively small part in a tradition more important than themselves alone.

There has never been a cricketing occasion like it. Two hundred and fourteen former Test cricketers, seventy-one of them flown over from England, spent two weeks wallowing in nostalgia, remembering their own moments of triumph or despair, reading and hearing about, in a plethora of publications and programmes, the most dramatic moments of a century of sometimes glorious, sometimes ignominious, occasionally bitter confrontations. There were innumerable receptions and dinners, and if these were affairs strictly for the initiated it was still a fascinating time for the cricket fanatic to be in Melbourne. With so many celebrities present it was as if the place were a cricketing department of Madame Tussaud's, with all the wax models come to life. Many were familiar faces, but many others had emerged from obscurity, come out of hibernation as it were, to be present at this unique match. Age and, in some cases, idle living had taken their toll, and many an athletic body had run to seed; here too was a reminder to the players of the present that their own time on the stage would be limited. Two of England's oldest surviving players, Tiger Smith and Frank Woolley, were unable to make the long journey to Australia because of their frailty, but Percy Fender, born in 1892, was there, as instantly recognisable with his long moustache as he had been in the days when he led Surrey with such dash and inventiveness. His 13-year-old grandson accompanied him to describe the events, which, with his eyesight fading, 'P.G.H.F.' was able to see only imperfectly.

A parade of present players and past captains began the proceedings on the cool autumn morning of Saturday 12 March, with Jack Ryder, captain against Percy Chapman's team in 1928–29, proudly leading the way for Australia only a few days before his death and R.E.S. Wyatt leading for England. Of Ryder's nine successors, only Bill Woodfull had died. Sir Donald Bradman, Lindsay Hassett, Ian Johnson, Richie Benaud, Bob Simpson, Bill Lawry and the Chappell brothers were all present. Chapman, Douglas Jardine and Wally Hammond had gone from England's ranks, but eleven of Chapman's fourteen successors paraded in front of the Melbourne pavilion – Wyatt, Gubby Allen, Norman Yardley, Freddie Brown, Sir Leonard Hutton, Peter May, Ted Dexter, M.J.K. Smith, Colin Cowdrey, Mike Denness and Tony Greig. Only Ray Illingworth amongst the living captains was unable to join in this happy, yet tear-jerking, reunion.

It was soon time to snap out of the mood of nostalgia and to switch back to the present. Greg Chappell tossed a specially minted commemorative gold coin; Tony Greig called correctly and, taking a gamble which had more often backfired than succeeded in the 224 contests which had gone before, asked Australia to bat. Greig was motivated by the attacking thought that the pitch was likely to have more moisture in it on the first day than on any other – S.F. Barnes's immortal spell on the first morning of the 1911 match at Melbourne and Peter Lever's success there on the 1974–75 tour were only two instances of this – and also by the defensive thought that Lillee might settle the game in a few overs if he were to be let loose on nervous and uncertain English batting at the start of the game. In the event, what Lillee and Walker might

have done to England, Willis, Lever, Old and Underwood between them did to Australia. All the confident predictions of the
local writers were made to look foolish by a performance of sustained excellence by England's bowlers and fielders and a generally indifferent one by Australia's batsmen. The Melbourne
crowd, 61,316 of whom had paid 66,345 Australian dollars to
watch, could hardly believe what they saw.

England's tour selectors, consisting of Ken Barrington, MCC's
manager through India, Sri Lanka and on this final two-week leg
in Australia, their captain Tony Greig, vice-captain Mike
Brearley and two of their senior professionals, Alan Knott and
Keith Fletcher, had announced a surprising team after a meeting
lasting just under two hours the previous day. It had generally
been expected that Fletcher, after a disappointing tour, would
give way to one of the younger players who had been doing well in
recent weeks, Graham Barlow or Geoff Miller, and that Bob
Woolmer, though he had scored a century in his last Test against
Australia, would also be left out of the side because of his recent
poor form. But English professionals in committee are more conservative than retired colonels, and they now ignored the claims of
both the younger men, preferring to rely, as usual, on experience.
It was almost certainly the opposite course to the one which Australian selectors would have taken in similar circumstances. Australia had, in fact, decided to give a first Test cap in this exacting
match to 21-year-old David Hookes, the fair-haired left-hander
from Adelaide who in his last three Sheffield Shield matches had
scored five centuries in six innings, four of them in succession. His
actual scores were 163, 9, 185, 101, 135 and 156. England's preference for Fletcher and Woolmer was perhaps less surprising than
the decision to drop Dennis Amiss down the order from number
one to number four just a few months after he had scored a
double-century opening the batting against an attack more hostile
than even Australia could produce – Holding, Roberts, Daniel
and Holder, the all-conquering West Indian quartet. Amiss had
followed this triumphant return to Test cricket at the Oval in 1976
with a highly successful tour of India in which, opening the batting as he prefers to, he had scored 417 runs in the five Tests, averaging 52 and having a great deal to do with England's success.
But a single match in Australia, the warm-up game before the
Centenary Test held in Perth against Western Australia, had been
enough to panic the selectors into trying to protect Amiss from the

new ball. The reason was another double failure by Amiss against his arch bogeyman, the saturnine, magnificently hostile fast bowler, Dennis Lillee.

Lillee's two successes against a nervous, bemused-looking Amiss at Perth added to his already remarkable tally of successes against England's premier batsman of recent years. In the fifteen first-class innings Amiss had played against Australian opposition since Lillee's own return to Test cricket after a serious back injury in late 1974, he had been out to Australia's number one sporting idol ten times. Yet, wherever Amiss batted in the order, both he and Greig knew that Lillee would be waiting for him. It was arguably putting even greater strain on him to ask him to come in at number four after a public admission from Greig that he was being protected 'for as long as possible because he is one of our best players'. An out-of-touch Bob Woolmer was given the opener's job instead, but for both him and Amiss the confrontation with Lillee was mercifully postponed and it was the opening pair from New South Wales, Ian Davis and Rick McCosker, who walked out on a cool, cloudy Saturday morning for the first ball of this historic encounter.

John Lever, unknown to the general world of cricket before his successful first series for England on the tour of India, was given the honour of bowling the first over, a maiden to the young New South Wales right-hander Ian Davis. Rick McCosker got the innings launched in the next over from Bob Willis, but England's big woolly-haired fast bowler twice beat Davis in the same over and there was a general air of hesitation about the batting which was indicative of the surprises which lay ahead. In the fifth over of the innings, with the crowd still making their way into the open spaces of the vast stadium, Lever pierced Australia's armour for the first time. Davis came across his stumps and shaped to leg-glance a ball which bent a little in the air and hustled through to strike his pad on a line with his middle and leg stumps. Tom Brooks, Australia's respected umpire, raised his right index finger and Davis was on his way.

Two runs later, and in the next over, Australia received a double blow of much greater significance. McCosker, generally a safe and confident hooker of the short ball, moved much too late to a rising delivery from Willis; he was struck on the jaw and, to add insult to a painful and serious injury, the ball was then deflected onto his stumps via his arm and bat. He was led off the field in great pain and put under sedation in hospital, where an X-ray revealed a fractured jaw which would take five weeks to mend. The jaw was later wired and McCosker told that he might bat again only in an emergency. Fortunately for Australia, as it turned out, he was to disobey the doctor's orders. Melbourne crowds are great and loyal supporters of the many spectaculars that take place at their famous stadium, but there are times when the cricketing judgment of the beer-swilling masses who soak up the sun at the southern end of the ground (the popular stand there alone holds 48,400 people) is apparently negligible. It was from this section that earlier in the season they had chanted 'kill, kill, KILL' as Dennis Lillee was tearing up the Pakistan batting in one of his peerlessly ferocious spells, yet now they began howling and booing at Willis as if the bowling of bouncers were something no decent Australian would ever stoop to do.

The frenetic atmosphere to which they contributed was combated by the calm figure of Australia's captain, Greg Chappell, who settled in to play a long and composed defensive innings which, fortunately for England, never got out of first gear. But Cosier, batting at number three for Australia for the first time, a tall, raw-looking red-haired right-hander who had scored a century in his first Test match against the West Indies the previous season, was anything but calm. He played an intentional upper cut for four over slips' heads off Willis, and in the same over square-cut him for four. Then Lever surprised him with a sudden bouncer. The batsman belatedly got into position to hook, making no attempt to roll his wrists and keep the ball down, and was caught off the top edge of his bat by Fletcher at leg-slip.

So, with Australia in trouble at 23 for three, David Hookes came in to play his first Test innings before some 60,000 people at 11.50 on a cloudy Melbourne morning. With his long fair hair jutting out from behind his baggy green cap, his battered old red-handled bat held together by binding which had once been white but was now grey, he looked every inch the tyro he was. But he found his first ball with the middle of the trusted blade and was off the mark with a leg-glance to his second delivery. He then produced a pleasing drive, hit on the up off Lever, which brought him three runs to deep mid-off; but his first four was a fast edge past Amiss in the gully, played all along the ground. Then he hit a cracking off-drive off Lever to leave Australia much more healthily placed after an hour's tense cricket at 41 for three from nine overs. Chappell, however, though he had looked in no trouble, was only four not out and both Willis and Lever had kept him on the defensive by bowling an excellent line and length.

When Old relieved Willis at the southern end at the start of the second hour, his line and general control were just as good and he moved the ball off the seam more than either of the openers. It was, however, the extra lift of a straight ball to Hookes which ended a promising innings as the batsman found himself committed to playing a stroke and he could only edge the ball to Greig at second slip.

Doug Walters is too old to change his ways. A score of 45 for four is as much an invitation to him to attack as one of 245 for four. Willis was brought back by Greig to greet him and as soon as he pitched the ball short Walters attempted to hook from well wide of his off-stump and top-edged another catch to Greig. So Australia, on a pitch of generally easy pace if occasionally producing uneven bounce, took lunch at 57 for five. The Melbourne crowd could hardly believe it.

Their digestion was improved, however, by the sight of Marsh and Chappell doubling the score in the sunlit afternoon before England broke through again. From the first over after lunch Marsh and Chappell took 15 runs off Old, Marsh playing three pugnacious straight drives, two of them hit in the air and on the up past the bowler. But Old forced him to be more respectful, twice getting in-cutters between his bat and pad and missing the off-stump by a coat of varnish. Chappell hoisted the first fifty partnership of the match with a typically elegant, lazy-looking stroke to mid-wicket, but then Old got his man as another off-cutter to the left-hander was superbly caught off the inside edge of Marsh's bat by Knott, diving to his right. It is customary to state on these occasions, when a wicket-keeper holds a catch off the inside edge, that he 'changed direction'. But the remarkable point was that this time Knott had not gone across to the offside to take the ball, but had waited for Marsh to play a shot before darting across to his right to pluck the ball inches above the ground.

The end of the innings was in sight now but, as England remembered well from the tour two years before, an Australian tail never gives up easily. Moreover Chappell was still in residence, looking to have much more time for his shots than anyone else had. However, Gilmour, who had recently scored his first Test century in New Zealand, never looked a match for Old, who has always bowled well at left-handed players. As with Marsh, Old kept piercing a gap between bat and pad before finally finding the outside edge of the bat, and Greig, diving in front of first slip, latched on to a superb low, right-handed catch.

This was followed by an equally inspired piece of fielding by the vice-captain. Underwood by now had been called into the attack, a wonderful man for Greig to have at his command because he could be certain that, with Underwood bowling, the pressure on the batsmen would not be relaxed through any loose deliveries. O'Keeffe, back in favour with the Australian selectors now that Mallett had retired, and bowling better than at any time in his chequered career, pushed forward and got an inside edge which brushed past Knott and carried in a parabola behind the wicket. Brearley launched himself from first slip and held the ball in mid-air in his left hand, somehow keeping hold of it despite falling with the whole weight of his body on his left arm. So, by outstanding, even inspired fielding, Australia's afternoon recovery was arrested.

Lever replaced Old after tea, his first over lasting eight minutes due mainly to a pitch invasion by a lone drunk, unusual in modern times in that he was fully clothed. The cloud which had made the Melbourne ground a grey and gloomy place, with its concrete stands and grey corrugated iron roofs, was gone now and the light was perfect for batting, which made it important for England to finish their first job in the field quickly and so give their batsmen a chance to launch their innings in favourable conditions. Chappell had taken one desperate swing at Underwood shortly before the interval – he missed, but survived the l.b.w. appeal – but he made no serious attempt to hog the bowling afterwards. Lillee, indeed, had helped Australia off the hook at Lord's in 1975 with a spectacular 73 not out and he fought with characteristic determination now, having come in ahead of Max Walker, who had enjoyed a long run of success with the bat in Australia's last home series with England. Lillee this time was to bat for an hour and it was Chappell who was out next as he aimed another uncharacteristic legside heave and was bowled, presenting the admirable Underwood with his 250th Test wicket. He was to take two more in the match to draw level with Brian Statham's final tally and so to set out, at the end of his most successful overseas tour, on the final leg of his journey towards the records of Gibbs and Trueman. His accuracy, more reliable than a machine, accounted for Walker as he too swung towards mid-wicket and missed. So, incredibly, Australia were all out for 138, Underwood finishing with the best figures of 3 for 16, but all the four bowlers used being able to look with pride at their figures, printed in red and white on the huge black scoreboard.

The distinguished pundits grinned and chatted from their privileged positions in the pavilion. The odd thing was, they believed, that the pitch was a good one for batting. Greig's gamble had paid off handsomely, but his opposite number attributed the failure of his batsmen more to the pressure of the occasion than to the two-paced pitch. 'I don't think Tony Greig or myself really thought that the festivities and the atmosphere of this celebration would affect our players to this degree,' said Chappell coolly. He was happy, too, to pay tribute to the England bowling and fielding. But Ken Barrington's pre-match penknife test on the pitch had revealed more moisture than many people imagined.

It was not long before Chappell's magnanimity had its reward, although England's reply on the first evening began solidly enough. In an hour they scored 29 and lost only one wicket. Brearley and Woolmer had a torrid time, however, and it was Woolmer who calmly bore the brunt in what for him was a crucial innings. Lillee, magnificently hostile as always, bowled rather too short to him at first but Walker twice beat him in his first over with big swing in both directions. Lillee soon found the right length and he knew the line (off-stump) instinctively. He appealed furiously when a vicious rising delivery glanced off Woolmer's shoulder and was caught by slip; he glared his disapproval at the umpire's refusal, then barked another imperious appeal as an outswinger slipped past the outside edge of Brearley's bat. The pressure was mounting and it was Woolmer who succumbed, flicking away from his body at another outswinger and glancing behind him to see Chappell clasping on to a sharp, low chance.

The pitch was still inclined to produce an uneven bounce when England resumed at 29 for one on the second day, but in pace it was easy, even slow. The only explanation for England's disastrous collapse, in which in the two-hour morning session they lost seven wickets for 54 runs, was superb bowling by Dennis Lillee and Max Walker supported by catching just as brilliant as England had produced the day before. Thomson was not present but in every other respect it was as if the two years between this match and MCC's last visit to Australia had never been. Of the eight England wickets which had fallen by lunch, only Greig did not succumb to a catch behind the wicket on the offside.

The sorry story for England supporters looking for a commanding first-innings lead began in the opening over when Brearley, going back across his stumps to fend off a rising ball from Lillee, could not control it and edged to third slip where Hookes joyfully accepted his first Test chance. The sun was shining, and the crowd, which later in the day would rise to 62,505, did not need any beer (it is not on sale in Melbourne on Sundays) to stir them to wild excitement. Lillee and Walker were their alcohol today. Walker followed up Lillee's crucial early blow with a smaller, but still significant one, when he removed the night-watchman, Underwood, who can be a stubborn enough sticker, with the aid of a low, diving right-handed catch at first slip.

So, after two overs in the morning, England were 30 for three and Amiss and Randall were together. For just a while they played quietly but safely, getting across and middling the ball with their defensive strokes although both were alarmed by two of Lillee's more wicked bumpers, the kind that keep on coming at the batsman's head rather than curving away. Randall, in his first attempt to amuse the crowd, stood to attention when he had ducked under his bouncer and doffed his cap to Lillee. But there was no relaxation or levity from Lillee.

Amiss, perhaps unsettled by the bouncer from his bogeyman, which he had evaded only at the last moment, losing his cap in the process, drove firm-footed at a half-volley from Walker in the next over and sliced the ball with an angled bat to O'Keeffe in the gully. Randall soon followed him, playing at a rising delivery outside his off-stump instead of leaving it alone as he should have done. Lillee seemed somehow to mesmerise the batsmen into doing this: in fact, it was possible to fault his bowling on this occasion for being directed too much down the offside, but whenever he found the right off-stump line he looked likely to strike. From their nadir of 40 for five England reached 61 before the next wicket fell, due to some belligerent blows from Greig.

England's captain began with two unsuccessful attempts to drive Lillee on the up through the covers. But he got off the mark in the next over with a firm off-drive for four off Walker. In the same over Fletcher too got off the mark, with a clip in the air which almost gave Walker a caught-and-bowled chance as he drove too soon at a ball which appeared to stop. Could these two great friends pull England at least level with Australia? Greig brought the fifty up with an off-driven four off Lillee and then with a magnificent, full-blooded swing of the bat he cover-drove Walker for four more. But these strokes were like small, barely visible stars in the dark night of England's innings. In the same over Greig drove again at Walker but this time a booming in-swinger came through between bat and pad to bowl him.

Knott and Fletcher were England's last hopes, but Fletcher followed another ball from Walker which went the other way and Marsh, diving across in front of Chappell at first slip, took a low catch in his right glove. Gilmour, who sadly was no longer the confident, menacing bowler he had been in England in 1975, was in the attack by now, delivering some wild full-tosses which England's batsmen seemed too bemused to punish, but as soon as Lillee returned to the fray he removed Old with a rapid rising ball that Old simply could not avoid. When England's dismal morning came to an end they had lost seven wickets for 54 runs in two hours, four of them to Walker at a personal cost of 31 runs from eight overs.

The end came swiftly after lunch. Knott is quicker to get across to the offside than most of his colleagues, but he starts with an open stance and is thus square on to the bowler when he plays his defensive strokes to straight deliveries. This leaves him open to l.b.w. decisions and he is out in this way more often than almost any other. In Lillee's first over after the interval he came across in front of his stumps, shaped to leg-glance, was beaten for pace and given out. This was Lever's cue to garner what runs he could by 'having a go', and he became the fourth man to reach double figures before touching Lillee to Marsh to enable the chunky West Australian to surpass Wally Grout's record of 187 Test victims. Later in a triumphant match he was to become the first Australian wicket-keeper to score a hundred against England. Only Leslie Ames and Alan Knott had achieved the honour for England against Australia. England's total of 95 was their third lowest against Australia since the war. It was lower than any Thomson and Lillee's combined forces had inflicted on them during the 1974–75 series and it was all the more humiliating after the heady success in the field the day before. The gentle dream through a sub-continent of spin had ended with the well-remembered nightmare of Lillee at his most fearsome. Yet though his figures were so dramatic Lillee had bowled better and more fiercely before. He and Walker had been relatively tame compared to Holding, Roberts and Daniel on some occasions the summer before.

England had lost nine wickets for 66 runs in two and a half hours. Australia would gladly have settled for a deficit of 50 when the day began. As it was, they began their second innings, still blinking with disbelief, forty minutes after lunch with a lead of 43. McCosker was unable to bat because of his fractured jaw, but this time Davis played soundly and very straight to make sure of his place in the touring team to England. O'Keeffe, deputising as opening batsman, did a good job for nine overs against an England attack which not unnaturally looked a little deflated. What early luck there was went with the batsmen, Davis hooking Lever close to the hands of Amiss on the deep square-leg boundary and O'Keeffe snicking Willis only inches in front of Greig at second slip. O'Keeffe was eventually caught at third slip off Old, who, having one of his very best matches as a bowler, then produced an off-cutter which carved a path through Chappell's tentative forward push and onto the stumps. It was a great feather in Old's cap and a great shame for the crowd who had wanted to see a thoroughbred performance from Australia's premier batsman. There were those who now despaired of the Centenary Test producing any outstanding batting, but they need not have worried: this was to be a game true to the great traditions it was celebrating, a match with a little bit of everything.

England did, however, have one further success, soon after tea, when Cosier, apparently a believer in lightning not striking twice, attempted to hook Lever exactly as he had done the day before. As then, he made no attempt to roll his wrists to hit the ball along the ground and, also as before, a slight error in timing resulted in the ball taking the top edge of the bat and skying this time to Knott.

Walters, too, had perished in just such a rash fashion in the first innings but this time, though Greig did not fail to test him as soon as possible with some overs from Willis, he was determined to be prudent. He was getting a good example from his partner, Davis, who was playing altogether more impressively than he had on the opening morning. There was still an hour and a half of the second day left when Walters joined him; 23 wickets had already fallen for less than 300 runs and the almighty extravaganza was in severe danger of subsiding in an atmosphere of anti-climax. But the moisture in the pitch had now gone and Walters and Davis proved that the bowling could be tamed. Davis was the more convincing and stable of the two. His attacking strokes were decisive when he chose to play them, mainly firm off-drives, well-controlled cuts and the occasional strong and correctly played hook. It was a neat leg-glance, however, played to a rare overpitched ball from Old, which made him, at 41, the highest scorer in the game. The stroke marked the watershed between the bowler's match and the batsman's match it was to become in its later stages.

England ought to have taken a fourth wicket before stumps were drawn, but Walters, as ever fallible around his off-stump, was missed off Old in the gully. The unfortunate fielder was the normally reliable Willis, and instead of being rid of the dangerous 'Dougie' at an important psychological moment late on the second day the England players were to find themselves clapping him into the pavilion still undefeated at lunch on the third. Davis and Walters had scored 51 together in ninety minutes at the close and a relieved Chappell stated that evening that the partnership might decide the match. England would now have to score the highest total of the game to win it and Chappell believed that if his side could reach 300 in their second innings they would be un-assailable. Strange game that cricket is, they were to exceed 400 and still to find themselves, for a time, assailed on every side.

There was another huge crowd on Monday, which was a public holiday, Labour Day. They were hoping, no doubt, for some glorious batting to relieve the almost monotonous supremacy of the bowlers. For 45 minutes they saw batting which, if not exactly glorious, was certainly as confident and composed as anything that had gone before in the match. It came mainly from Ian Davis, who reached the first 50 of the match with an off-drive off Willis and who kept the scoreboard ticking over with some attractively played drives, glances and cuts. The late-cut was clearly his favourite stroke but at times it came near to being an obsession, and although he kept his bat right over the ball in the text-book manner he also left himself open to an off-cutter or in-swinger by sometimes attempting the stroke when the ball was dangerously close to his off-stump. Still, he was the dominant partner as Walters concentrated on getting himself set, refusing any invitation to repeat his first-innings indiscretion. The bowling, moreover, demanded respect. Willis, in his attempt to bowl a yorker, overpitched at times, but there was very little off a good line or length from himself or Lever, who opened, or from Old and Greig, who took over from them.

It was Greig, bowling controlled medium pace, who got rid of Davis as he followed a ball moving away from his off-stump and nicked it to Knott. He had batted for four hours, made sure of his trip to England and immeasurably strengthened his side's position. Greig might twice have followed up by dismissing Hookes before he had scored but the new batsman was not afraid to go for the hook when Greig pitched short to him, and a glorious off-drive showed Greig he could not overpitch and get away with it. At the other end Walters reached 50 with another perfect off-drive, although Old forced him to check his stroke to every one of his next seven deliveries. He was still moving the ball more than most, although his knee strain was worrying him. Lever and Underwood, England's main bowling successes on the tour of India, were in harness by lunchtime, but they could not break through. Walters, admirably disciplined and using all his experience, was 66 not out at lunch, with Hookes 20 not out and the lead extended well past 200. By slow but sure degrees the game was being tugged out of England's grasp.

During the lunch interval the 1500 metres Olympic gold medallist and world mile record-holder John Walker of New Zealand coasted away from his challengers in the invitation 'Centenary Mile'. If this event seemed a little incongruous in the middle of a Test match it certainly wasn't entirely out of place, for Walker was following in the footsteps of great long distance runners like Zatopek, Kuts, Landy and Delany who had figured in the 1956 Olympics held at the Melbourne Cricket ground, thought by many Olympic veterans to have been the happiest of the modern Olympiads. Walker was clearly excited at running before a crowd as big as this one, and the enjoyment was mutual.

But there was even greater excitement to come. Walters was out in the first over after lunch, when Greig got a ball to leave him and Knott took a good right-handed catch. Marsh was the new batsman, but for the moment it was young Hookes who took over the centre of the stage and in the middle of a sunny afternoon he suddenly produced an array of strokes which brought an emotional crowd to its feet.

Greig was by now bowling off-spinners from the pavilion end and to the third ball of an over Hookes lent forward to give his answer to the England captain's decision to bring up a short extra-cover to discourage him from driving. He did not get to the pitch of the ball, but he swung the bat through just the same and lifted the ball over the top of mid-off for a powerful four. The next ball was short outside the leg-stump: a bad ball which Hookes duly hit to the fine-leg boundary. Now Greig bowled a half-volley on the off-stump and this time Hookes drove him classically through extra-cover for a third four to take him to 48 not out. Greig changed his direction and pitched the next ball on his leg-stump on a good length. Hookes opened his body and hit the delivery firmly to the mid-wicket boundary off the front foot. The applause for his fifty was still ringing in his ears as Greig ran up again, bowled a good length ball on the off-stump and watched in astonishment as the tyro drove him on the up through the gap between cover and extra.

There was all the innocence of youth in these shots, all the splendid simplicity of a talented young batsman playing his natural game in a totally uninhibited way. There was no calculation or tactical awareness, just an instinctive and spontaneous response. Greg Chappell saw it as the moment that Australia really took control of the game. Many a watcher compared the effortless, leaning power of the strokes to that of the great South African left-hander, Graeme Pollock. The swaying, delirious masses in the southern stand saluted a new hero. An over ago Hookes had been a promising young batsman, 36 not out. Now he was 56 not out and a star.

He got no further, however. In the previous over from Underwood there had been an appeal for a bat-pad catch to Greig at silly-point, and now Hookes turned Underwood to the onside where Fletcher dived forward to hold a brilliant one-handed catch at short-leg. Spitefully Greig said a sharp word or two, Hookes looked astonished and umpire Brooks rightly told Greig to 'cool it'. It is an exciting thing when a young player makes an impact like this, and the context of the dazzling sequence of strokes played by Hookes made it all the more dramatic. Here was a 21-year-old smashing the England captain for 20 runs in five balls in the Centenary Test when, by rights, he ought to have been over-awed. Not since Doug Walters had scored successive hundreds in his first two Test matches against England in 1965–66 had a young Australian made quite such an impression. It was lucky for Hookes that he was a left-hander or he might have been dubbed the new Sir Donald Bradman there and then. He was not yet, of course, even the new Doug Walters (they had called *him* the new Don Bradman once) but it had been a most thrilling début and a tour of England now gave him an ideal opportunity to develop his skill and reveal his true worth. (In fact, he had already had some experience of English conditions through playing club cricket for Dulwich the season before in the Surrey League.) The doyen of the Australian press corps, Ray Robinson, ferreted out the fact that Hookes's 56 was the highest score by a left-handed Test débutant since Joe Darling's 53 against England at Sydney at the age of 24 in 1894.

The fall of Hookes, sixth out at 244, gave England the chance to keep Australia's second-innings score within reasonable bounds, but the more experienced Marsh now kept the impetus going expertly as yet a third left-hander, Gilmour, settled in, hopeful that he might extend the batting successes he had recently enjoyed in New Zealand and so save his place for the forthcoming tour of England. Having shaved off the beard he had recently acquired before coming in to bat, Gilmour hit one or two good offside strokes before playing on to his wicket a ball of full length from Lever.

Australia, however, were powerfully placed at tea, 302 for seven, and in the remaining time they were to take a still stronger grip. Marsh was the central figure as he pressed on from his tea score of 43 to within a few runs of his third Test hundred. Apart from his tendency to play outside the ball when forcing on the off-side off the back foot – he was lucky more than once, notably against Old – he defended solidly and occasionally unleashed a stroke of rugged power. If Old was the bowler who looked most likely to dismiss him, he was also the one who felt most strongly the weight of Marsh's bat as he straight-drove anything over-pitched with the relish of a forester felling a tree. England were tiring now and they had to settle for a policy of containment. The growing docility of the pitch was emphasised by the way that Lillee settled in and played with time to spare against the quicker bowlers. On a good batting wicket Lillee can sometimes look a stylish player and, like Marsh, who had until now had a poor season with the bat for Australia and for his own all-conquering state side, he reserves his best for England. 'Dennis we all love ya,' proclaimed a notice printed in red on white cloth, and he added more adoring members to his fan club with an innings which lasted an hour and a half and which helped Marsh add 76 for the eighth wicket. He was dropped by Old off Willis when 16 but Old himself eventually had him caught at cover to pave the way for a bizarre finale to the day.

It had been expected that Walker would come in at number ten and that McCosker, there now being no question of emergency, would not bat. But, with Australia's lead already 396, in he came, his jaw wired, his cheek cruelly bruised and swollen and his whole face so bandaged that he looked like the 'invisible man' beneath his green Australian cap. And, to add insult to England's unseen injury and glory to McCosker's all too visible one, he batted calmly through the best part of an hour, to extend Australia's lead by the end of the day to an apparently invincible 430.

England treated McCosker chivalrously. Since he had come in at such a stage Greig had every right to bring back Willis, the man who had broken his jaw, and to test him at once with bumpers. But he no doubt took into account the spirit of the occasion as well as the potential hostility of a crowd of 55,000, and Willis did not bowl again that evening. O'Keeffe acted as McCosker's runner and cheers greeted the new batsman as he calmly got into line to his first ball from Old. The ball was kept up to him initially but when he had made seven quiet runs Lever bowled two bouncers in an over, the second of which McCosker firmly and bravely struck for four.

The England bowlers were tired and the wicket was now placidity itself, and the nearest thing to a wicket in the final stages was from a typically swift pick-up in the field by the irrepressible Randall. If he had hit the stumps with his throw he would have run out Marsh for 85. But his accuracy, not for the first time on the tour, was less than his speed, the chance passed, and England's weary players left the field with the rest day ahead of them during which to ponder the extreme doubtfulness of their being able to break a world record fourth-innings score to win.

From the opening day one thing in particular had worried the organisers of the Centenary game. Her Majesty Queen Elizabeth II was due to visit the ground at three o'clock on the last afternoon of the match during the course of her Jubilee tour of Australia. It was apparent after the collapse of the two sides on the first two days that it would need a small miracle for the game to be in progress at such a late stage. But after a rainy rest day Melbourne produced another fine day, if a little cooler than before, on the

Wednesday, so no articifial (or natural) aid arose to extend the duration of the match. There was, however, plenty of help for the batsmen from a pitch growing steadily quieter, and it was this which gave the administrators and England supporters hope that the improvement shown by Australia's batsmen would be maintained by England's.

First, however, there was an hour of the Australian innings to go before Chappell decided to declare. The gallant McCosker defended skilfully whilst Marsh got the five runs required to make him the first Australian wicket-keeper to score a hundred against England. It was his third Test century and his rugged style had seldom served his side better. Two bouncers from Willis had McCosker, his face still monstrously swollen and his jaw wired, ducking low and he may have decided that his job was done when he perished to the second of two legside hooks off Old. The first brought him runs, the second he skied to Greig, who made no mistake with a swirling catch at midwicket.

Walker, who had been such a thorn in the flesh of the England bowlers of Denness's side, batted for 29 minutes without much trouble, indicating the increasingly benign nature of the pitch. However, Lillee has made the friendliest pitch look suddenly unplayable and Chappell decided at the end of the first hour that the time had come to let him loose.

England's theoretical target was 463 runs in ten hours and fifty minutes. Woolmer and Brearley were entrusted with the task of getting their side off to a good start and, with a little bit of luck, they survived some high-quality overs with the new ball from Lillee and Walker. Woolmer turned Lillee twice in his opening over for five runs in all but he was also beaten by a diabolical lifting outswinger. He played and missed once or twice more but generally batted well and took the brunt of the attack until in the last over before lunch, bowled by Walker, he pushed forward to an inswinger and looked a little unlucky to be given out by Max O'Connell. So his tour ended on the disappointing note with which it had begun and continued.

Woolmer's personal disappointment was soon forgotten as England batted through the remainder of the day and lost only one more wicket. It was just what the match needed to keep the interest alive, and it made for one of the most heartening days throughout the long MCC tour. Mike Brearley and Derek Randall were the two batsmen mainly responsible. They batted through the two hours of the afternoon with admirable devotion to a cause that history suggested was a hopeless one. Only twice in Test cricket had a side scored more than 400 to win. Bradman's Australians had scored 403 to beat England at Leeds in 1948, and Sunil Gavaskar and Gundappa Viswanath had piloted India to a remarkable 406 to beat the West Indies at Port-of-Spain two years before. Yet the length of time available meant that England were bound to get close to winning if they were to save the game, and there was never a time during the afternoon, in which Brearley and Randall added 85 runs, that they became totally bogged down. Indeed, thanks to some wayward overs after lunch from Gary Gilmour, they scored for a while at a very good rate. Gilmour, his confidence gone and his rhythm disrupted, partly because of an Achilles tendon injury, was hit for 29 in four overs, and Randall, often a nervous starter, was able to get his strokes going before Lillee was reintroduced into the attack.

The return of Lillee was sure to be a crucial point in the game and he soon had Brearley fending a ball just in front of the close fielders and both batsmen avoiding rapid short-pitched balls at the very last moment. But they survived and when Lillee was next brought into the attack for a short spell (with O'Keeffe settling into a long and steady one at the southern end) Randall became the first man in the match to hook him. His first hook brought him two, his second four to midwicket. Then he cut right off the meat of the bat but in the air. O'Keeffe in the gully did not see the ball which struck him full-toss on the wrist. Randall was then 42 not out and this was technically a chance, but it did not dissuade him from playing his shots for when Lillee again pitched short outside his off-stump he cut once more with perfect timing and this time the ball carried for four. He had scored 12 off the over and the spell cast by the ogre had, for the moment at least, been broken. The pitch, of course, was in the batsmen's favour now and soon after this surge of runs Randall, face red and cap askew, was cheerfully acknowledging the applause for his first Test fifty. It was a great and significant moment for English cricket. With his ability in the field, Randall had already impressed himself on Australians and now his timing, which had throughout MCC's tour suggested a class batsman, impressed them too. Frank Hayes had been the last relatively young English batsman to make a major impact and he had turned out to be a disappointment, but hope was growing all the time that there was a solid silver base to

Randall's glitter.

England were 113 for one at tea but in the first over afterwards Brearley's patient defensive innings of 43 ended when he was l.b.w. to a straight fast ball from Lillee. It was the fourth ball after the interval and England with two good men already gone were still 350 runs away from victory. In this sense, the pressure upon Dennis Amiss, as he came in to face his tormentor, was as great as ever. It was another crucial point in the match.

It certainly cannot be said that Amiss completely laid the Lillee bogey. Indeed, he was hustled into an unwise slash when he had scored only four and was missed at third slip by Hookes. He had hit the ball so hard, however, that it carried for four and with this little bit of luck Amiss settled in to weather the initial storm from Lillee and bat for the rest of the day. He watched with as much delight as any other Englishman as Randall continued to bat with authority at the other end. When the umpires intervened to stop play twenty minutes early, with the shadows of the stands covering the pitch, Randall was thirteen short of his first Test hundred; he had hit eight fours (two each off Lillee and Walker) and England's target had been reduced to 272 in six hours. The impossible was now merely the improbable.

The final day began with one of cricket's classic situations, and although the vast stadium was quickly filling with people there was an unnatural hush around the ground as Lillee opened the bowling to Randall. The new ball was due after thirteen overs, so it was mildly surprising that Lillee should have been unleashed at the start. On the other hand Chappell clearly wanted a quick wicket. It was soon evident that Randall and Amiss had no intentions of becoming bogged. Randall scored his first run of the morning with a cut in the air past gully, but the usual slips cordon was missing and the danger of such a shot was correspondingly less.

It was Randall, too, who hit the first four of the morning, a sweep to the fine-leg boundary off O'Keeffe, who then beat Randall with a leg-break and off the next ball appealed for a bat-pad catch to Cosier at short-leg. Randall was unconcerned. In the next over he cut Lillee in the air to third-man for four, a streaky sort of shot perhaps, but it took him to 99 and he dabbed the next ball towards fine-leg for his first Test hundred. Randall, just turned 26, had arrived and the game the world over had found a real character who could only enrich it.

If Amiss was overshadowed and betrayed a certain nervousness when he called Randall for a hasty and dangerous single to Cosier at midwicket, he still settled in safely and solidly. As an older war veteran than Randall he must have winced in sympathy when his partner drew away too late from a Lillee bouncer and was struck flush on the left-hand side of the head. Amiss insisted on Randall composing himself again, and after a five-minute delay he continued, apparently none the worse.

Amiss had just reached 50 in 148 minutes with three fours out of a stand of 112, taking the score to 225 for two, when sensational news which had been half-expected was announced by Australia's chairman of selectors, Phil Ridings. Dennis Lillee would not be going to England. Australia were simply half the side without him and later in the day he was to underline the profundity of the loss. But an X-ray which revealed a reopening of one of the stress fractures in his back which had first interrupted his career in 1972, plus the desire to see more of his wife and two young children and to take up his contract with Mr Packer, all combined to decide Lillee that a long rest was in every way in his own best interests. If he had gone to England with a suspect back he might have broken down irretrievably.

The news about Lillee seemed to have deflated his team-mates, but they looked to him again to use the new ball to break through. At first he ran in with all his old menace and no hint of pain. But this time Walker's support was inadequate; Randall cover-drove him handsomely for four, then repeated the shot with slightly less force but still enough to earn him an all-run four. After only two overs Walker was replaced by Walters and Randall greeted his medium pace with yet another glorious cover-drive. Soon Lillee shortened his run; even so Amiss looked apprehensive against him and Lillee once angrily shuffled his feet in imitation of Amiss's anxious foot movement across his crease. Still, however, it was the perky little figure of Randall, five foot eight inches and eleven stone of Nottinghamshire cheek, which held the stage. In the last over before lunch Lillee bowled a bouncer which narrowly evaded him as he backed awkwardly out of line at the last moment. Randall carried on backwards and casually continued the movement to execute a perfect back roll, pads, gloves and bat notwithstanding, before leaping to attention as if taking part in a gym display.

At the interval England were truly for the first time within sight

Above Amiss is yorked by Thomson in the first innings at Lord's and England are off to another bad start. *Below* Woolmer is run out by Walters, sprinting in from the covers – also in the first innings.

Above Hookes sweeps on the way to his 50 in the second innings; and Bob Woolmer hooks with Cowdreyesque authority in the course of his second Test hundred against Australia. *Below* Lever bowls Robinson for 11 in Australia's first innings.

of an amazing victory. They had batted through the morning as they had needed to without losing any wickets and they had managed to score 76 runs at a healthy enough rate as well as successfully negotiating the new ball. The score at lunch was 267 for two with Randall 129 not out and Amiss 63. Randall, in another purple patch straight after lunch, hit ten runs off an over from Lillee but soon afterwards Amiss's quiet but typically staunch and valuable innings came to an unexpected end when Chappell, who had introduced himself mainly to try to put pressure on the batsmen by cutting down their rate of scoring, got a ball to cut back off the seam and to whisk through low past Amiss's defences.

It was a surprising bonus to Chappell in the course of a crucial spell of steady medium-pace bowling, in which he took one for thirteen in ten eight-ball overs. Randall reduced the pressure with a superb force off the back foot past cover for four, a stroke of serene timing, but he was then dropped off Lillee with his score on 146 when he clipped a ball off his toes through the hands of Cosier at midwicket. This might have been an important nail in Australia's coffin if only Fletcher had been able to settle in and get going. But not for the first time Lillee produced a special delivery to dismiss him, a snorting ball which lifted steeply from just short of a length to take the edge of the bat and whistle through to Marsh. Thus, it seemed, did a disconsolate Fletcher, a cricketing enigma, depart for ever from the Test arena.

Greig walked out at 290 for four and immediately imposed his authority. He also made his plans clear enough by twice off-driving Lillee for majestic fours in the first over which he faced. A disaster nearly followed soon afterwards which might have resulted in Randall being run out for 160. Chappell roughly pushed him aside as he followed through to recover a ball played gently to mid-on by Greig. Randall turned to recover his ground but had not done so when Chappell's throw hurtled past the stumps. It would have been a most difficult decision for umpire Tom Brooks. When he was 161, Randall was actually given out by Brooks but then recalled when Marsh nobly admitted that he had not taken a catch off Chappell cleanly. Lillee by now was off and despite Greig's belligerent intentions his opposite number in company with Walker at his best again were making it very difficult for the batsmen to keep up the required rate. In eight overs only three scoring strokes were played, but then Randall broke the spell with two more sumptuous cover-drives. It was the cue for

Chappell to rest himself and to bring O'Keeffe into the attack, the signal for the final act of this intensely dramatic game.

To add further adornment to an unforgettable day's cricket (listened to through the night on radio's ball-by-ball commentary by many English listeners who could not bear to switch off) the Queen, in the course of her Jubilee tour of Australia, had arrived at the ground for a brief but exciting visit. She had just invested the ailing Sir Robert Menzies with the insignia of the Order of Australia and settled into her seat when, ten minutes before tea, Randall played forward to O'Keeffe, snicked the ball via his pad onto the legside and saw Cosier flop forward to hold the ball brilliantly in his outstretched left hand. Randall had batted for seven and a half hours. He had hit 21 fours and had really made the match. He walked back to deafening applause and, typically, got lost as he reached the shadow of the pavilion, walking towards the place where the Queen was sitting and then having to turn when he realised he wasn't heading for the dressing-room.

When Knott joined Greig, with only the tail to come, England's need was for 117 more runs in two hours and ten minutes. At tea the target was 109 in two hours with five wickets to fall, and with a splendid if foolhardy disdain for history the remaining batsmen decided during the tea interval that they would not allow the occasion to die by putting up the shutters and playing for a draw.

The teams were presented to the Queen during the tea interval, and the nerveless Lillee was brash enough to ask her, vainly, for her autograph, before going out again to have a decisive say in the last phase of the match. There are two schools of thought about England's approach after tea. One was that the glorious attempt to go for victory at all costs was in the proper spirit of the great game, which should apply in all Tests. Had the Ashes been at stake one doubts whether England would have continued to attack, but no one blamed them for doing so. The other opinion, with which I agreed, is that whilst Greig was right, certainly from the teatime position, to keep victory as his main aim he might actually have achieved it if only he and his other remaining batsmen had gone about attaining the runs with the same calculated approach with which so many one-day matches have been decided. But the policy was 'hell for leather', and the law of history, so firmly in favour of the bowling side in such a situation, was to triumph again.

Greig was out in the second over after tea, like Randall caught off bat and pad by Cosier òff O'Keeffe. This might have been the moment to switch policy if a draw had been of any interest to England, but Knott kept on swinging the bat daringly and, thrillingly, the runs kept coming. But, alas for England, they came only from one end. Old, whose immense cricketing ability is undoubtedly greater than his cricketing 'nous', did not give himself a chance to excel. With his powerful hitting he could have been the man to finish Australia off if only he had played himself in, but he tried to swing at once and the return of Lillee was all that was needed to end his brief innings. He was smartly taken by Chappell at first slip and Lever and Underwood soon followed, the first l.b.w. going back to O'Keeffe and the second bowled by Lillee, who, appropriately, was going to have the final word.

Since this was such an extraordinary contest there seemed only two ways now that the god of cricket might aptly finish it. The first would have been a fairy-tale last-wicket stand, with Lillee being hit for improbable fours by Willis before being recalled in desperation by Chappell to take the final wicket with the scores level and the match finishing in a tie. The other alternative was for the game to finish in a win for Australia by 45 runs, exactly as the first Test match had done 100 years before. And, as everyone knows, this is what happened. Knott was l.b.w. to Lillee very much as he had been in the first innings, and Australia had won at last the victory which had looked certain to be theirs from lunchtime on the third day. In the event they did not achieve it until ten past five and the second of the compulsory last fifteen overs of the final hour.

Lillee, with match figures of eleven for 165, was the hero and his colleagues carried him off in a triumph that was bitter-sweet. The summer ahead in England was bound to be less spectacular for his absence. It was difficult to believe that, after all his achievements, he was still only 27 years old, and everyone except those who have to bat against him will hope that he is fit to resume his Test career later. It was partly Lillee's decision not to tour and partly Randall's great innings which made one feel that, although Australia had deservedly won the Centenary Test match, England's team emerged from the unique occasion in higher spirits. Only a few hours after Randall had been given the 1,500-dollar award as man of the match, Australia's players had collected

9,000 dollars as winners and England 4,500 as losers, and the crowd of 31,000 had dragged themselves home, the Australian selectors announced their touring party of seventeen, and attention turned from the breathless drama of Melbourne towards the matches which lay ahead in England.

Melbourne March 12, 13, 14, 16, 17

Australia won by 45 runs

Australia

First Innings		Second Innings	
I. C. Davis lbw b Lever	5	c Knott b Greig	68
R. B. McCosker b Willis	4	(10) c Greig b Old	25
G. J. Cosier c Fletcher b Lever	10	(4) c Knott b Lever	4
*G. S. Chappell b Underwood	40	(3) b Old	2
D. Hookes c Greig b Old	17	(6) c Fletcher b Underwood	56
K. D. Walters c Greig b Willis	4	(5) c Knott b Greig	66
†R. W. Marsh c Knott b Old	28	not out	110
G. J. Gilmour c Greig b Old	4	b Lever	16
K. J. O'Keeffe c Brearley b Underwood	0	(2) c Willis b Old	14
D. K. Lillee not out	10	(9) c Amiss b Old	25
M. H. N. Walker b Underwood	2	not out	8
Extras (b4, lb2, nb8)	14	(lb10, nb15)	25
Total	138	(9 wkts dec.)	419

Fall of Wickets
1 – 11 2 – 13 3 – 23 4 – 45 5 – 51 6 – 102 7 – 114 8 – 117 9 – 136 10 – 138
1 – 33 2 – 40 3 – 53 4 – 132 5 – 187 6 – 244 7 – 277 8 – 353 9 – 407

Bowling	First Innings				Second Innings			
Lever	12	1	36	2	21	1	95	2
Willis	8	0	33	2	22	0	91	0
Old	12	4	39	3	27.6	2	104	4
Underwood	11.4	2	16	3	12	2	38	1
Greig					14	3	66	2

England

First Innings		Second Innings	
R. A. Woolmer c Chappell b Lillee	9	lbw b Walker	12
J. M. Brearley c Hookes b Lillee	12	lbw b Lillee	43
D. L. Underwood c Chappell b Walker	7	(10) b Lillee	7
D. W. Randall c Marsh b Lillee	4	(3) c Cosier b O'Keeffe	174
D. L. Amiss c O'Keeffe b Walker	4	(4) b Chappell	64
K. W. R. Fletcher c Marsh b Walker	4	(5) c Marsh b Lillee	1
*A. W. Greig b Walker	18	(6) c Cosier b O'Keeffe	41
†A. P. E. Knott lbw b Lillee	15	(7) lbw b Lillee	42
C. M. Old c Marsh b Lillee	3	(8) c Chappell b Lillee	2
J. K. Lever c Marsh b Lillee	11	(9) lbw b O'Keeffe	4
R. G. D. Willis not out	1	not out	5
Extras (b2, lb2, nb2, w1)	7	(b8, lb4, w3, nb7)	22
Total	95	Total	417

Fall of Wickets
1 – 19 2 – 30 3 – 34 4 – 40 5 – 40 6 – 61 7 – 65 8 – 78 9 – 86 10 – 95
1 – 28 2 – 113 3 – 279 4 – 290 5 – 346 6 – 369 7 – 380 8 – 385 9 – 410 10 – 417

Bowling	First Innings				Second Innings			
Lillee	13.3	2	26	6	34.4	7	139	5
Walker	15	3	54	4	22	4	83	1
O'Keeffe	1	0	4	0	33	6	108	3
Gilmour	5	3	4	0	4	0	29	0
Chappell					16	7	29	1
Walters					3	2	7	0

Umpires: M. O'Connell and T. Brooks. Toss won by England.

Chapter Two
A WEATHERBEATEN START

The absence of Dennis Lillee made the choice of Jeff Thomson for the tour of England all the more important. With these two in harness Australian teams had proved virtually unbeatable. They had overcome England 4–1 under Ian Chappell in 1974–75 and a year later overwhelmed the powerful West Indies batting to win the series 5–1. Another very talented batting side, Pakistan, toured Australia whilst MCC were in India. In the opening Test match at Adelaide Thomson had taken two early wickets when he ran to catch a ball skied into 'no-man's land' off his own bowling. Alan Turner, the thickly built New South Wales batsman, had also gone for the catch and the two collided heavily with their eyes still locked on the descending ball. Both were hurt but Thomson's injuries proved much more serious; dislocated joints in his right shoulder necessitated the insertion of a metal pin. He missed the remainder of the series, the Australian tour of New Zealand and the Centenary Test, and had Lillee been available to tour England it is less certain that Thomson would have been an automatic choice. As it was, the selectors demanded several rigorous fitness tests of his shoulder. He passed these to the satisfaction of everyone and took his place with the rest of the team just a month after having the metal pin removed.

In support of their main strike bowler the Australian selectors picked four other fast or fast-medium bowlers, but the name of Gary Gilmour was not amongst them. Gilmour was dropped ruthlessly but no doubt realistically after a poor display in the Centenary Test, when he had scored only 4 and 16 and, more significantly, had failed to take a wicket in the nine overs which Chappell had dared to give him. The sad fact was that Gilmour – who had first been capped against New Zealand in 1973 and then made a dramatic impact on the 1975 tour of England, where he had bowled the old enemy out with a superb display of swing bowling at Headingley in the semi-final of the Prudential World Cup when he took six for 14 and scored 28 not out and eventually forced his way back into the Test team – had completely lost his bowling rhythm, and with it all his confidence. So, after fifteen Tests he was discarded, just a few weeks after hitting his first Test century against New Zealand. In all Gilmour had scored 483 runs in his Tests at an average of 23 and taken 54 wickets at 26.04 runs apiece. I well recall Ted Dexter eulogising one day on Gilmour's rare ability to swing the ball late both ways. And here he was, out in the cold at the age of 25, but bolstered by the knowledge that he was safely inside Mr Kerry Packer's fold of rebellious sheep.

Gilmour's replacement was a steadier and more experienced version of himself, the greatly respected Geoff Dymock. He had played in one Test against England before, at Melbourne in 1975 when Thomson was unfit, Lillee broke down, and Denness and Fletcher made merry as England won by an innings. It was customary for people thereafter to sympathise with Dymock for 'choosing the wrong game to play in'; to which this cheerful Queenslander would reply: 'Rubbish; I'm just glad I played at all.' His reply when he was told that he was on the plane to England was equally forthright: 'You have to be bloody joking.' He was all the more amazed since only that week he had announced his retirement from first-class cricket because it was costing him too much money. Indeed he had had to borrow 400 dollars to pay for his visit to Melbourne to watch the Centenary Test. Yet though this well-built, honest performer with the fair curly hair and sparkling blue eyes was a surprise selection, he was also a thoroughly sound one. He had first appeared in Test cricket in 1973–74, taking seven wickets against New Zealand in his first game at Adelaide, and he appeared in the first two Tests in New Zealand in 1974 before losing his place to Gilmour, whose better batting always gave him the edge. When Thomson was injured early in the 1976–77 season, Dymock became Queensland's main spearhead (Tony Dell, another Queensland Test seamer, had also left the scene) and he responded by taking 35 wickets in nine Sheffield Shield matches at an average of 24.66. In truth, his selection was much less of a gamble than those of many others: he was a well-proven bowler with the great virtues of strength, an ability to bowl a persistent length and line and the added advantage of two seasons' experience in English conditions bowling for Milnrow in the Lancashire League.

Dymock, however, knew he would have to bowl very well in England this time to earn a Test place. His rivals were Thomson,

Max Walker and two bowlers quite new to English conditions, Len Pascoe and Mick Malone. Walker's qualities as a tireless, invariably dangerous swing bowler were universally known. It says much for his reputation, indeed, that he should have been considered a disappointment after taking 36 wickets on his first English tour at 29 runs each and 14 wickets in the four Test matches. My impression was that in 1975 Walker had been a slightly jaded cricketer. His performance in the Centenary Test proved that he had regained all his natural zest and was in itself a warning to England to beware complacency in the absence of Lillee.

Pascoe was the quickest of the bowlers after Thomson, whose friend he had been since they had opened the bowling together for the New South Wales club, Bankstown. On the recent tour of New Zealand Pascoe had been omitted in favour of Alan Hurst from Victoria, who had toured England successfully in 1975 but whose 1976–77 form was unimpressive. Another genuinely fast bowler, Wayne Prior (known, engagingly, by the nickname 'Fang'), was also in the running, but he too had been a disappointment of late. Pascoe, on the other hand, had taken 35 wickets at 19 runs each for New South Wales in the Sheffield Shield despite having to watch the first two games as twelfth man because Andy Roberts of the West Indies was bowling for the side as a hired mercenary – a young Australian thus held back by an overseas star as so many Englishmen have been in recent years. Now Pascoe was picked as the form horse at the age of 27, with the advantage of a six-feet two-inch, fourteen-stone frame which had stood up to hard treatment without any suggestion of a breakdown. The son of Yugoslav immigrants to Australia, who had changed his name from Durtanovitch, Pascoe's main passion off the field was surfing and like Thomson he had nearly given up cricket at one stage for the less demanding pleasures of the beach.

The fifth seamer in the party was the least experienced and, in a way, the most interesting, because he was essentially an English-style cricketer, a specialist swing bowler. Before the tour Australians freely compared him with another West Australian, Bob Massie, whose prodigious swing at Lord's in 1972 had reaped him sixteen wickets in the match. Malone, a six-feet three-inch schoolmaster, had been the outstanding bowler in Australian State cricket in 1976–77, taking 48 wickets in ten games, more than anyone since Sir Gary Sobers bowling for South Australia thirteen years before. He had done much, as an ideal foil to Lillee, to win the Sheffield Shield for Western Australia.

The bowling hand was completed by only two spinners. Kerry O'Keeffe, the senior one, had played with mixed success on his previous visits to England. Appearing for Somerset in 1971 he took 77 wickets, a very good performance for a young leg-spinner in his first year in county cricket, but he was not selected to tour with the Australians the following year and for Somerset this time could take only 19 first-class wickets. He returned to Australia having apparently lost the art of flight and bowling more off-spinners than orthodox leg-breaks. He came to England again in 1975, the year of the next Australian tour, but again he was not in the official party. This time he played under contract for the Lancashire League Club, East Lancashire, and more than earned his keep with over 1000 runs and 68 wickets. His performances for New South Wales improved, and when Ashley Mallett substituted the typewriter for the cricket ball as the main tool of his trade O'Keeffe returned to the Australian side in the absence of his other main rival, the leg-spinner Terry Jenner, who had also retired. Although he was only 27 when he arrived in England in 1977, O'Keeffe was by now an experienced cricketer, with 21 Tests behind him, and he was fortified by the knowledge that of his fifty Test wickets his dismissal of Greig and Randall in the Centenary Test had virtually decided the issue of that game in its final stage.

Ray Bright, a cheery, bulkily built young Victorian, began the tour with little chance of making the Test team as an orthodox left-arm spinner, and he therefore had everything to gain. But he had been chosen as a reliable bowler who had already made two successful tours of New Zealand and who also had the advantage of some experience in English conditions. In 1974 he took 73 wickets at an average of nine each for Ramsbottom in the Lancashire League, and for good measure he averaged 30 with the bat as well.

Potentially, indeed, this Australian team possessed a very capable bowling attack, though much was clearly going to depend upon Thomson's ability to act as the main cutting edge. It was a similar story with the batsmen, and in this department it was the captain Chappell who bore the main responsibility. He was the one specialist batsman who would, when the series began, have earned an automatic place in the traditional world eleven against Mars. Without the cares of captaincy he had batted brilliantly in

England in 1972, averaging 70 over the whole tour and 48 in the Test series, scoring memorable hundreds at both Lord's and the Oval. But after dominating the series in Australia in 1974–75, when he scored 608 runs, he made only 106 more runs in the four Tests of the English summer which followed. An operation to end persistent tonsillitis soon after this tour successfully recharged his batteries and in his first series as captain, against Clive Lloyd's West Indian touring team, he was once again the outstanding Australian batsman: cool, courageous and masterly. He had the ability to dominate the series which now lay ahead in England and, even more than Thomson, the key to the issue this time therefore lay in the hands of this quiet, slim man of military bearing. His captaincy had been generally successful, though questions were raised after defeat at the hands of the talented Pakistan team in Sydney in Australia's season just past, and he had earned the respect of his players not by words but by actions. Like his brother Ian, Greg Chappell does not waste words; he has always been self-possessed and visibly, yet also unostentatiously, tough.

Only two of the other batsmen had previously toured England. Doug Walters had frequently been a matchwinner all over the world, an Australian Denis Compton capable of turning games by daring, exuberant strokeplay and by scoring his runs that much faster than the average mortal. Yet in England in 1968, 1972 and 1975 he had been by any standards a disappointment and by his own a failure. This was assuredly his last chance to put the record straight. Something about England's green turf and cloudy skies had enabled the exponents of cut and swing to find the flaws in his technique which on faster or truer wickets abroad were masked by the quickness of eye and foot which make the sight of Walters in full flow one of the wonders of modern cricket.

The dark good looks and quiet, almost gentle mien of Richard Bede McCosker had first attracted notice in 1974 when, rather later than most Australians, he forced his way into the national team with a spate of high scores for New South Wales. He was an immediate success in Test cricket both at home and in England in 1975, and his broken jaw in the Centenary match at Melbourne was the first serious setback to his career. As an experienced opening batsman McCosker's batting expectations and responsibilities were second only to Chappell's. He arrived two weeks after the rest of the team, with the wire removed from his injured jaw, which was pronounced entirely mended.

The really exciting part of the Australian selection lay in the choice of the five young batsmen whose success or failure would in all probability make or break the tour. It is always said that Australian selectors give their players a longer chance to prove themselves than their English counterparts, but they proved ruthless enough on this occasion, discarding three players from the side which had recently toured New Zealand under Chappell. Gilmour and Hurst have already been mentioned. In addition, Alan Turner was left behind, although this solid, determined left-handed batsman had been a reasonable success in recent Australian Test sides. Bruce Laird, who had enjoyed a useful tour of England in 1975 as an opener without actually earning a Test place, was also overlooked, as were the claims of Martin Kent, an attacking right-hander who had greatly impressed other Test players when playing with an international touring team in South Africa, and Graham Yallop, discarded after a promising start to his Test career as a middle-order left-handed bat against the West Indies the season before. Instead the five men chosen to supplement Chappell, Walters and McCosker were three with brief Test experience – Ian Davis, Gary Cosier and David Hookes – and two with none at all, Craig Serjeant and Kim Hughes.

Davis had hitherto had a topsy-turvy career, playing his first Test at the age of only 20, losing his place for a time but then regaining it and gradually growing in confidence. The Centenary Test had been his twelfth for Australia, and although this neat and attractive strokeplayer had looked very vulnerable in the first innings against the moving ball he had sealed his place in the team with a steady and sensible knock in the second.

Although Cosier, like Gilmour, had fared so disappointingly in the Centenary game, he was retained in the team on the wider evidence of his 522 runs in nine Tests at an average of 40. He had already scored two Test hundreds, one against the West Indies in his first Test and the other a big innings of 168 against Pakistan. Moreover this solidly built redhead had been groomed for a place in Australia's team since his schooldays when he had represented national youth teams. He had much still to prove, but he had already shown himself to be a tough competitor.

One felt of both Davis and Cosier when the tour began that their potential was limited: it was the three virtually untested batsmen, Hookes, Hughes and Serjeant, who gave the side its novelty and youthful vitality. All were young batsmen of exciting ability.

Hookes had announced himself to the world in the Centenary Test and with the five Sheffield Shield centuries which had earned him his place. But he was not new to English cricket. Playing for one of the strongest of England's southern clubs, Dulwich, in 1975 he had at the age of 19 scored 1408 runs at an average of 83.52 and at a rate which had helped his club to win the Surrey Championship. Against Bexley he hit six sixes in an over off an unfortunate but experienced club bowler, Geoff Burton, and went on to score 125 in 78 minutes, turning probable defeat into victory. In addition Hookes took 78 wickets and held 23 catches for Dulwich that season.

Hughes had also played one season in the United Kingdom when spending a term as PE teacher at George Watson's College, Edinburgh. For Western Australia on the fast Perth wicket he had quickly developed as a commanding young player and he had done well on the tour to New Zealand without managing to force his way into the side for any of the three Tests. With his sunny temperament and fair curly hair and his expertise in the field, he was destined to be a popular tourist, not least with female spectators.

Serjeant's appearance had been relatively late by Australian standards, largely because he had put his career as a pharmacist before his career as a cricketer, but his rise from the time that he found a place in the powerful Western Australian team had been almost meteoric. He had played only ten first-class innings by the time he got to England but these had brought him 730 runs at an average of 66, and of his two centuries one had been a most impressive one against MCC. An alert, personable, mature 25-year-old, he was quickly to make an impact when the tour began.

The party was made up of two batsmen-wicket-keepers of great experience and high quality. Rodney Marsh was universally respected, but nowhere was his stock higher than in England. He had always seemed to reserve his finest performances for the old enemy, having begun with some erratic wicket-keeping displays against them in 1970–71 when he had been dubbed 'iron-gloves' because of all the chances that bounced out of his hands. These days he was a slimmer and a wiser cricketer. As brother of an equally talented international golfer it was the comparison between his earnings of about £16,000 a year and brother Graham's estimated £100,000 which was to strengthen the case of the cricket mercenaries.

Marsh's deputy was Richie Robinson, who had been to England on the previous tour and who, as captain of Victoria, had just had an outstanding season in the Sheffield Shield with four centuries. No one had played Dennis Lillee with such authority, and though his chances of displacing Marsh as wicket-keeper were slim he had every reason to hope that he might earn his first Test cap as a batsman, in the same way that Alan Knott's deputy, Roger Tolchard, had done for England in India the previous winter.

This, then, was the team which flew into London in late April, the lucrative contracts of thirteen of their number with a television company still at this stage a closely guarded secret. Any flight from one side of the world to another is gruelling, but the Australian party seemed to have come through their thirty hours in the aircraft remarkably well as they attended an opening press conference at the Waldorf Hotel in London. The manager, Len Maddocks, and captain Greg Chappell were in charge of proceedings and handled all the questions with patience and good humour. They had vocal encouragement from the two old sweats, Walters and Marsh, who, with a glass in each hand (and in Walters' case a cigarette hanging from his lips making him look like the original cartoonist's drunk), cheerfully yelled 'hear, hear' to everything that was said from the stage. Marsh's wits were sufficiently sharp, however; when Chappell was asked if he would be bowling much in the Test matches his vice-captain quickly cracked: 'I hope not.' The whole occasion was cheerful and friendly, almost an extension of the atmosphere which had attended the Centenary Test the previous month. I found myself wondering why one should think it amusing and in character for a couple of Australian cricketers to have made the most of the free drinks on the aircraft, whereas if MCC cricketers had so openly displayed their merriment at the start of a tour of Australia certain journalists and officials would at once have been carping at the deplorable lack of discipline being shown. This Australian side was dressed in anything that took their fancy; there were no team blazers, which is the least uniformity an MCC manager would have demanded of a side meeting the press on the first day of a tour. Yet one somehow knew of the Australians that on the field, unless Chappell were to lose his grip altogether, there would be discipline and uniformity enough.

Chappell said amongst other things that the chances for the

coming series were 'fifty-fifty', that Thomson was, yes really was, fully fit, and that he would not himself be retiring at the end of the tour although he might miss the tour of the West Indies for personal and business reasons. Maddocks soon made himself popular by having the good sense to agree that for once Australian players would not be barred from making statements to the media if they had done something outstanding on the field of play. Meanwhile, the first match of the domestic season was being played out in cold grey weather before a few spectators at Lord's. For those of us who genuinely believed in the abilities of the young batsmen gradually forcing their way into the County sides it was an encouraging game, even though the very first day of the season was, in traditional manner, a washout. Against the champion county, Middlesex, almost all the young hopefuls representing MCC played worthwhile innings. Bill Athey showed the soundness of his technique and a good range of strokes in his 20 and 33; Brian Rose, in two mixed innings of 30 and 44 not out, occasionally timed the ball very sweetly; David Gower, run out when going beautifully for 25, again looked to have an exceptional talent, and Ian Botham hit the ball with robust power in making fifty off 65 balls as well as taking five wickets for 60 in the match with his medium pace. Peter Willey, the most authoritative batsman in the game with 20 and 44 not out, Geoff Miller who struggled but stuck to it in now familiar vein in making 24, and the five Middlesex men in the running for a Test place – Brearley, Edmonds, Selvey, Barlow and Gatting – were all reminded of the extent of the competition.

Willey and Edmonds had the first chance to impress themselves on the Australians when they opposed them in the opening match of the tour at Arundel. Almost miraculously in a week of bitter weather and April showers, which were more like December downpours, the Duchess of Norfolk's match was blessed with a day of unrelieved sunshine. The day before, many cricket journalists had met in a mood of melancholy at the funeral of the greatly loved and respected cricket writer Clive Taylor, but at Arundel all was leafy hopefulness. This most beautiful of all cricket grounds does not attain its full majesty until the middle of the summer, when all those splendid trees are at the height of their glory and one looks through the gap between them to the mellow and unblemished folds of the Sussex countryside. But what a setting for the start of a tour of such great expectations!

It was decided to play a game limited to 45 overs per side, and the Australians opened with some attractive batting and a victory. Serjeant, opening the batting as an experiment, made the first impression on English spectators, hitting the ball solidly and with great assurance as befitted a player mature beyond his ten first-class matches. Chappell also began authoritatively. Hughes played one or two imperious strokes in the short stay at the wicket which the overs limit allowed, sparkling during an innings notable for quick footwork. The bowling figures suggest that Cosier was in devastating form – in fact he was rewarded for performing tidily at the crucial stage of the opposition's innings – but he, Dymock, Malone and Pascoe all made encouraging starts. For the Duchess's side Willey led the way with a succession of brilliant strokes, Randall also played well, and although the venerable Cowdrey, M. J. K. Smith and Murray did not get going, the result was in doubt long enough to keep a crowd of 5,000 or so in contented suspense about the outcome.

The first-class section of the tour began altogether less happily. Saturday, the last day of April, dawned bright and sunny in the Surrey countryside, though it was no surprise to me when I arrived at the Oval to find that the start of play had been delayed owing to rain and hail the previous day. There was a remarkably enthusiastic crowd there by the standards of the Oval, where the diehards tend to treat their cricket as a rather serious business. They had been told that play would start at twelve noon. A sharp downpour prevented this, but there was first surprise and then fury on the part of many when at about two o'clock it was briefly announced that the ground was now so wet that play was out of the question. The Surrey Secretary, Warren Sillitoe, a man used to dealing with awkward problems in his previous role as Army PRO in Northern Ireland, spent an unpleasant afternoon staving off irate Surrey members, whilst the Australians cheerfully exercised on the outfield in bright sunshine. Certainly, remembering the extraordinary end to the Oval Test of 1968 when the outfield was under water in the morning yet mopping-up operations by the crowd and the groundstaff proved so successful that Underwood was given time in the evening to bowl Australia to defeat, one wondered why no attempt to mop up the saturated turf was made on this occasion. The main difference, of course, was that in 1968, though it had been a wet summer, the ground had been drier before the downpour in question, whereas the Australians now were the victims of a wet spring which meant slow-drying grounds even when the rain abated. There were two positive results following from everyone's disappointment at the Oval: the Surrey committee decided to look into the antiquated mopping-up equipment at the command of Harry Brind and his groundstaff, and it was decided in future to give the crowd 'pass-out' tickets in the event of their paying in future for no entertainment.

Actually, on this occasion, those who stayed did get *some* recompense by watching the Australians whiling away the afternoon in their own special way. Greg Chappell conducted a rigorous fielding practice, which was followed by an energetic game of 'catch football' – an impromptu game played with a cricket ball and two goals. The participants may pass the ball forward or back whilst running at speed, and it looked good fun to play unless you happened to be the goalkeeper. It was a game played by frustrated men destined to become even more bored as they dodged the cold, relentless showers of a less than merry month of May. One wondered if in future it might not be better for a touring side spending the whole summer in England to arrive at the end of May rather than the end of April. The 1975 Australians were luckier in this respect, not beginning their official tour until the end of the Prudential World Cup in June. That competition was played in perfect weather despite the fact that on 2 June 1975 play had to cease at Buxton in Derbyshire because the ground was covered by an inch of snow.

The second day of the match against Surrey was played in gloomy light and a cool temperature. For Surrey it was a day of useful batting practice, for the touring team a badly needed work-out in the field. Walker, with a 14-over spell of three for 31 in the afternoon, confirmed his status as the side's most reliable bowler, but the two other seamers made a good impression as well. Dymock looked the experienced cricketer he is, bowling 24 overs of tidy line and length. Pascoe, his run-up looking like a combination of Dennis Lillee and Alan Ward but his delivery stride lacking the magnificent final stretch of Lillee (and most other truly fast bowlers), nevertheless bowled with some hostility and it was not hard to imagine him being a useful support for Thomson if the latter really started to fire later in the tour. (Thomson had withdrawn from this game having jarred his right elbow, the result of trying to bowl too fast too early during net practice.) O'Keeffe, likely at this stage to be the only spinner in the Test side, also bowled well against Surrey, flighting the ball and occasionally getting his leg-spinner to turn and bounce on a generally unresponsive pitch.

Two England Test players excelled for Surrey. Graham Roope, who had a poor 1976 season after an unnerving experience early on against Michael Holding – when he seemed to be playing more balls with the back of his head or his back than with the bat – played this time more like the man who had helped to fight England out of a deep hole against Lillee and Thomson at the Oval in 1975. He timed the ball increasingly sweetly in his 107 not out, hitting twelve fours and reaching his century with the second of his sixes. He drove with splendid freedom, cut and hooked too, and at the end of the grey day he was batting really magnificently, though he had begun in such a sticky way that his immense natural talent was well concealed and his sixteenth first-class hundred looked very unlikely to be reached. In contrast, John Edrich had earlier looked as though he was going to get *his* 100th first-class century, against an Australian touring team – the ideal opponents to concede him that honour bearing in mind his remarkable record against them. He had, for instance, scored a century against them in 1972, when Surrey had last played an Australian touring team, and he had hit seven Test hundreds against Australia. But this time, after nudging his unspectacular but infuriatingly solid way to 70, he drove at a wide slanting delivery from Walker and edged to Marsh.

We were all looking forward to seeing the Australian reply to Surrey's good score on an Oval pitch that was even slower, according to Roope, than the one on which Australia and England had ground out their high-scoring draw two years before. But it was not to be. The rain returned. Nor was it confined to London: when the Australians arrived, eager now to the point of desperation, at Canterbury, they were granted just 135 minutes to bat after Chappell had won the toss, before rain set in again. Ian Davis, receiving his first ball in first-class cricket in England, played across an outswinger of full length from Kevin Jarvis and was bowled. But Serjeant confirmed the good impression he had made at Arundel. He hit 55 at a healthy rate with several potent drives and was particularly severe on the legside. Hughes, neat and balanced, struggled through a bad patch to reach 34 not out, and then, when play resumed two days later, he batted with greater freedom to total 80 before falling to the off-spin of Graham

Johnson on a drying pitch. There was time on the last afternoon for the faithful and hopeful Canterbury folk to see Jeff Thomson bowl his first ball in first-class cricket for five months. He operated at little more than half-speed for three overs, but in the last of them fell foul of umpire Bill Alley, who called him four times for overstepping the front crease, a problem which had plagued him on his last tour of England.

As for Kent, who had beaten the 1975 Australian team when Colin Cowdrey suddenly shed his years and played an innings of genius, there was little to rejoice about this time except perhaps for a distinguished first scalp for Colin's son Christopher who had Doug Walters caught at slip. Jarvis, too, now established as one of the best young seam bowlers in the country, must have been encouraged by dismissing both Davis and Cosier for ducks with the new ball.

Hove in Sussex was the next port-of-call, and the weather proved equally squally. A crowd of some 5,000 waited patiently between persistent showers on the Saturday, but all they saw was 35 minutes' cricket, in which time the hapless Davis succumbed again, this time to one John Snow, and Serjeant gained more good marks by resolutely hooking both Snow and Imran Khan, the Pakistan Test bowler who had humbled Australia at Sydney a few months before and who was now playing for Sussex after leaving Worcestershire in an atmosphere of some bitterness. Khan was not to take a wicket in this match; Serjeant was to continue between the interminable showers towards another fifty – his third in as many innings – but all that happened at Hove and everywhere else on the cricket fields of England in the next few days was to be robbed of significance by the shattering news which burst like a shell upon a little-suspecting world on Monday 9 May.

Chapter Three
THE EARLY MATCHES
AND THE ONE-DAY
INTERNATIONALS

Not until the initial hullabaloo surrounding the astonishing announcement of the challenge to Test cricket by the 'Packer circus' had died down did the English weather relent and the Australian touring team begin to get down to serious match practice. The game against Hampshire was a complete washout, making a total of eight blank playing days out of a possible thirteen. Instead of the 78 scheduled hours of first-class play, the Australians had been in action for only thirteen hours by the time that the first day of the Glamorgan match at Swansea had also been rained off. But at last the clouds lifted, and in two full days against the Welsh county batsmen and bowlers alike brushed away some of the cobwebs.

For some time, however, the combination of scant practice, inexperience and the worry over what might happen to the players when they got home conspired to produce performances which were barely recognisable as those by an Australian touring team following in the footsteps of the Bradmans and the Ponsfords long ago. At Swansea the bowlers did well enough, dismissing the opposition cheaply despite good innings from the unrelated Jones's – Alan, the experienced craftsman, and Alan Lewis, the promising apprentice – but the skilful late swing of Malcolm Nash undermined the batting and only Cosier reached fifty in the Australian innings. Indeed, in their second innings, after Alan Jones had boldly declared, visions of famous Glamorgan victories against Australian sides of the past (in 1964 and 1968) were aroused, until the spinners O'Keeffe and Bright saved the day with an undefeated seventh-wicket stand.

At Bath there was no such escape. This time the touring team encountered a true wicket and three sunny days. Chappell won the toss and, playing against his old county, scored a lordly century, failing by only one run to reach his hundred before lunch. He was especially severe on the enormous six-foot eight-inch Barbadian Joel Garner who, maturing with his experience in Lancashire League cricket, had stepped into the breach left by injuries to Holding and Daniel the previous winter and who, with another new fast bowler, Colin Croft, had kept his country on the winning trail. This was his first appearance as a midweek signing for Somerset, and once Chappell had impressed his world-class abilities upon him Garner responded effectively to finish with four good wickets. That loyal man of Somerset, Graham Burgess, mopped up the tail with his medium-pace swingers to finish with five for 25, and but for Chappell's innings a barely respectable total would have been paltry indeed.

When they batted Somerset emphasised that no blame could be laid at the door of the pitch at the Recreation Ground, once a familiar place to Bert Lock in his role as inspector of pitches. The main contributors in Somerset's first innings were both young Englishmen in their twenties – Brian Rose, who made a steady and at times elegant century, and Ian Botham, who hit 59 at a run a minute with three powerful sixes and six fours. Botham is both a no-nonsense cricketer and a no-nonsense character. The previous winter, whilst he was on a Whitbread cricket scholarship in Melbourne, he warned Ian Chappell that if he continued to bait him he would have to 'belt him one'. He was as good as his word.

After Botham had impressed himself firmly on the occasion Philip Slocombe, who batted so well in his first year for Somerset in 1975 that he was picked for the MCC side against the Australians at Lord's and thoroughly justified his choice, also made an attractive fifty. Slocombe, like so many cricketers who make an impact in their first year, had been much less successful in his second, so this was an especially encouraging performance. Close declared, with typical enterprise, with Slocombe and Rose in full cry. The Australians accepted the challenge, Serjeant making another fifty and Hookes getting going for the first time, stroking four sixes and 13 fours in an elegant innings of 85 not out. He proceeded to his hundred next day, remarkably off only 81 balls, but the last six Australian wickets fell in the first session of the third day and Somerset were left with 182 to make in 220 minutes. Despite some overs from Thomson at something like his full ferocious pace, Viv Richards contributed a timely fifty and Botham knocked off the runs with great confidence and maturity at the end. Since 1893 and before this match Somerset had entertained Australian touring teams on 21 occasions, losing twelve times and never winning. It was one more feather in Brian Close's copiously plumed cap.

The Australians pronounced themselves to be quite unworried. They had come to win Test matches. In any case they soon rebounded with a win themselves, defeating Gloucestershire at Bristol by 173 runs with a day to spare on a pitch of uneven bounce which helped to produce some extraordinary bowling performances. On the first day Brian Brain, rejected by Worcestershire, yet still on his day as hostile a fast bowler as any in England, took seven for 51 and Max Walker retaliated with seven for 19. Greg Chappell then demonstrated his cool mastery over bowlers and conditions alike by scoring his second century in successive games, and he paid particular attention to Brain, hitting him for five fours with pulls, drives and a typical clip off his legs during a spell of six overs which clearly showed who was the real master. Julian Shackleton, son of Derek of Hampshire and England, and a bowler of similar type, had the satisfaction of taking Chappell's wicket in both innings. Gloucestershire never looked like getting anywhere near the 342 they needed to win, and this time it was Pascoe, fiery and accurate, and Bright, benefiting from some rash batting, who did the job. Having beaten Gloucestershire in the serious contest, the touring team asked for an extra 45-over match on the third day and won this one too with Doug Walters finding something like his true form at last. They then travelled back to London for the first important match of the tour, the three-day game against MCC at Lord's.

The England selectors had picked an interesting MCC side, captained by Mike Brearley, who was officially appointed England captain for the three One-Day Internationals on the second day of the Lord's match. His opening partner was the 19-year-old Yorkshireman Bill Athey, and they were followed by a string of promising batsmen in their twenties, Randall, Barlow, Willey, Miller, Botham, and Edmonds. A reserve Test attack was chosen with Mike Hendrick, still to do himself justice at Test level, asked to open the bowling with Allan Jones, the lanky fast bowler who had at last found a home at Middlesex under Brearley after a chequered career at Sussex and Somerset. The spinners were Miller and Edmonds with Willey's off-spin in reserve, and Botham lent support to the front-line seamers. Competition amongst them was heightened by the fact that on the day before the match Chris Old strained a muscle behind his left shoulder while playing a Benson and Hedges match against Essex and was pronounced unfit for the One-Day Internationals. It turned out that the prognosis was unduly pessimistic but this was apparently a severe setback for English hopes. A fit Old was an automatic choice, and he had just been approaching his best form with some fine bowling performances for Yorkshire.

One man's misfortune, however, is often another's good luck and on the first day of the match at Lord's Mike Hendrick bowled himself back into England contention with a performance of sustained, accurate and hostile bowling. Hostile is not an adjective one usually uses in connection with Hendrick, but with a strong gale behind him from the Nursery End and a pitch as fast as any first-class cricketer had seen all season, his deliveries from a model high action were both quick and bouncy. Jones also bowled very well and Brearley was able to keep the seamers going down wind whilst using Edmonds and Miller into it. It was Miller who had the greater success, and the two men from Derbyshire took seven Australian wickets between them.

McCosker gradually got the feel of things again before contributing to his own downfall with a lamentable steer into the slips. Chappell also got past 20 but the only innings of substance was played by Kim Hughes, who kept his head down and worked hard, reaching 60 before he danced down the pitch and tried to hit Miller where Albert Trott once hit Monty Noble. MCC were soon taking their turn on the lively pitch but only twice in their brief innings did it look as though the batsmen might settle. They began disastrously, losing Athey to a catch at the wicket off Walker and Brearley brilliantly run out by Serjeant as he pushed a ball from Thomson just wide of gully's right hand and meandered up the pitch looking for a run which was not there. The fact that Thomson was the bowler may not have been insignificant and although he did not get a wicket on the first day he began to fire on all cylinders on the second morning. Randall and Barlow played him well during an attractive stand of 46 at a run a minute which, as it transpired, was to be the best of the innings. Barlow was l.b.w. to Dymock, the fourth time in six innings that he had been leg-before this season, and MCC finished the first day at 70 for three.

There was still enough wind cutting down from the Nursery End for Thomson to be a hasty proposition on the gorgeously sunny second day. Randall, who had been missed by Chappell at slip off Walker the previous evening, played some glorious off-drives but just when he had reached a fine fifty with his seventh four he was l.b.w. to a ball which Thomson got to move back and keep a little low. Willey and Miller both laid the foundations of an innings, but both got out, Willey to a slip catch off Thomson and Miller to a legside tickle off O'Keeffe. The latter had his best bowl of the tour from the Nursery End, and with Hendrick unable to bat after cutting the little finger of his right hand whilst fielding, the MCC innings ended with a deficit of 58.

This time the Australian batsmen buckled down to batting on the dry pitch with sterner application. The cricket during the second afternoon had a Test match feel about it, although Serjeant got a touch as he flashed at Jones. Before an admirably polite crowd McCosker and Chappell batted with almost grim resolution through most of the sunlit afternoon. Chappell was moving into top gear when he drove a ball from Edmonds high into the onside and saw Athey run to his left from deep mid-on to take a brilliant diving two-handed catch. Cosier decided that the afternoon merited some entertainment from the batsmen and hit both Edmonds and Miller for six over the close Tavern boundary. But he perished attempting an encore and the day ended with the bowlers back on top as Botham removed McCosker for 73 and Hughes for five in a hostile spell.

The Australians were strongly placed when the third day began but they lost their last five wickets for 62 in an hour and ten minutes, during which the MCC bowling and fielding maintained the very high standard it had set from the start. Botham shone brightest with three catches, the last a beauty low to his left at second slip. Hendrick, the thankful bowler, continued to keep a model length and line, picking up three more wickets with the new ball, and Miller's off-spin was again tidy and testing. So MCC were left with the task of scoring 294 in about 270 minutes on a pitch still full of pace and life which was giving a chance both to batsmen and to bowlers.

They started well despite the disappointment of losing Athey, caught behind the wicket again as he was beaten for pace by Thomson. So ferociously fast was this delivery that Marsh took it one-handed over his head and was almost knocked off his feet by the ball's impetus. After this, Randall and Brearley settled down to play some attractive cricket, although England's newly appointed captain was often late to pick up Thomson's flight: when you have only a third of a second to make your mind up you need to have very sharp reactions to be *early*. But Brearley is, and always has been, a worker, and he battled through the dangerous period with the new ball to add exactly 100 with Randall, who again played beautifully: Randall scoring 51 in 92 balls, Brearley 47 in 126. When the former was out to O'Keeffe (Chappell taking a lovely diving catch in the deep) and the latter to Dymock, MCC's chances of recording their first win in this fixture since 1909 receded.

Willey disappointed, as in the first innings, but Barlow and Miller got the scoreboard moving again, Barlow thumping the ball away across a fast outfield with great panache and Miller accumulating in his calm, stylish and orthodox manner. With Barlow leading the way they put on 45 together in a mere 22 minutes, but the return of Thomson signalled the end of the fun. He yorked Miller l.b.w. and two balls later took revenge on Botham, who snicked a rapid off-stump delivery to Marsh.

An entertaining match was still not over because in the second of the last twenty overs Edmonds drove O'Keeffe handsomely into the pavilion and then for four to the Tavern to take MCC past 200. Barlow reached a well-merited 50 with a typical quick single in the next over, and with 17 overs left the touring team needed to get four more wickets, MCC 92 more runs. From the moment, however, that Barlow stepped out to hit O'Keeffe and was smartly stumped by Marsh, the game was over because three genuine tail-enders were now exposed. O'Keeffe again served his side well at a crucial moment and with plenty of time to spare the Australians had won the first major match of their tour by 79 runs. They now travelled up to Worcester to do battle with a largely young and enthusiastic county side still doing its best to recover from the shock of losing its star overseas player, Imran Khan, and of hearing that the Cricket Council had, on appeal from Sussex, overruled the registration committee of the TCCB and permitted him to play for his new county from the end of July.

Worcestershire were also without Basil D'Oliveira, but they still managed to draw the match honourably with their loyal and consistent opening batsman Alan Ormrod scoring fifties in both innings and Glenn Turner also getting one. Chappell called correctly when he tossed up with Worcestershire's respected captain Norman Gifford, and on a beautiful Saturday morning was soon personally testing whether or not Worcester's pitch, in the shadow of the cathedral beside meadows leading from the tranquil sweep of the River Severn, was still one of the best in the land. Chappell came in after a pedestrian opening partnership between McCosker and Davis, the latter determined to play a long innings, and at once the captain's batting was seen to be on a higher plane. He made a sumptuous and commanding century, then retired with a bruised knee. Hookes failed once again but Robinson and Walters played in characteristically buccaneering vein before falling respectively to the experienced left-arm spin of Gifford and the developing off-spin of Dipak Patel. (Patel, an East African-born all-rounder of great promise who had come to England as a child, has the ability to become the first such immigrant to win a Test cap.)

Davis and Chappell again made some runs in the second innings and Cosier scored 44 but without doing enough to maintain his place in the representative team. He was replaced by Serjeant in the side for the first of the 55-over One-Day Internationals for the Prudential Trophy, played in hot sunshine at Old Trafford on 2 June before an enthusiastic crowd which appeared to be in excess of the official estimate of 15,000. This was the only change in the Australian batting line-up compared with the team for the Centenary Test, but stiffness and soreness in Thomson's right arm just above the elbow prevented him leading the attack, and the places occupied at Melbourne by Lillee and Gilmour went on this occasion to Pascoe and Malone, with O'Keeffe and Walker making up the attack. Without Thomson, with Walters so unreliable and the batting so heavily dependent on Chappell, it was not an Australian side to make the opposition blanch, and England duly won the first of the £2,000 prizes.

Captained by Brearley for the first time, England left three of the younger men out of their squad of fourteen – Hendrick, Botham and Miller. Of those who had played in the Centenary Test, Fletcher and Woolmer, the latter being penalised for his disappointing tour of India despite a good start to the season with Kent, were omitted. Only five of those in the England squad had said goodbye to their twenties, and with Barlow and Randall at numbers three and four in the order we knew that this team would lack neither enterprise with the bat nor dash in the field. It was in the field, indeed, that England won the game, only for brief moments relinquishing the firm grip they took when in the first three overs they dismissed Davis and McCosker with only two runs on the board. Lever captured the first wicket with the aid of a beautiful low left-handed slip catch by Greig, and McCosker fell to a short delivery from Willis and a smart catch by Knott. The more significant event was Greig's catch. The British public were still furiously debating the rights and wrongs of what he had done vis-à-vis Packer, and it was uncertain how the crowd would react when he took the field, physically dwarfing his successor, who had clearly said that he respected Greig as a captain and would not hesitate to take advice from him now. This early flash of brilliance from the self-conscious 'super-star' won the crowd to his side and when he came out to bat later in the day the noisy reception he received was mostly in his favour. Had he dropped that chance and bowled badly when Brearley turned to him as his sixth bowler, he might have been less popular. Indeed it was a bad day altogether for those who believed that the established form of Test cricket was threatened by the coup by the leading players, because Kerry Packer appeared that night on David Frost's television programme and was allowed to say what he wanted without effective counter-argument. Greig had been cheered by a cricket crowd in the day and Packer was now cheered by a non-cricket studio audience in the evening. But the main debate had hardly begun.

England's players, rebels and otherwise, were presenting a united front. Whether or not any resented what Greig, Knott, Underwood and Snow had done, or rather the way they had done it, there was a universal determination to rekindle the great spirit of the winter tour when Greig's power and popularity had been at their brief zenith. They all owed it to Brearley, of course, to play as a team, and none can have envied him his task, taking on the leadership in these embarrassing circumstances while at the same time needing to justify his place in the side as a batsman and concentrating on the problems of 55-over cricket.

Brearley began well. After the two early breakthroughs he kept the pressure on the Australian batsmen, and although Chappell and Serjeant patiently played their way out of trouble, tight bowling and razor-sharp fielding eventually caused both to perish in a desperate search for quicker runs. Walters was confronted by Old when he came in, and two gullies were especially posted for his streaky shots on the offside. He dutifully obliged by hitting the ball straight at one of them before he had scored. Brearley now introduced Greig and in his first over he persuaded Serjeant to hit a catch to midwicket and had Hookes caught behind, much to Greig's exaggerated delight and the batsman's ostentatious fury. Australia were reduced to 94 for six. However Marsh, with legside hitting of brutal force, made a game of it. In 29 balls he scored 42, twice driving full-length balls from Lever over long-on for six. But Lever never lets himself be panicked into forgetting the basic rules. He kept on bowling straight and attacking the stumps and soon enough Marsh swung across a yorker and missed. His batting was thrilling whilst it lasted and it made the match, so that Geoff Pullar's decision to award him the £200 prize as Man of the Match was absolutely justified.

For all Marsh's muscular mayhem, Australia's total of 169 for 9 was less than adequate. England knew that with no Thomson to trouble them they merely had to play sensibly to win. Amiss, alas, was in one of the streaky moods he often seems to reserve for Australia. He began by flailing furiously at anything near his off-stump, and one felt that his dismissal was as inevitable as Walters' had been. For some reason his many failures against Australia seem to have dissuaded him from grafting against them in the way that he usually does against other teams. On this occasion he fell to a superb diving catch by Serjeant, right-handed and at full stretch. Walker was the bowler and the dismissal was similar to many which had occurred in Australia on the last MCC tour, when Amiss had so often been the victim of brilliant catches off Walker or Lillee.

Randall made an immediate impact. He leant forward to the first ball from Walker and steered it through the covers for four, almost unintentionally, then swayed into the next ball, a half-volley on his leg-stump, and creamed it for four more to midwicket. Brearley, apart from two risky upper-cuts off Pascoe, who was doing his best to look as hostile as Lillee and not playing the part at all badly, also batted well. Then Malone came on from the Stretford End. With his mop of black curls and powerful build, Mick Malone looks like the Irish labourer his name suggests. He has perhaps the finest action of any medium-fast bowler playing international cricket, and Alec Bedser must have seen in him one of his potentially authentic successors. A lovely late outswinger found the edge of Randall's bat and gave McCosker the chance to take a good slip catch, and when Brearley tried to pull a ball barely short of a length he was l.b.w. This was a pity because England were well up with the clock and their new captain was gathering runs at a perfectly healthy rate. Normally a slow scorer, he may subconsciously have been trying to press for runs unduly because of press comments that he was not the right sort of player to open in a one-day match.

Brearley's fall at 71 kept Australia in the game, and when Willey, who was going through an unlucky phase, top-edged a sweep off O'Keeffe straight to Walker at fine-leg they were in with a chance of winning for the first time. Enter Greig, to a mixed reception, though Barlow stole his thunder somewhat, counter-acting Malone's basic swing into the left-hander by swinging several fours hard and high to the onside boundary. Greig played his part too, hitting one magnificent off-drive off O'Keeffe, and England were sailing home on a fair breeze. But Greig, who might have been expected to attempt a low profile for a change in Brearley's first game as captain, was starting to play to the gallery and he now committed suicide by dashing up the wicket to run an impossible leg-bye. He turned to see the bowler, Pascoe, pick up the ball, sprint to the stumps at Greig's end and remove the bails with the batsman beaten by a neck to the winning post.

This was quite an original way of getting out, but Barlow was not to be outdone. He played a ball to Malone at fine-leg, took a safe single, walked up the pitch a few yards whilst he considered the second and rejected it as Malone's throw came over the stumps to Marsh. He then sauntered towards his crease like a man going for a peaceful stroll in the park, unaware of the fact that Marsh was taking aim from the far end. The wicket-keeper's throw shattered the stumps a split second before Barlow completed the formality of putting his bat down and suddenly the cruise towards an impressive victory became an exciting scramble towards a tight one. Forty-four runs were still needed by England with 11 overs in hand but only four wickets to play with and two new batsmen at the crease. Fortunately for England, the last two players with serious batting pretensions restored their team's advantage with some bold hitting, and by the time that Old was caught off a long-hop from Walker, having driven and cut his way to a handsome 25, Australia were looking for miracles again. Lever was out quickly with two runs still wanted but Pascoe bowled a bouncer to Knott which umpire Constant adjudged a wide under the Prudential's special rules, and a cracking square-cut two balls later assured England of the £2,000 cheque. Or did it? Since the Prudential Internationals began in 1972 it had usually been the custom to share the prize-money regardless of the result, which the sponsors quite rightly deplored. The matches this time were played seriously enough, but one got the impression that when the Australians lost the series they did not consider that the end of the world had come. For an Australian to lose and decide that the world is still in existence is against the natural order of things.

Australia

R. B. McCosker c Knott b Willis	1
I. C. Davis c Greig b Lever	1
*G. S. Chappell lbw b Underwood	30
C. S. Serjeant c Randall b Greig	46
K. D. Walters c Amiss b Old	0
D. W. Hookes c Knott b Greig	11
R. W. Marsh b Lever	42
K. J. O'Keeffe not out	16
M. H. N. Walker c Barlow b Underwood	5
M. F. Malone c Brearley b Underwood	4
L. S. Pascoe not out	4
Extras (b4, lb4, nb1)	9
Total (9 wkts, 55 overs)	169

Bowling
R. Willis 8–2–16–1, J. K. Lever 10–1–45–2, D. L. Underwood 11–1–29–3, C. M. Old 11–3–30–1, P. Willey 11–1–30–0, A. W. Greig 4–0–11–2.

England

D. L. Amiss c Serjeant b Walker	8
J. M. Brearley lbw b Malone	29
D. W. Randall c McCosker b Malone	19
G. D. Barlow run out	42
P. Willey c Walker b O'Keeffe	1
A. W. Greig run out	22
A. P. E. Knott not out	21
C. M. Old c Hookes b Walker	25
J. K. Lever c Walters b Walker	1
D. L. Underwood not out	0
Extras (b1, lb3, w1)	5
Total (8 wkts, 45.2 overs)	173

Bowling
Pascoe 10.2–1–44–0, Walker 7–3–20–3, Malone 11–1–37–2, O'Keeffe 11–3–36–1, Chappell 6–1–31–0.

Fall of Wickets
1 – 2   2 – 2   3 – 55 4 – 62 5 – 93   6 – 94   7 – 145 8 – 152 9 – 156
1 – 17 2 – 51 3 – 70 4 – 71 5 – 123 6 – 125 7 – 160 8 – 168

Umpires: D. J. Constant and B. J. Meyer.

Although the tour had begun earlier than the Australians would have wished in order to accommodate matches against all seventeen first-class counties, plus the international matches, the itinerary had been skilfully planned to cut travelling to a minimum, and it was only a relatively short hop down the motorway from Manchester to Birmingham, where rather than taking anxiously to the nets after their defeat the Australians instead made eagerly for Edgbaston Golf Club. I was fortunate enough on the same day to go round the newly opened Brabazon Course at The Belfry in Sutton Coldfield, remarkably well established considering the exceptionally arid and then unusually wet weather in which it had perforce to grow up. The PGA now have their headquarters here rather than at the Kennington Oval, where for years they were tucked away incongruously, and the plan is for the American-style course to stage major tournaments in the future including the Ryder Cup match with the United States. It is unusual too in that it is a club without members where any itinerant player is welcomed. But occasional golfers such as myself, more prone to strike the small white ball through the covers along the ground rather than straight back over the bowler's head and far over the sightscreen, should be warned that cavernous water hazards apparently possess remarkably powerful magnets.

It was back to work for everyone on Saturday. Though it was grey and cloudy in Birmingham, though England's and Scotland's footballers were doing ridiculously belated summer battle at Wembley, and though the Jubilee celebrations were moving into full swing in parishes large and small throughout Britain, there was still a large crowd at Edgbaston's superbly appointed ground to see England proceed to another victory.

From an early stage an air of unreality hung about the game. Chappell won the toss and asked England to bat, correctly anticipating that the ball would swing under cloudy skies. Amiss and Brearley started confidently enough against Thomson and Malone, the former playing after an announcement the previous night that he would not be fit, but Chappell brought himself into the attack early and soon got his away-swingers to bend. He began an efficient morning's work by trapping Brearley with a ball which kept low and cut back, and next ball delivered a speculative bouncer to Randall who, unable to resist, went for the hook and snicked to Marsh.

Amiss and Barlow, with many good strokes, took England to 67 before Barlow spooned a catch to wide mid-on. Cosier now joined the attack, bowling late in-duckers from a deceptively dilettante action, and suddenly a rash of over-ambitious strokes led

England into serious trouble. Willey, Amiss, Greig and Knott perished in quick succession and at lunch England were 90 for seven after a mere 28 overs. Chappell had taken four for 12 off eight overs and Cosier three for four from four. Thomson alone had been expensive, frequently overpitching, and it had really only been by chance that Malone and Walker had not picked up any wickets between them. Nor did they do so after lunch, when the sun came out and England eased themselves off the hook by dint of fierce and enterprising driving by Old and a canny, calm, defensive innings by Lever. They put on 55, joyfully cheered by a warm-hearted Midlands crowd who seem to enjoy their big occasions at Edgbaston although for so long they have been starved of a really memorable game of cricket at international level.

A total of 171 should have been enough, we thought, to make a game of it on this occasion. The actual target Australia faced demanded a steady start and a controlled batting performance. But they again failed to get a proper start, and with Lever to the fore, golden hair flying in the breeze, England steamrollered their way to a victory which for their opponents was nothing short of humiliating. There were two decisive moments: first when Willis got his second ball to bounce steeply and Davis could only fend it to gully; then seven overs later when Chappell had already begun to play with the lofty disdain of a Prussian general and Lever swung a well-pitched ball in past his driving bat.

When Willis's fiery opening burst was over Old replaced him and bowled almost as well as Lever at the other end, and one by one the young and inexperienced Australian batsmen came and went, their technique against high-class fast-medium swing bowling, supported by aggressive fielding, proving quite inadequate. Two run-outs both compounded and reflected their general confusion. It really was unreal: Australia all out for 70! But it was not, of course, a Test match. R. E. S. Wyatt, his round face very little changed since his Test days, gave Lever the Man-of-the-Match award, and a strange game was over.

It had been watched by Kerry Packer, the guest of the Warwickshire Club, and this massive Australian, who had stirred such deep emotions in the world of cricket, watched and talked with Doug Insole, Donald Carr and Peter Lush, men from the privy council of English cricket. But the burning issue of the day was left to sizzle. Mr Packer announced to BBC radio that he had no intention of bringing his players to England or of interfering in any way with Test and County cricket in England. He may have looked, in Neil Allen's picturesque phrase, like an 'amiable hammer-headed shark', but he was prickly and defensive when faced with any questions which did not enable him to present his own case unopposed. Mr Packer was tired, he said, of being asked 'loaded questions'. It happened that I was the one who was asking them on this occasion, and my impression was that he was a tough but devious man, who did not really 'feel' for the game or fully understand the defensive passions it aroused.

England

D. L. Amiss c Marsh b Chappell ...	35
J. M. Brearley lbw Chappell	10
D. W. Randall c Marsh b Chappell	0
G. D. Barlow c Hughes b Chappell ...	25
P. Willey c Marsh b Cosier	6
A. W. Greig c Chappell b Cosier ...	0
A. P. E. Knott lbw Cosier	0
C. M. Old c Hughes b Chappell	35
J. K. Lever not out	27
D. L. Underwood b Cosier..............	0
R. G. D. Willis c Marsh b Cosier	7
Extras (lb15, w4, nb7)	26
Total...	171

Overs: 53.5.

Bowling
Thomson 9–0–46–0; Malone 11–2–27–0; Chappell 11–5–20–5; Walker 11–3–29–0; Cosier 8.5–3–18–5; Bright 3–0–5–0.

Australia

I. C. Davis c Old b Willis	0
C. S. Serjeant b Willis	2
G. S. Chappell b Lever	19
G. J. Cosier lbw Lever	3
K. J. Hughes c Knott b Lever	2
R. D. Robinson b Old	12
R. W. Marsh c Old b Lever	1
R. J. Bright not out	17
M. H. N. Walker run out	0
M. F. Malone run out	1
J. R. Thomson b Greig	3
Extras (b4, lb5, nb1)	10
Total ...	70

Overs: 25.2.

Bowling
Willis 6–1–14–2; Lever 11–2–29–4; Old 7–2–15–1; Greig 1.2–0–2–1.

Fall of Wickets
1 – 19   2 – 19   3 – 67   4 – 84   5 – 84   6 – 84   7 – 90   8 – 145   9 – 160
1 – 0   2 – 27   3 – 31   4 – 34   5 – 35   6 – 38   7 – 58   8 – 58   9 – 60

Umpires: W. E. Alley and H. D. Bird.

The third of the One-Day Internationals was for various reasons the most memorable. Indeed it finished in a way which was utterly unforgettable. But one must begin at the beginning with Chappell once again calling right and for the second successive time asking England to bat on an overcast morning. The Oval was at its drabbest in the grey light, yet the crowd was the largest of the three and at last they had some strokes of high quality to applaud. Amiss in particular, though an impending family bereavement was on his mind, settled in quickly to play a flawless innings, rich in crisply timed strokes off his legs and through the covers. Brearley manfully kept pace with him, equally severe and decisive whenever the fast bowlers overpitched. He did, however, need some luck against Pascoe, snicking him off the inside edge past his leg-stump for a rapid boundary and then using the outside edge to frustrate the bowler further as Thomson dived in a vain attempt to accept a fast-moving slip catch.

These, however, were fleeting moments of error in a stand of great authority which ended in the early afternoon as Brearley advanced down the pitch to drive O'Keeffe. Records of the short history of Prudential matches mean little, but it should be recorded that this stand, worth 161, was the highest for any wicket to date. Brearley was out in the 38th over; sixteen overs later nine more wickets had fallen and only 81 more runs had been added. Most of these were scored by Amiss, who was seventh out after reaching his second hundred in Prudential games against Australia. His first century, at Old Trafford in 1972, was also a brilliant innings which started him off on his long run as an established England player. The Oval's slow pace has always suited him and on this occasion the Australian fast bowlers pitched the ball up obligingly, enabling him to show the best of his magnificent array of front-foot strokes. It remained to be seen whether in the Tests themselves they would attack him with slightly shorter-length balls on or outside the off-stump, as Lillee, and to a lesser extent Walker and Thomson, had so successfully done in the past.

It needed an innings of special quality to surpass what Amiss had achieved, and Greg Chappell produced it. He came in after an unhappy McCosker had been l.b.w. to Old and whilst Robinson was still miscuing many of the aggressive front-foot strokes he was to play with increasing certainty. Chappell was, from the moment he entered, playing on a different level to the others and he soon hit Old, who was bowling well, for sixteen in one over with a rat-a-tat-tat of superlative strokes. 155 runs were needed with nine wickets in hand – a scoring rate of 4.8 an over – when the black clouds which for some time had enveloped the Oval began to deposit their contents. The game at this point was well balanced, but so set did the weather look that over threequarters of the crowd made their way home, wondering no doubt whether to return next day when national attentions would be switched to the main events of the Queen's Jubilee celebrations.

Unhappily for those who left, but mercifully for the remainder, the clouds lifted, the sun came out, and an hour and five minutes after the players had scurried for shelter they were renewing the battle in the middle. The wet ball counted against England's bowlers now, and Chappell continued to command the situation. Only Underwood caused him any trouble, packing his legside field and as ever bowling with impeccable control. There was a more speculative air about Robinson's batting but he kept the runs coming with his full backlift and generally buccaneering approach, pulling one immense legside six off Lever just short of the scoreboard by the gas-holders. At last he mishooked but, after Hughes had been l.b.w. to Willis, Walters came in, whereupon Willis, instead of bowling to the attacking offside field he was given, delivered a succession of overpitched balls down the legside. Walters was out at 209 in the 48th over and the game then ended in an atmosphere of high farce.

Soon after half-past seven, when most cricket matches have reached the stage of bar-side post-mortems, the rain began again — at first just a shower, then more heavily. Everyone, however, was determined to play on, despite the abysmal light. The sun came out, dazzlingly low, from just over the line of the Vauxhall stands. Still it rained. The outfield became slippery, the ball wet. The bowlers cut down their runs, the fielders and batsmen slithered. The victory target came nearer as Chappell, with raindrops dripping in front of his eyes from the peak of his cap, batted serenely on, as if indifferent to the extraordinary goings-on around him. In the fiftieth of the permitted 55 overs Hookes had a swing at Lever and missed. In the fifty-first Bright hit a searing drive inches off the ground to the left of Randall at cover. Somehow the comical genius, who could hardly be expected not to have a say at the height of the farce, clutched onto the ball with both hands. In the fifty-second and fifty-third overs O'Keeffe and Thomson were run out, this time thanks to Barlow's brilliance in the field, and it was only at a quarter-past eight, with nine balls left, the sun still glinting and the rain still teeming down, that the drenched cricketers were able to cease their bizarre and highly entertaining capers. Peter May gave Greg Chappell the Man-of-the-Match cheque, and as he soaked himself in his hot bath even this outwardly emotionless man must have allowed himself a smile.

England

*J. M. Brearley st Robinson b O'Keeffe	78
D. L. Amiss b Pascoe	108
D. W. Randall c & b Bright	6
G. D. Barlow run out	2
A. W. Greig c Robinson b Thomson...	4
†A. P. E. Knott c Robinson b Pascoe...	4
G. Miller c Robinson b Pascoe	4
C. M. Old c Thomson b Chappell......	20
J. K. Lever b Thomson	2
D. L. Underwood c Pascoe b Dymock	5
R. G. D. Willis not out	0
Extras	9
Total...	242

54.2 overs.

Bowling
Thomson 11-2-51-2; Dymock 10-0-39-1; Pascoe 11-0-43-3; O'Keeffe 11-0-43-1; Bright 11-1-56-1; Chappell 0.2-0-0-1.

Australia

R. B. McCosker lbw b Old	11
†R. D. Robinson c Brearley b Willis...	70
*G. S. Chappell not out	125
K. J. Hughes lbw b Willis	3
K. D. Walters c Brearley b Underwood	12
D. W. Hookes b Lever	3
R. J. Bright c Randall b Old	0
K. J. O'Keeffe run out	0
J. R. Thomson run out	3
G. Dymock not out	2
Extras (b1, lb14, nb1, w1)	17
Total (8 wkts)...	246

53.2 overs.

Did not bat: L. S. Pascoe.

Bowling
Willis 11-0-49-2; Lever 10-0-43-1; Old 10.2-0-56-2; Underwood 11-2-21-1; Miller 5-0-24-0; Greig 6-0-36-0.

Fall of wickets
1 – 161 2 – 168 3 – 179 4 – 196 5 – 203 6 – 207 7 – 217 8 – 227 9 – 241
1 – 33   2 – 181 3 – 186 4 – 209 5 – 225 6 – 228 7 – 228 8 – 237

Umpires: H. D. Bird and K. E. Palmer.

Chapter Four
LORD'S: A PROMISING START

It was perhaps odd that, having won the Centenary Test, however narrowly, Australia should have made four changes in their side for the Jubilee Test, while England made only one. On the eve of the game at Lord's Australia decided to omit Cosier and Davis after their parlous start to the tour, and to introduce two new batting caps in 25-year-old Craig Serjeant and 30-year-old Richie Robinson. Both were players of sound temperament and mature character, but with the coltish Hookes and the unpredictable Walters also in the first six it made for a vulnerable batting line-up, heavily reliant upon the supreme Chappell and to a lesser extent on McCosker's ability to lift his form for the big occasion.

The Australian selectors omitted Dymock but otherwise left their bowling options open until the morning of the match, when they also left out Bright and Malone. The seam attack therefore comprised Thomson, with only seven wickets to his credit at this point on the tour at a cost of 36 runs each; the reliable Walker; and Pascoe, narrowly preferred to Malone but deservedly so after taking wickets consistently on his first tour and bowling with more hostility than anyone else. O'Keeffe was, as expected, preferred to Bright as the spinner. England's only difference from their Centenary Test side was the replacement of Fletcher by Barlow, a change which might well have been made anyway before the game at Melbourne. Miller, who had also narrowly missed selection for the Melbourne match, was picked in England's twelve but left out on the Thursday morning. Woolmer, who had enforced his own return by scoring three centuries in successive Championship matches for Kent, was the only one in the England eleven who had not taken part in the One-Day Internationals.

The fact that ten of the Australian and four of the England team were prepared to risk their Test careers for forty pieces of silver, and the general uncertainty and nastiness in the air engendered by the Packer crisis, undoubtedly took away some of the spice from the traditional atmosphere of the Lord's Test. It was essential, one felt, that we should have a match worthy of the occasion.

The ground was still filling on a bright morning when Thomson bowled the first ball of the match to Amiss, a slow full-toss which was gently glanced square by the batsman for two runs. The pitch was a pale brown, a sharp contrast to the deep velvety green of the outfield which a few nights before had been saturated by a heavy storm which had actually flooded the basement of the pavilion. Though the new £5,000 covers had successfully kept away the torrents of water which had rushed down the famous Lord's slope during the storm, with the devoted groundsman Jim Fairbrother calling out his staff in the middle of the night to help direct the water away from the square, it did seem that one or two damp spots were affecting the wicket early on as Pascoe and Thomson got the ball to bounce at different heights. Pascoe looked the more hostile as Amiss and his new captain launched the innings steadily and with the utmost caution, but it was Thomson who got them both out. Off the last ball of his fifth over Thomson dismissed Amiss with a ball of yorker length. Amiss tried to drive with his weight on the back foot but succeeded only in deflecting the ball off the bottom inside edge onto the stumps. With his next delivery, the first of the eleventh over of the innings, Thomson had Brearley caught at short-leg as he fended off a lifter near the top of his bat. The England captain would have needed luck to have survived that particular ball.

England were 13 for two with Woolmer and Randall the new batsmen. When Randall had safely negotiated the remainder of his sixth over Thomson was rested after taking two for eight; he had already rendered irrelevant his modest start to the tour. Pascoe replaced him and Woolmer relieved the pressure by stroking him through mid-on for three. Randall, starting with suitable circumspection, nevertheless hooked and missed twice at rising balls from Pascoe before a classical downward-aimed hook brought him the first four of the morning. He repeated the shot soon afterwards off Walker, and after 21 overs Chappell called up O'Keeffe to bowl the first overs of spin. He caused the batsmen no serious problems, although Randall hit a full-toss through Serjeant's upstretched hands at midwicket. He was 33 not out at lunch, with Woolmer, who had got his head down patiently, 13 not out. He had been hit on the pads more often than he would have wished, but as usual had played calmly, giving an impression of almost leisurely control.

Randall had timed the ball impeccably before the interval. After it, he played with less fluency, Woolmer with more. During the course of a fine spell from the Nursery End, Walker several times got balls to nip back late to find Randall's inside edge or Woolmer's pads, but it was with a wide half-volley outside the off-stump that he had Randall beautifully caught by Chappell at first slip. Randall slashed at the ball and edged it very fast into the safest pair of hands in modern cricket. With Woolmer the lad from Retford had put on 96 in just over two hours and when he had gone for 53 the situation swiftly changed.

Greig was caught at second slip off his first ball, fortunately for him a no-ball. His second ball was well up to him on the off-stump and with splendid flamboyance he drove it through the covers for four. But Walker was one proposition, Pascoe, bowling from the Pavilion End, another. He was always the master of Greig during their brief duel and after hitting him on the shoulder with a bumper he bowled him two balls later as Greig drove without conviction.

Barlow, given a great opportunity to shine in his first Test in England on his own ground, settled in solidly but pushed forward to Walker without getting to the pitch, edged and was caught very low down at second slip. One's immediate impression was that the ball had not carried but the Australians appealed to a man when they saw that Barlow was not walking, and after consulting his colleague, Lloyd Budd, at square-leg Harold Bird gave Barlow out. Knott stayed with Woolmer until tea, when England were 155 for 5, but as if giving fielding practice he hit the first ball after 'tiffin' straight to Walters at cover.

This uncharacteristically suicidal stroke put paid to any English hopes of a recovery, because the contest between Chris Old and good fast bowling is rarely an even one, and there can be no doubt that this was high-quality bowling by the three Australians with Thomson maintaining a full length and an excellent off-stump line, Pascoe bowling the occasional delivery exceptionally fast and Walker battling away remorselessly. It was the latter who got Old, nicking a lifting delivery, and now it was a question of whether Woolmer would be able to raise his game one stage higher to take control whilst the tailenders stayed as long as they could. Hitherto Woolmer had only attacked the bad balls, striking them away with admirable certainty and otherwise defending soundly except when the ball moved excessively. He played and missed frequently but was eventually out not through any technical failing. Instead, he pushed Pascoe into the covers off the last ball of an over, set off for a run, realised that Walters was converging on the ball from cover, hesitated in mid-pitch, ran on again and saw Walters hit the stumps at the bowler's end from point-blank range. He had made 79.

Pascoe soon induced Lever to play on for a well-deserved second wicket, but a spirited last-wicket stand of 27 by Underwood and Willis made a disappointing batting performance look a little better than it was. Thomson struck Willis's off-stump at twenty past six and the touring team returned to the Waldorf Hotel well contented with a good day's work. England, all out 216, had perhaps not helped their own cause very much at times, but the Australians had bowled and fielded quite excellently.

The outcome of the match would probably depend on how substantial a reply Australia could make, but they awoke on the Friday morning to overcast skies and intermittent drizzle. Play began an hour and a quarter late before a shivering but patient crowd. The light was poor, but Robinson, opening the innings in his first Test though normally a middle-order batsman, was breathing healthy Australian competitiveness from every pore. He got one wild spar out of his system before clipping a confident single off Willis's second ball, and McCosker, after ducking below a bouncer designed to invite an injudicious early hook, was soon pushing the ball through wide open spaces on either side of the wicket. Robinson, escaping one confident l.b.w. appeal by Lever, looked for runs equally eagerly, and Randall and Barlow were soon haring in all directions.

It was too much for Australians to hope that the levity would last. Robinson was batting more like a club player than a man burdened by the honour of opening for Australia in his first Test match at the Mecca of cricket. It was almost improper that he should not be just a little overawed, experienced Sheffield Shield cricketer though he was. At any rate, his fun was shortlived. He drove optimistically towards mid-on at a good-length ball from Lever; it swung in late and his off-stump cartwheeled joyously.

There was not long to go before lunch, but Chappell did not hold himself back. Underwood was brought on almost immediately to greet him, more for psychological reasons than for any hope that the pitch might have some dampness in it, and both Underwood and Old, who relieved Lever at the Pavilion End, were treated with the greatest respect, so much so that six overs went by after the interval without a run being scored from the bat. This was, as everyone recognised, a crucial phase in the game. So much depended on Chappell, and McCosker was the person most likely to stay with him and build a position of dominance.

The advent of Willis and an injudicious bouncer caused a hurried consultation between umpires Bird and Budd (a satisfying pair to pronounce, sounding more like solicitors than umpires, and a nice contrast in appearances, Budd tall, balding, calm and genial, Bird small, dark, nervous and self-conscious), and the batsmen quickly agreed with them that the light was not good enough. The players came on again for a time but in mid-afternoon the light was again considered too bad for play and very soon the rain came down to put its damp seal on a dismal day, with Australia 51 for one.

It did not rain hard enough, however, for play to be called off until five past six, and though the pitch was covered from the moment that the decision was made, the long period of inaction was not without significance, because, though not exactly soaked, the pitch received enough rain to make sure it would gain in liveliness when play resumed.

For a time it seemed that any new terrors in the pitch were mere imaginings of the mind as the third day began in grey light with the clouds a little higher and a 25,000 crowd so silent that the tap of ball on bat was clearly audible from every seat. The atmosphere was tense and England quickly took the early wicket they craved for.

The first few balls of the day by Willis and Old were speculatively short, but there was no question of anything lifting or flying. With their experience of faster pitches Australian batsmen tend to be strong off the back foot, and it was significant that the first time that McCosker was brought forward he was bowled by Old: a beauty which swung in between bat and pad and knocked back the middle stump. Old again bowled on an admirable off-stump line and with perfect rhythm. It needed all Chappell's skill to keep him out and all the self-possession of the new batsman, Craig Serjeant. This tall, dark, personable Perth pharmacist played with astonishing maturity for a man in his first Test. With

Old at one end and Underwood brought on at once from the Nursery End, conditions were not easy. Yet, though he took 38 minutes to get off the mark, a fact which, significantly, did not bother him as it might have done a man of lesser patience, he looked if anything rather safer than his captain. Chappell, in fact, should have been out for 13 but Underwood in his second over was unable to recover from his follow-through in time to hold on to a straightforward caught-and-bowled chance. For an instant he may have thought it a bump-ball, because he stuck out his right hand apparently casually.

Old was rested after an hour, his figures at this point being 15–6–15–1, and the quality of his replacement, Lever, was at once obvious as he came within a whisker of bowling Serjeant with a late inswinger. The inside edge of Serjeant's bat got the faintest of touches which took the ball fractionally wide of the leg-stump.

The light remained dim; Underwood plugged on remorselessly from the Nursery End with subtle variations; the sternly disciplined Chappell was unable to break his grip. The crowd looked quietly on in their macintoshes. It was cricket for the connoisseur, as different from a Sunday League match as Lord's from Lahore. The crowd were roused from time to time, however. Serjeant hit Underwood for two clean, uncomplicated boundaries over the top of the legside field and then watched Underwood leap in vain appeal as Greig at silly-point juggled with and triumphantly caught a ball which had popped – but in the batsman's and the umpire's opinion off Serjeant's pad rather than his bat.

Twenty minutes before lunch, Willis was recalled for a pre-prandial burst. Twice his extra pace almost caused Serjeant to play on to his stumps, but at lunch he was still there, 17 not out, Chappell, yet to hit a four, 39 not out, and Australia had inched their way to 99 for two, having scored just 48 runs in the two hours.

Chappell's first boundary was almost worth waiting for, a glorious off-drive off Old in the first over after the interval, and he gradually began to open out despite a half-hour interruption due to bad light. He reached 50 after 213 minutes of gritty application, but Serjeant continued to intersperse healthy legside clouting with extraordinary good fortune, especially against Willis. Ironically, it was Chappell, not Serjeant, who fell first, Willis getting the scalp he so thoroughly deserved when Chappell tried to drive on the up and edged to Old in the gully. The captain had scored 66.

Enter Walters, to be greeted by four slips, two gullies and Willis and Old fancying their chances, with good reason. The advent of Walters induced a feverish rash of injudicious strokes by Serjeant, plus one solid and worthy hook, as his curate's egg of an innings continued.

Walters, his feet immobile, looked as frail as ever around his off-stump. He edged Willis through the slips for a streaky four, groped agonisingly time and again, and was dropped by Brearley at slip off Woolmer when by means legitimate and lucky he had already scored 21. Despite all this, he scored at about twice the rate of anyone else. Apart from a rasping square-cut and a fine on-drive, both off Woolmer, one was at a loss to recall where his runs had come from, but as tea approached so too did the probability that Australia would now achieve a substantial first-innings lead. At the interval they were only 26 away from England's total; Serjeant was 50 not out after three and a half hours at the crease and Walters was 29 not out.

The hard work had been done; Australia were now in a position to capitalise, and so they did. Serjeant played his best stroke, a controlled drive between mid-on and the stumps, Walters whipped Lever off his toes to the Mound Stand, then handsomely square-cut him to the Grandstand. Despite England's excellent ground fielding (even in the absence of Randall, who was in the pavilion all day nursing a sore elbow), the Australians ran excellently between the wickets. Now the new ball was England's only hope of salvaging much from a fairly fruitless Saturday's work.

As so often happens, however, the new ball at first proved only that much easier to see and that much easier to strike. Serjeant tucked into Lever with such relish that he hit three successive fours: a wristy flick off his toes, a solid off-drive and a rustic pull. Perhaps he got just a little over-confident, however, because he was out in the next over, aiming to square-cut a ball from Willis which bounced a little higher than Serjeant had expected. It had been an invaluable and wholly admirable innings of 81.

Walters reached fifty with another streaky slash over the slips before Willis had his deserved revenge, Brearley clutching with relief onto a low, fast chance at first slip. One should not only dwell on Walters' good fortune: he had played some magnificently timed cuts and drives in between the gropes and slashes and as usual he had scored far faster than anyone else. It is the fast scorers who give the time for bowlers to win Test matches.

Hookes came in on the grey evening with little to gain from the situation. Both Old and Willis were bowling exceptionally well with the new ball and neither Marsh nor Hookes played with any great confidence. Hookes did play one streamlined cover-drive off Old, but next ball went onto the back foot and unhappily steered the ball to slip. At the other end Marsh shuffled across in front of his stumps to gain the first affirmative decision after many hopeful shouts from bowlers of both sides. Thus, in the end, the new ball had done the trick for England and they were able to take their Sunday rest with rather greater peace of mind. Australia's score stood at 278 for seven, 62 runs ahead of England.

The London weather was again cold and grey when the fourth day began before a slightly smaller crowd, still wrapped up in coats but looking forward to a day which was likely to be decisive in the outcome. It was not the sort of weather for a merry tailwag and it was only a matter of time before Willis and Old polished off the innings. Old was as much out of luck as he had been on the Saturday and he was forced to wait for his 100th Test victim as Willis proceeded towards his best Test figures. Bowling very fast and straight from the Nursery End he got more bounce than he had on Saturday and the wicket generally looked more lively, perhaps because it had not been mown since the Saturday morning and a thin green growth was starting after the rain on Monday. Or perhaps it was more simply that the pitch had now completely dried out. At any rate Willis soon had Walker caught behind, followed up by inducing O'Keeffe to play a hurried hook which directed the ball off the top edge into the sure hands of Alan Ealham, Randall's exceptionally capable fielding substitute, and then bowled Thomson to become only the third Englishman (after the Yorkshiremen Ulyett and Verity) to take seven wickets in an innings at Lord's for England against Australia.

Australia's lead was 80 and in an instant the team gathered around their opening bowler, joyously anticipating the possibility of yet another Australian victory on the ground where they had lost only one match during the twentieth century. Thomson versus Amiss was, on this occasion, no contest. Amiss played and missed at the first two balls, which missed the off-stump as well, made tentative contact with the third and was bowled by the fourth as he pushed the bat across the line, possibly anticipating that the ball would swing away past the off-stump. It did not do so, and Amiss walked home, inwardly groaning, no doubt, at the situation his team was now in and at the prospect of having to open the innings frequently against Thomson and Lillee in the Packer circus.

Randall was still under the weather with a mysterious blood infection, possibly bursitis, which had resulted in a swelling the size of a golf ball above his left elbow. So it was Bob Woolmer who walked out to face the fifth ball of the innings. The finest hour of his career to date was about to begin. It was imperative for England that Brearley and Woolmer should make a solid stand against the Australian fast bowlers. Pascoe shared the new ball with Thomson and the pace of both was furious. But Brearley relieved the pressure somewhat with a smoothly timed push through the covers for four off Thomson, who next overpitched to Woolmer and watched the new batsman play the first of his fours confidently and expertly off his toes to square-leg.

Woolmer and Brearley played with great resolution in the crucial period until lunch, when England were 29 for one, and the game now hung on whether they or their immediate successors could avoid one of those famous English collapses against fast bowling. Woolmer's talent and character were equal to the situation. Brearley's character was too, although his technique was tested to the limit and he needed luck to survive. Once Walker, cutting the ball about lethally from the Pavilion End, sent a booming inswinger between Brearley's bat and pad. Marsh and the close fielders went up in instantaneous appeal, and Marsh threw the ball away angrily when it was turned down. The omniscient television playback seemed to confirm that the ball had evaded the bat. When he was 19 Brearley might have been out exactly as he had been in the first innings as he fended a lifter from Thomson to the left of Robinson at short-leg. 'Action Man', as the England team had christened the delightfully keen Victorian, dived to his left but could not quite grasp the chance. In the very next over Woolmer had his one great slice of luck when he failed to get over a ball from Walker and gratefully watched Serjeant fumble the chance in the gully. It was not appreciated until later that these two chances were the last that Australia would have to win the game.

At the time, of course, England's situation was still critical. Woolmer was playing with the skill and confidence of a class batsman in good form. There was no playing and missing from him as there had been in his worthy first innings. But Brearley was merely hanging on. Walker kept finding the edge of his bat or just evading it with his leg-cutters, and Chappell moved from slip to close silly-point, the further to fence in his opposite number. But Brearley, struggling as he was, looked anything but miserable; he was clearly relishing the battle, and calmly and decisively evaded the four bouncers in five balls which Pascoe hurled at him, without interference from Lloyd Budd. Perhaps Pascoe was keen to impress his hostility on everyone because he had been understandably stung by allegations made by Ted Dexter in his Sunday newspaper column that Pascoe 'chucked' some of his faster deliveries. At any rate Pascoe overpitched as he tried to follow his bouncers with a yorker and Brearley calmly drove the ball back towards the pavilion.

Greg Chappell came on at the Nursery End in an endeavour to break through and more than once he beat Brearley with a late outswinger or an off-cutter which rapped the front pad. But Australia's luck was as bad as England's had been on the Saturday, and Woolmer was always the master. He saw Pascoe out of the attack with a firm hook and a smooth turn off his legs, then despatched Chappell to the Grandstand with another crisp hook and, after Brearley had joined in with a cover-driven four off Chappell, he raised the 100 partnership with a cover-drive off Thomson which was pure Cowdrey.

Woolmer, his cheeks rosy as a Kent apple, reached his 50 off just 91 balls and, apart from his one escape off Walker, his first misjudgment came when O'Keeffe was called up for the fortieth over of the innings. Woolmer played over the top of a looping leg-spinner in his first over, which went through Marsh as well for byes, but thereafter he dealt with O'Keeffe as authoritatively as he did everyone else. One especially remembered a scything mow through the covers off a wide half-volley, a swift, swivelling hook and a glorious force off the back foot through the covers. How marvellous it was to see him play like this after all the disappointments of his tour of India!

The advent of O'Keeffe did, however, rid Australia of Brearley's limpet-like innings. Just before tea he pushed forward and turned the ball low in front of Robinson, who took the chance well. Woolmer was 76 not out at the interval and he proceeded serenely enough to his second Test hundred, another classical drive off Pascoe helping him on his way. There were twelve fours in the century which was his fourth of the season and which, rather surprisingly, was only the fifteenth of his career. One regretted again the years he had been languishing in the depths of the Kent batting order.

Woolmer held the stage until the day ended forty minutes early because of bad light, at ten to six, but Greig played a responsible supporting role. He looked completely out of touch, which indeed he was because he had scored very few runs for Sussex. But, granted a little luck outside the off-stump against Pascoe, he battled through, and had not only scored 18 but begun to play rather better when the umpires offered him the opportunity to come off. Caution always tends to triumph in such circumstances. If England were going to win they needed all the time they could have, but after going so far to make the game safe they could not be blamed for avoiding any risks at this late stage. At the close England's score stood at 189 for two, with Woolmer on 114.

The roles of Greig and Woolmer were reversed when the final day began before a disappointingly sparse crowd in the same cold temperature and dim grey light. The few hardy thousand who made the journey to St John's Wood were rewarded with a day full of excitement and unexpected twists.

Woolmer added only six more runs in 45 minutes at the start of the day before he drove at a rising delivery and was snapped up by Chappell at first slip with that cold, almost mechanical efficiency which makes him the surest slip catcher in the world and the best Australian exponent of that most difficult art since Bobby Simpson. Woolmer's innings overall had lasted five hours and 248 balls and had been a triumphant demonstration of his ability and temperament, as well as an example of how quickly fortunes change in cricket: after his winter tour one of the England selectors was prepared to write him off for the future. He was duly left out of the One-Day International matches, a decision which hardened his determination further, and now he was apparently assured of his place all summer long. One had only to study Woolmer closely in India to realise that his easy-going nature was mistaken by some for complacency and that the real problem with his batting there was not any lack of talent nor even, generally speaking, of concentration. It was simply that as a 'touch' player, who loves to deflect and caress the ball, he was never at home against subtle spin bowling on slow pitches.

Fortunately for England, Tony Greig was, like Woolmer, required to make a point to selectors and critics. Several people questioned his right to be in the England side, apparently ignoring the fact that his form at Test level had always been more reliable than his form for Sussex. He played with an assurance, on this fifth day, which belied both his form and the precarious nature of his place in the side, hitting Pascoe off his toes for the first boundary of the morning, inside-edging another chancier one off a full-toss from the same bowler and reaching his fifty not long after Woolmer's departure with a characteristically savage slash to backward point off Thomson.

The new ball was taken at the first opportunity by Chappell (after 85 overs) and poor Barlow, needing an innings to consolidate his place in the team, had come in just as it was due. Thomson's pace at one end and Walker's movement at the other (although the latter bowled very wide of the stumps for much of the time) provided a testing combination which he never looked like dominating, although he hung around for just under an hour and was only out when Pascoe took over from Thomson and claimed his second wicket of the morning with a straight ball. Barlow apparently misjudged the line and was thus l.b.w. for the sixth time in twelve innings during what so far had been a disappointing season for him.

Greig, meanwhile, was scoring four after four with a mixture of crashing drives through the covers and brutally hit cuts, many of them through or over the slips. He still looked vulnerable to the good-length ball and Walker more than once had him groping around the off-stump. But it was Pascoe who eventually prevented Greig from getting a hundred, the second time in successive Lord's Tests that he had narrowly missed one. He went for one ambitious drive too many, did not get to the pitch and sliced the ball to backward point where O'Keeffe judged the catch nicely, holding on two-handed over his head.

Having deprived us of one of their collapses at the start of the innings, England obliged with one at the end. Without it there would not have been such an exciting conclusion to the match. Starting with Greig's demise, England managed to lose four wickets with the score on 286 and to lose their last six wickets in all for 19 runs. Knott and Old hit Walker straight to the sure hands of Walters at cover, the one just before and the other just after lunch; the injured Randall received a nasty lifter from Thomson and was very well caught low at second slip by McCosker, and Lever and Willis nicked rising balls to the wicket-keeper. England were grateful for twelve brave runs from Underwood, but with the innings ending so smartly at a quarter-to-three Australia were left the not impossible target of 226 in an hour and three-quarters plus the last twenty overs.

It was an intriguing prospect, and with laudable enterprise Greg Chappell told his men to go for the runs. Robinson, of course, needed no persuasion. This was his game, but he was going to need luck to get the quick fifty which might have set Australia up for a win. He got four runs from a top-edged hook over slips' heads off Willis and then in the second over pushed Old into Woolmer's hands at short-leg. Willis followed up in the next over by bowling McCosker with a well-pitched delivery which beat a tentative forward stroke, and Australia were five for two. Chappell showed his attacking intentions by sending in Hookes rather than Serjeant at number four and by his own batting, for he was soon acquiring runs all round the wicket. A superb hook off a not very short ball from Old was followed by two lordly cuts off Willis, the first backward of square, the second in front. But the excitement was two-way because in the same over he played across an outswinger and was perilously close to being bowled.

Hookes joined in the fun with a crisp hook off Willis which carried over the boundary in front of the Mound Stand, then took a risky single and would have been run out if Barlow had hit the stumps after a quick pick-up on the run from mid-off. But Australia were scoring almost effortlessly at the required rate of four an over when Chappell, rather surprisingly, was out. He tried to hook a ball from Old which perhaps was not quite short enough and dragged the ball wide of mid-on where Lever clutched the ball safely to his chest.

Still Australia attacked, sending in Walters at number five, and at tea they were 64 for three, Hookes 22 not out, Walters 10 not out. Old had at this point taken two for 23 from nine overs. A draw was still overwhelmingly the most likely result, but a win for both sides was still just possible and it was sad that only a few thousand spectators were there to see the final outcome. England felt that, with Chappell safely in the pavilion, there was no one who could win the match for Australia, and Brearley accordingly set attacking fields, employing Lever for the first time from the Pavilion End with Underwood, as usual, using the slope from the Nursery End. Excitement grew as Underwood took two more wickets. Whenever one has seen Underwood successfully attacked – and it is a rare occurrence – it has been by batsmen prepared to hit in the air either straight or to the offside. Swinging across the spin to leg is nearly always fatal, and so it proved on this cold, drab evening as first Walters and then Serjeant swept deliveries away off the line of the stumps in an attempt to clear the onside field. First Alan Ealham, for many years one of the finest outfielders in the land, sprinted from midwicket to hold a well-judged catch on the run, and then Amiss, making even greater ground, took a superb catch as he galloped towards the Grandstand from mid-on with his back to the wicket.

Australia were now in trouble and they knew it. Marsh approached the wicket like a particularly indolent tortoise and there was time for only one more over before the start of the mandatory final twenty. Marsh, by nature a controlled hitter, now began an admirable defensive innings which saved his side the embarrassment and disappointment of a defeat they did not deserve. Hookes played coolly too but his defence was altogether looser. For the second time in his innings he survived a concerted appeal from the England team and looked with relief at the motionless figure of the avuncular umpire Budd. Before tea Old had been convinced that he had got Hookes caught behind: now Woolmer dived close to the bat as Hookes pushed forward to Lever, but the claim for a bat-pad catch was ruled to have been pad only.

If any fault could be found with Brearley's captaincy it lay in his continuing rather too long with two left-handed bowlers to two left-handed batsmen. Old and Willis were entrusted with the final fling, but Hookes reached a mettlesome 50, scored out of 99, with a flick to midwicket off Old. His innings contained a six and three fours, but there was an element of over-confidence in his attempt, a few balls later, to hook Willis. He was duly caught and bowled, and with a possible nine and a half overs left England now needed just four more wickets.

Both Marsh and O'Keeffe, however, are cricketers who love a challenge. O'Keeffe might have been caught low to his left at slip by Brearley off Willis in the fifteenth of the last twenty overs but otherwise looked safe; this was the last piece of excitement because a bouncer from Willis to Marsh who, gifted actor that he is, subtly indicated by half-ducking into the ball that the light was getting impossible, induced an immediate

Old Trafford: *Above* Hookes is caught behind off Lever in Australia's first innings. *Below* A brilliant reflex catch by Woolmer gives his Kent colleague Underwood yet another Test wicket. Serjeant is the victim.

Above Woolmer drives O'Keeffe during his 137; and Randall on-drives the same bowler during his brilliant stand with Woolmer which signalled the start of England's supremacy in the series. *Below* Chappell drives Underwood during his masterly innings of 112.

All the balance and authority of Greg Chappell's batting are typified in this hook off a
Willis bouncer.

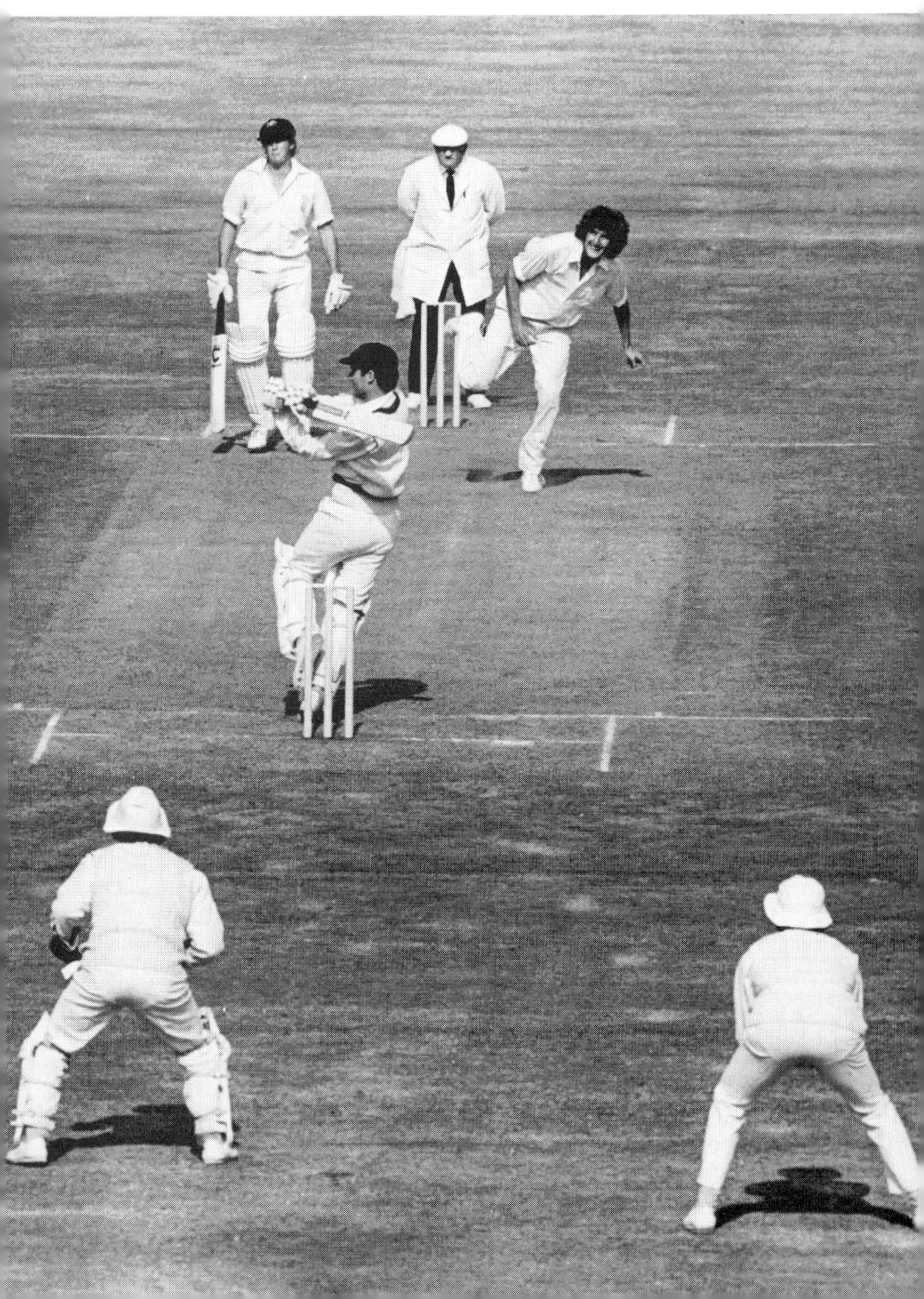

Mixed memories for Dennis Amiss of what seems certain to be his final Test. *Above* He is about to be caught off bat and body by Chappell (first slip) as he mishits a hook off Walker. *Below* He scores the winning runs to register England's first home win in a Test match for three years.

conference between the umpires. They had no sooner asked the batsmen whether they wished to continue than Marsh was off to the pavilion at approximately ten times the pace he had left it the best part of an hour before. There were five overs remaining for play but it was highly unlikely that England would have taken four wickets in that time.

A good cricket match was over, with honours exactly even. Both sides had bowled well on a good wicket, and both had fielded well apart from two important missed catches each. England's first-innings batting was inferior, but in the second they recovered with spirit and, in the case of Woolmer, with an innings of the very highest Test quality. Had not six hours, exactly one day's play, been lost in the miserable gloom of so-called midsummer, one or other of the sides must have gained a narrow victory. Only the weather, and the thunderclouds of the Packer crisis still banking up around the headquarters of cricket, prevented the Jubilee game from being the classic encounter which the Centenary Test had been.

Chapter Five
VICTORY AT
OLD TRAFFORD

The breakdown of the talks between Kerry Packer and the ICC at Lord's soon after the first Test spread further gloom around the Australian tour. Against the counties, however, the form of the Australians was becoming steadily more impressive. Marsh, with a rapid 124, which included 15 fours and four sixes, Hookes and Serjeant had all batted well against Essex in the match before the first Test, another game curtailed by indifferent weather, and after Hookes, Hughes and Davis had all made good fifties against the Oxford and Cambridge Combined side the potential of the team was fully realised for the first time in the match against Nottinghamshire.

No county has a prouder record against Australia than Nottinghamshire, who had beaten seven previous touring teams, but after an opening day which produced 415 runs on a good Trent Bridge wicket with a fast outfield the 1977 encounter was simply no contest. Nottinghamshire were without Randall, whose swelling above the left elbow was still alarmingly large but whose spirit as ever was unquenchable, and without him their batsmen fared moderately. It was not that the Notts batting lacked ability but that they were at this stage collectively out of form. In any case the Australians bowled well. Thomson got some of his early deliveries to lift off a length in that old disconcerting way, almost as if he were bowling back in Brisbane; Malone after a disappointing first spell was deservedly destructive in his second; and the two spinners, Bright and O'Keeffe, with little to choose between them now as far as selection for the Tests was concerned, were as good as each other.

The touring team made a brisk enough start shortly before tea on the first day, but when McCosker was out, leaving an inswinger from the otherwise erratic Hacker, Chappell came in and in half an hour's lordly batting once again lifted the proceedings from the banal to the sublime. Three of his first four balls from the left-handed Hacker were imperiously despatched for four and he continued to dominate the Nottinghamshire bowlers as if they were schoolboys until, hitting across Doshi, he was bowled and the crowd's enjoyment was unexpectedly truncated. However, his example was contagious. Davis, at last getting into form, began to pull with almost as much power as his captain and generally to play prettily and well. Serjeant was even more impressive, with his powerful figure and delightfully clean hitting, his big backswing and his straightforward method.

After a Sunday rest he proceeded to make his first century of the tour, and in reaching 159 with another outstanding display of effortless batting he recorded his own personal best in 15 first-class innings and the highest individual score of the tour to date. At one point he took five fours in an over from Birch, all well-timed strokes between cover and midwicket. Hughes scored only ten of the fourth-wicket partnership of 78 in 63 minutes with Serjeant, but he now became the senior partner and with Cosier settled down to another productive and attractive partnership. Cosier, looking gauche and overweight, still showed the extent of his ability, thumping the ball in all directions with special decisiveness whenever he could get onto the back foot – which was frequently. Hughes deserved to become the third century-maker of the innings but perished attempting to get to his target in the grand manner.

There was time for Thomson to take the first wicket before a rousing second day of the match ended, and in only three and a half hours of the third Nottinghamshire were soundly tanned. Malone, O'Keeffe and Bright shared the bowling honours on the last day, Thomson once more overstepping and taking his tally of no-balls on the tour past a hundred as well as bowling too short at the husky South African, Clive Rice, who took thorough recompense.

No one in the Australian party was now worried. Thomson was a big occasion man, and the team as a whole was improving all the time. They had another good game against Derbyshire at Chesterfield, although the weather deprived them of another possible innings victory. Pascoe managed to peg back the sustained challenge to his Test place from Malone by being the bowler chiefly responsible for Derbyshire's lowly first innings total of 126, and the Australians hardly noticed the absence of Dymock, who injured himself after bowling only five overs. Poor Dymock, a thoroughly worthy cricketer, was becoming one of those inevitable passengers which almost every touring party has.

O'Keeffe, under as much pressure for his Test place from Bright as was Pascoe from Malone, also responded well to the challenge, taking four for 21. Then Davis, Hughes, who again narrowly missed a century, Robinson, Marsh and O'Keeffe all batted well, although Hendrick, with 2 for 61 from 29 overs, came through with his reputation unimpaired. He would have had more wickets with greater support from the slip fielders. Miller, given a long bowl by Barlow as usual, did not take a wicket, which was disappointing because he had been taking plenty against the counties, but he bowled better than his figures suggested and at least batted long enough in both innings to know that Pascoe and Walker would be formidable opponents when his chance to return to the Test side came.

The Australians moved still further north for the last match before the Old Trafford Test, with just one matter causing them serious concern – disregarding for the moment the various statements of Mr Packer, which hung like a dark cloud above them wherever they travelled. The most pressing matter on the field was the miserable form of Rick McCosker. Many a batsman who has been hit on the head by a fast bowler has, not surprisingly, suffered a prolonged loss of form as a result, and everyone was now wondering whether McCosker's lack of confidence and clear vulnerability around the off-stump did not have something to do with his blow on the jaw from Willis in the Centenary Test. He was selected again for the match against Yorkshire, in a last attempt to get him back amongst the runs. This meant he had played in nine consecutive first-class games since his late arrival in England, but, in conditions enjoyed by the swing bowlers, he was to be twice out cheaply.

Speculation was rife in some quarters of the press that Geoff Boycott would, having announced his availability again, be picked for England for the second Test. The confrontation between him and Thomson was therefore eagerly awaited. In the event, Thomson again felt a twinge or two in his right arm and was kept on ice for Old Trafford, so the heavyweight bout was postponed. Boycott was fortunate enough to win the toss on one of those typical misty Scarborough mornings, and before an hour and a half's cricket had been played the Australians were 46 for six. Old, Arthur Robinson and Stevenson were the three seam bowlers who enjoyed the conditions, and it was only the admirable and defiant defensive batting of O'Keeffe and the other Robinson, plus some generous captaincy by Boycott, who bowled his spinners in conditions made for seamers, that enabled the Australians to recover. Having done so, there was no looking back. Walker and Malone, their barrel chests heaving with pleasure in the sea air which was so ideal for their particular brand of swing and cut bowling, whistled Yorkshire out for 75, the county's lowest ever against an Australian team since 1948. Boycott was the first to go, l.b.w. on Saturday evening, and by the middle of Sunday afternoon the Australian batsmen were improving their tans under the seaside sun and, thanks to disciplined and skilful batting by Serjeant and Hookes, simultaneously taking control of the match.

Another useful knock by Robinson on the last day, which came too late to save his Test place, enabled Chappell to set Yorkshire a stiff but not impossible challenge. One might have written 'Boycott' rather than 'Yorkshire' because the captain, having by now heard that he was not to make an immediate return to the Test team, was determined to make his mark on the game and to make the Australian bowlers pay for his first-innings duck. They duly did so, although Boycott's priority was that Yorkshire should not lose. He and Jimmy Love were, in fact, going well enough at one point for a Yorkshire victory to be possible. But Love was out for 59, an innings marked by some belligerent driving, and with Walters directing affairs in the field because Chappell was in the dressing-room resting an aching head after making unintended contact with a low beam, Boycott went single-mindedly and skilfully towards his century target. When he got there he lifted his arms in the air twice in slow, deliberately triumphant gestures to a warmly appreciative crowd. A firm on-drive had seen him to his target after 18-year-old Kevin Sharp, the promising left-hander who was soon to captain Young England against Young Australia in two Junior Internationals, had twice refused desperately risky singles which betrayed the urgency of Boycott's need to make his point to the England selectors and the world in general. This, in fact, was classic Boycott: still a self-conscious, sensitive character relating almost every cricket situation to himself; still possessed of the outstanding ability to rise to the challenge to himself which he interpreted from the particular situation, and to come out on top. Thus, in the eyes of the public if not of the players, the match itself took second place to a personal victory, and although neither Thomson nor Pascoe was playing the point was clearly made that Geoff Boycott was still England's leading opening batsman.

To have picked him for Old Trafford would, however, have meant disrupting the harmony of the side which, although under new management (Brearley for Greig), was still living off the spirit which had developed during the MCC tour of India. There had been much baying for blood in some sections of the press, with Amiss and Barlow as the main targets. But Amiss had only a few weeks previously scored a very good hundred at the Oval in the One-Day International, while Barlow had fared well in those games too and his fielding and general attitude of bustling enthusiasm were positive influences for good in the side. He was not in very good batting form for Middlesex and his Test innings so far had been single-figure failures, but, apart from his first innings in Delhi, he had not yet batted on a batsman's wicket in a Test and he deserved one more chance to show whether he could play a substantial innings in Test company. If Boycott had played at Old Trafford Amiss or Brearley would have had to have dropped down the order, but both had been in recent good form and they had looked in recent Tests to be developing a settled English opening partnership, although they had only once reached fifty in six starts together to date – their 146 in the fifth Test against India at Bombay being the only England opening partnership of 100 or more since that of Edrich and Wood at Lord's in the second Test of 1975.

These figures spoke eloquently enough for the recall of Boycott. But apart from the disruption his selection would have caused in a side which had not done badly in the first Test, there was a moral question to be answered. How could those players who had signed with Kerry Packer be condemned, as they were sure to be by the ICC later in the month, and Boycott not be condemned, simply because he personally had not signed for Packer? The fact remained that, though his reasons for turning his back on England were not so simple – his main problem was that he could no longer stand the mental strain of all the fierce publicity he was getting – he had declared himself unavailable to play for his country and had, whilst Greig and company were sweating out their series in India, been playing cricket for very substantial rewards in Australia. Was this not precisely what Greig and the others were about to do? In any case, was Boycott prepared to take the rough with the smooth again and to declare himself available to play not just against Australia but also against Pakistan in the winter? These were questions to which Boycott would give decisive replies before long, but the selectors could not be blamed for wanting to think hard before they put him back into the team. After all, they would probably have to make enforced changes for the winter tour.

So it was an unchanged England twelve which made its way, under morning sun, to Manchester as the golfing Open Championship was beginning at Turnberry and the last words were being spoken and written about the victories of Virginia Wade and Bjorn Borg at Wimbledon. In the fields by the sides of the motorways which took the cricketers to Old Trafford the tractors were out and the hay bales were piling up, but the arid brownness which had already taken the gloss off the English countryside by this same stage of the previous summer of drought was happily absent.

The pitch the cricketers found at Old Trafford, however, looked quite dry enough, and the immediate prognostications were that it would help the spinners sooner or later. The pitch had been prepared in controversial circumstances. For some years wickets had been declining in quality, but Gordon Prosser, the new head groundsman appointed at the start of 1977, had been sorting out the problems, levelling out undulations on the square and promoting a more even growth of grass, before leaving the club abruptly at the end of May after a disagreement with it over the domestic arrangements made for his family. So John Taylor, an assistant groundsman for twenty years at Old Trafford, was pitched in at the deep end. The wise guidance of Bernard Flack, groundsman at Edgbaston and the TCCB's inspector of pitches, was sought and the only worry about the hastily prepared final product was that it contained cracks at each end of the wicket.

Pundits have often been confounded by the way a wicket plays, and cracks on the surface of a pitch are often deceptive – all depends on whether or not they crumble – but after much agonised deliberation on the glorious Thursday morning on which the match began both captains decided to include a second spinner. Thus, Ray Bright earned his first cap for Australia and Geoff Miller his second for England. Bright replaced another bowler, the unfortunate Pascoe, but Miller, with his reputation as an all-rounder, replaced Barlow, a specialist batsman. One felt at the same time sorry for Barlow, who was in danger now of being cast aside without another chance, and glad for Miller who had been on the point of getting a place more than once the previous winter, only to be disappointed at the last moment.

The choice of five specialist bowlers – Willis, Old, Lever, Underwood and Miller – meant that England were better insured than they usually were against losing the toss, as lose it they did. With the prospect of considerable help for Bright and O'Keeffe later in the match it was a lucky break for Australia and their job now, of course, was to capitalise upon it by making as large a first innings score as possible.

Australia had made one change to their batting, bringing back Davis now that his form was so much better, in place of 'Action Man' Robinson. But there was quite as much pressure on his opening partner McCosker, whose form was such that had he been an Englishman on tour he would not have played. Certainly Hughes was unlucky, after several good innings, not to earn his first cap and certainly too the unfortunate McCosker was unable to justify his selection. Willis, bowling with his usual whole-heartedness from the Warwick Road End, got quite alarming bounce with the hard new ball in his first few overs, and after one delivery had carried from Davis's gloves just short of first slip a ball in Willis's third over was edged by McCosker to third slip where Old caught the ball at stomach height at the third attempt.

For a long time – he scored only three singles in 80 minutes – Davis did no more than hang on to the lifeline of the crease, but Chappell was soon in polished control. He glanced Willis for the first four of the innings in the seventh over and a few balls later drove him past cover for four more. A third four followed from a superb force off the back foot past cover.

Lever's opening overs from the Stretford End were straight and accurate but if anything his bounce was low. Old, too, looked more innocuous than usual when he replaced Lever, and Chappell was ruthless with any ball even fractionally short or overpitched. Davis, a model of patience, gradually gained in confidence and hit one rousing pull off the back foot to a short ball from Old which he picked up so early he was able to hit past mid-on. Underwood bowled at first from the Warwick Road End, where the fast bowlers were getting some help; they certainly got little from the other end where Old and Lever were toiling in vain. Nor was there any turn this early in the game for Underwood, and it was only when

Brearley turned to Greig, to see if his great height would result in the same bounce achieved earlier by Willis, that England had their second success. In fact Greig was not looking any particular threat to the batsmen, and Chappell had just hit his seventh four, a crisp on-drive between the bowler and mid-on, when, out of the blue, he got a ball of good length to move fractionally away from a slightly crooked defensive push by Chappell and Knott gratefully accepted the surprising chance right-handed in front of first slip.

Australia lunched, therefore, at 80 for two, and with Chappell disposed of for 44 on a day when he looked sure to score a hundred, England must have felt that more than a fifth of their work had been done. The Australian innings, indeed, went into decline in the early part of the hot afternoon before the absorbed gaze of a crowd of just under 20,000 protected from the burning glare of the sun by a colourful array of straw or cotton hats.

Davis is a good cutter but almost a compulsive one, and he fell to a good low catch by Knott off the inside edge as Old made a ball cut back under the batsman's blade. It was the movement of the ball rather than any fault in the execution of the shot which caused the wicket.

Walters and Serjeant now joined forces, the one dashing, impatient and determined to attack, the other composed and happy to bide his time. Walters, as always, sparred and snicked outside his off-stump but with much less frequency than normal, and he generally played himself in sensibly, attacking the occasional bad ball with rapier speed. Serjeant played only one memorable stroke, a powerful pull, but was warming to his task well when a quicker ball from Lever moved just enough off the seam and trapped him l.b.w. on the back foot. Bowling with admirable pace and accuracy in the full heat of the mid-afternoon Lever followed up this important blow by having Hookes caught behind off the inside edge as he played an ungainly stroke on the back foot. Hookes, as immature in appearance as he is talented, departed furiously, though whether with the umpire or with himself one was left to guess.

At 140 for five the innings was at its nadir, but things looked up again for Australia as Walters suddenly blazed away with a succession of sparkling strokes before tea – savagely executed square-cuts and off-drives and the particular Walters speciality, the whip-drive through midwicket. Marsh was 4 not out at the tea interval, Walters 47 not out, and Australia 162 for five. The wicket was now playing quite easily, the bowlers were tired, if very far from exhausted, and with two belligerent strokemakers together the situation was ripe for a recovery. It duly came by dint of responsible cricket and many pleasing strokes.

Brearley's captaincy was sounder than his predecessor's, but he did make one decision after tea which, both at the time and with the benefit of hindsight, seemed strange. Miller bowled his first over of the day from the Stretford End immediately after the interval. It was not a particularly good one, Marsh punching several short deliveries hard into the covers although he gleaned only two runs from the over. But even professionals need a loosening over sometimes, and although Miller had not got any turn from his first six balls at the left-hander it seemed hasty for Brearley to decide that he was not going to trouble the batsmen and also unsettling for Miller when he was taken off and replaced by Underwood. In other words Miller was only being used to enable Underwood to switch ends. The latter was as tidy as ever, but the two experienced 'cobbers' played him easily enough and whenever Underwood tossed one up Marsh hit him safely away, as often as not in the air. He also produced a savage stroke or two against Old, once clubbing him past mid-on, then over mid-off, and a third time cutting with such force that Woolmer, struck just above the wrist on his right arm, had to go off for an X-ray. Walters continued to play beautifully, moving his feet decisively against Underwood and twice driving him past mid-on for cleanly struck fours.

It seemed that a century partnership and an overdue hundred by Walters in a Test in England were both safe bets when Brearley turned belatedly back to Miller. His first ball was short and punched through the covers by Marsh, but he then settled to a length and in his third over Marsh lost patience, aimed a massive blow whilst slightly off-balance, and the ball turned enough to take the edge of the bat and carry in a gentle parabola to cover-point. Miller naturally looked happier than he had all day and he followed his crucial blow with another rather more fortuitous one. After edging one drive past slip Walters, on 88, hit a low full-toss straight to Greig at extra-cover. So Miller ended the day with figures of two for 14, and Australia's hopes of a commanding total – they were 241 for seven at the close – were dashed.

As yet there can have been no serious complaints about the wicket, which made Greig seem all the more unwise for once again ruffling the feathers of the authorities by putting his name to an article in the *Sun* which was heavily critical of Old Trafford pitches in the past and called for an end to Tests on the ground if the pitch was as 'disgraceful' as the one on which the 1976 Test against the West Indies had been played. Apart from producing an angry reaction from the Lancashire Chairman, Cedric Rhoades, Greig's general condemnation of groundsmen, whom he felt were too lazy these days and too inclined to rely on machinery and modern science, must have hurt more worthy, hard-working groundsmen than it pricked the conscience of the few to whom his words might fairly have applied. As mentioned earlier, his county carried the can for his misplaced candour.

Brearley withheld the new ball in the morning, although it was now due. He has always been a believer in spin bowling, especially against tailenders, but on this occasion the much-criticised but perfectly reasonable decision to invite the tailenders to hit out or get out did not immediately succeed and twelve runs were added by Bright and O'Keeffe before Willis was let loose at them. He could not again summon the bounce and hostility of his opening overs the day before and it was fifty minutes before England broke a useful little stand which only underlined the feeling that the pitch was a friendly one for batsmen. O'Keeffe went first, giving a dolly off an attempted hook at a bouncer. Bright soon followed, slashing at a short ball that slanted across his body and seeing Greig at second slip hold on to the ball, travelling at bullet speed, high to his right. But Thomson, natural games-player that he is, hit anything pitched up to him with a satisfying crack, Walker also contributed some lusty blows and only when Brearley recalled Underwood after a last-wicket stand of 25 did a well-flighted ball do the trick. Australia were all out for 297.

England were left with twenty minutes' batting before lunch, and the innings began auspiciously with Thomson and Walker's opening overs safely negotiated without a trace of alarm. After lunch, however, Thomson worked up full speed and Brearley was simply beaten for pace as he went half-back to a ball of good length and edged to McCosker at second slip. The catch was dropped but Chappell with marvellous reflexes intercepted the ball before it fell to ground.

This was disappointing for England and for Brearley especially, but Amiss had begun so confidently that he looked like having one of his good days. Alas, not so. He had twice hooked Walker authoritatively before lunch, and it was almost an ironic overconfidence which led him to repeat the shot to a shortish ball. He misjudged the bounce and a catch lobbed up to Chappell at slip off pad, forearm and back of the bat. Amiss waited for Bill Alley to give him out, partly no doubt in his chagrin at getting out when playing so well.

Out he was, however, and England had once again got away to a miserable start. Yet this was the prelude to as handsome an afternoon of batting from two English players as had been seen for years. Twelve months before in the Old Trafford Test the ancient warriors Edrich and Close had been grimly resisting the rampant West Indies fast bowlers. The cricket then was painful and one-sided. Now two young men in their twenties, granted the help of a very much more agreeable wicket, embarked upon a carefree stand, so much so that in the middle of it Bob Woolmer, cheery soul that he always is, said to Derek Randall, the comic genius: 'I'm enjoying this.' 'Aye,' said Randall, 'I am an' all.' So was everyone else. It was high time for Test cricket to become, for an English team at least, an enjoyable exercise again.

Before the strokes began to flow the playing-in process was essential. This was not easy against Thomson bowling with great heart and splendid speed from the Warwick Road End. Randall got on his way with a four past cover off the back foot off Thomson, the prelude to a flurry of sweetly timed strokes off Walker at the other end. Woolmer took a little longer to get into his stride, but as at Lord's he was reassuringly solid and quick to pick up the line. Thomson bowled for a further seven overs before coming off an hour after lunch with impressive figures of one for 20. Already Chappell was missing the presence of Pascoe to help maintain the pressure and before long he was turning to Bright's tidy but flat left-arm spin. Woolmer would have been more seriously tested had the bowler given the ball more air; as it was he soon paddled him round the corner with that very late sweep shot beloved of Cowdrey and D'Oliveira. O'Keeffe came on to join Bright and both batsmen drove and swept him in turn. Fourteen runs were taken off two overs and Chappell was forced to recall Thomson, more to stem the flow of runs than anything else. But Randall and Woolmer were now in very clear control, Woolmer deft and masterful, Randall exuding pleasure as he punished every loose ball which came his way. Hitting the ball in the middle of the bat past groping fieldsmen is the essential joy of playing cricket, but of course the fielding side cannot be expected to share the pleasure to the full. 'You don't have to talk to me,' said the chirpy Randall at one point to the grim-faced Marsh. 'It's not a b. garden party' came the reply.

Randall reached fifty with another sweep off a wide legside half-volley from O'Keeffe. In the same over he played the flipper easily enough. Randall looked up the wicket to O'Keeffe and cheerily turned his wrist over, a gesture which showed his admiration for the ball but simultaneously let the bowler know that the batsman had read the delivery without difficulty. 'Cheeky little b . . .' said Fred Trueman in the commentary box with a delighted grin. England's batting that afternoon must have taken him back to the days of England dominance in the late 1950s when May and Cowdrey would take control of an attack with a not dissimilar mixture of Randall's natural brilliance and Woolmer's polished gentility. At tea, with the runs coming at almost a run a minute, the stand was worth 94, and 107 had been added in the session. The large and enthusiastic crowd rose as one to give the two batsmen a proper welcome to the pavilion.

Woolmer received his first important piece of luck soon after the interval when, very much as Brearley had done, he pushed forward around the off-stump against Thomson and snicked a fast chance to second slip, where poor McCosker muffed it again. This time there was no Chappell to reprieve him and he must have known that the only reprieve he *would* get now would be by means of a big second-innings score. The chance to achieve this was a long way off. Woolmer, 43 when he offered this opportunity, celebrated with one of the purple phases through which his long six-and-a-half-hour innings passed, cutting and driving his way to 20 of the first 29 runs made after tea. Hitherto the flawless Randall had scored appreciably the faster. He kept in the act now with the latest of cuts, deftly improvised, against Bright.

Woolmer offered a second chance when he drove without getting to the pitch of a ball from Walker, and Walters, diving at cover, got his fingers to the ball but could not hold on to it as he fell. Randall was less fortunate when he was given out l.b.w. for 79 to an inswinging yorker which gave Bright his first Test wicket and deprived Randall of a second Test hundred.

Greig came out to loud boos, only to be expected after his unwise criticism of recent Old Trafford conditions which, in this match anyway, were proving so excellent. But this is just the sort of thing which stirs Greig to produce his best, and by the time he was out the following afternoon he had silenced the boos and earned himself forgiveness from the always generous folk of Manchester. He was 16 not out, and Woolmer 82 not out, and England were most happily placed at 206 for three when a rousing day's cricket ended.

The first question to be answered on the Saturday was whether Woolmer would reach his second successive hundred against Australia; the next was whether Australia could break through with the new ball, due soon after the start. In the event Woolmer not only reached his personal goal but saw to it that his work was not wasted by batting through the dangerous period which followed. Yet with these two essential objectives achieved, England fell away and the day ended with Australia relieved that things had not gone worse for them and hopeful that they might henceforth improve.

Chappell gave Thomson and Walker a couple of exploratory overs first thing from the Warwick Road End and then took over for six overs himself until the new ball was available. From the Stretford End Bright was employed to keep things as quiet as possible and pick up a wicket if he could. He nearly did so, too, when Woolmer, after an exquisite cut for four off the front foot, the stroke of a confident batsman with implicit trust in the pitch, was beaten in the air and almost bowled. Thus encouraged, Bright bowled eight overs for nine runs and it was mainly at the expense of Chappell that Woolmer, with a mixture of drives, cuts and glances, had reached 99 when Thomson bowled the first over with the new ball. It was a good one. Woolmer set off on a risky run and was rightly sent back by Greig; he flirted absent-mindedly with a dangerous bouncer; then, off the final delivery, firmly cut past gully for the runs which gave him his third Test century. This was his fifteenth four but he now sternly and determinedly set himself to blunt Thomson and Walker, denying himself all excesses with admirable devotion to the cause of his team.

Greig's approach was different. He seemed out to irritate his opponents to the maximum. Every time he played a defensive shot he ran a couple of paces up the pitch as if looking for an impossible single, though this usually confused his partner more than it did the fielders. At anything remotely resembling a half-volley from Walker or Thomson he aimed a mighty drive, and at anything short he cut or slashed, trusting to luck that if he hit the ball on the edge it would go hard enough to be safe. Whilst Greig continued to carve and snick and occasionally to unleash a powerful and authentic off-drive, Woolmer persisted with calm defence, and before ten overs of the new ball had gone Chappell was being forced onto the defensive again – or at least away from all-out attack.

The Australian irritation was exacerbated by some untidy fielding and then by a definite piece of misfortune. When he was 40 Greig tried to avoid a nasty bouncer from Thomson and as he attempted to lift the bat out of harm's way his shoulder rose to obscure umpire Tom Spencer's view from a thin but clear deflection into Marsh's gloves. Never one to hide his emotions, Marsh mouthed a four-letter *cri de coeur* which the millions watching on television will have interpreted as easily as a deaf person reads the lips of an elocution specialist.

Everything continued to go England's way before lunch, and Woolmer again began to allow himself the luxury of run-scoring, so that at the interval Australia's lead had been cut to only nine runs and seven English wickets had to be taken on a wicket which still threw the words of its critics back in their faces.

To their great credit the Australian bowlers did hit back in the afternoon and indeed by the close had taken six of the wickets they needed and restricted England's lead to 139. Max Walker was mainly responsible with some lion-hearted bowling between lunch and tea, while O'Keeffe, wheeling away unchanged from the Stretford End for the entire session, was equally worthy. Woolmer could not hit the ball with the same sweet timing after lunch and quite suddenly he looked fallible. In a marvellous over Walker twice beat him outside the off-stump and twice smiled philosophically as Woolmer earned fours off the edge to the third-man boundary. At the other end O'Keeffe had him in trouble padding up to a googly which almost brushed the off-stump, then troubled him with a leg-spinner and finally, just before three o'clock, ended an innings of great importance with a ball which bounced enough to find the edge of the bat and carry via the pad to an alert Davis at short-leg. Woolmer had batted a little under six and a half hours for his 137, hit twenty fours and shared stands of 142 with Randall and 160 with Greig.

O'Keeffe, however, did not hold any fears for Greig whose confidence and aggression had grown as Woolmer's had waned. He took a couple of paces down the pitch and hit one enormous straight six which cleared the boundary to the offside of the sight-screen by at least twenty yards, then hit another scorching four down the ground past the bowler's left hand.

Knott took a good look at the bowling before attempting anything daring, but he got going through O'Keeffe's generosity in bowling three successive long-hops, two of which Knott pulled past mid-on for fours, the third being helped round to the long-leg boundary for the sake of variety. But Australia returned to the pavilion for tea with two more wickets in the bag. Greig checked an attempted drive and the deserving Walker ended his valuable if variegated innings of 76 by sticking out his left hand as he followed through and taking a fine catch which was made to look all the more spectacular by a subsequent somersault. He deserved to make all he could out of this sweet moment of reward for all his tireless endeavours. When he was finally rested after fourteen wholehearted overs he had bowled for an hour and forty minutes.

Miller, torn between playing a passive role and trying to inject some new life into a flagging batting rate, made six reasonably accomplished runs without ever looking like getting on top, then tried to hook a fast short ball from Thomson before he was ready to attempt anything so ambitious. The result was a top-edge and a disdainful dismissive gesture by Thomson which seemed to say: 'Give me men, not boys.' Miller will grow worthy of such exalted company before long.

England were 367 for six at tea and soon afterwards Australia got rid of the greatest menace in their way when Knott purposely sliced Thomson over the heads of the slips only to see O'Keeffe dive forward to take a brilliant right-handed catch at third-man. It was one of the bright moments of an uncharacteristically shoddy fielding performance by Chappell's team.

One's attention at this period was somewhat split between seeing how many the tailenders would muster and keeping an eye on the classic combat going on at Turnberry, where Jack Nicklaus was breaking the Open Championship scoring record by seven strokes, yet losing to his heir-apparent, Tom Watson. The duel between Jeff Thomson and Chris Old was something less than classic and certainly less equal, but Old, paralysed by very fast bowling as usual, somehow managed to avoid snicking anything to the wicket-keeper and, when he got down to the end where first

O'Keeffe and then Bright were operating, he unleashed some magnificent full-blooded drives. Walker returned to have him caught, driving a wide half-volley which Bright at slip dropped but diverted into Marsh's gloves.

Lever made a typically useful contribution but the day ended with Willis and Underwood holding out in order to give Brearley the right to use the heavy roller after the weekend. England's lead was now 139 and their total was 436 for nine. Their cautious progress through a mildly disappointing Saturday's play had earned them 230 runs for the loss of six wickets but they were now three-quarters of the way to a famous victory.

Manchester was excelling itself. Only in 1934, I am told, did England play Australia at Old Trafford without the weather intervening at some point in the game. Now for the fourth day running it was warm and sunny and so much the more enjoyable for coming after the grey gloom of Lord's.

Brearley batted on mainly so that he might use the heavy roller on the dry pitch. No doubt he also hoped for a few quick runs from Underwood and Willis. In the event England scored one bye, Underwood gave Bright his third Test wicket and by 11.45 a.m. Australia were starting their attempt to make the 140 they needed to make England bat again and the 300 which would have given them a chance of victory.

A good start seemed essential for them, yet to the third ball of the innings McCosker tried to hook a short delivery from Willis without moving his feet and Underwood circled under a gentle skier to mid-on. McCosker's nightmare match was over. He walked in, indeed, like a man in a dream and was replaced by the slim straight-backed figure of Chappell, marching purposefully out to play, albeit in a losing cause, one of the great captain's innings for Australia.

Willis was both fast and fiery in his opening overs, his awkward action strained to the limit as he varied his off-stump attack with the occasional bouncer. Chappell and Davis both snicked him close to the slips but both also played with spirit, and when Chappell was invited to hook he did so with such conviction and good timing that he lifted the ball clean over Lever's head on the long-leg boundary. The slightest mistiming and he would have been gone, but Davis did not read the danger signs, tried to emulate his captain by hooking up rather than down and was well taken by

Lever: 30 for two, in the eleventh over.

Underwood had been introduced at the Stretford End after only four overs from Lever and soon got some deliveries to turn a little, but Chappell, ice-cool as ever, was judging the length of the ball unerringly. Twice he on-drove Underwood past a groping Amiss at mid-on, and when Amiss was replaced by the more mobile Lever a third four flashed past Lever's right-hand side as he dived. The immaculate Old Trafford outfield continued to give no chance to a chasing fielder once a stroke had got through the inner ring. Old replaced Willis and he too was punished, this time for pitching fractionally short. Chappell hit him off the back foot past mid-off with a short-arm punch, and then with a full swing of the bat sent him crashing through the covers.

Serjeant stayed with the master for half an hour, hitting Old past mid-on for four and then glancing Underwood to fine-leg with a deft late turn of the wrists. But in attempting to repeat the shot he glanced straight to Woolmer, who took a fine reflex catch at close forward short-leg off the face of the bat.

Showing no outward sign of any emotion Chappell soon redressed the balance, a superb hook off Old giving him his eighth four and a flawless fifty out of 84 in an hour and a half. If Walters could only get going as he had in the first innings a sparkling afternoon's cricket was in prospect and a big enough Australian total to make England's second-innings task very difficult. Walters might have been caught when he edged a beauty from Old where a second gully might have been, but if Brearley made a rare error here he enjoyed a vital success when he called up Greig for the last over before lunch in Underwood's place and saw Walters shuffle behind an off-cutter to be trapped fatally in front of his wicket.

Australia, therefore, were 92 for four at lunch, of which Chappell had made 54. The gap between himself and his colleagues was almost embarrassing. But for 80 minutes after lunch young David Hookes, full of confidence in his own ability, played well enough to suggest that England's batsmen might yet face a severe test in the fourth innings. He was allowed to settle to a certain extent by means of three fairly friendly overs from Greig after lunch. Underwood and Willis proved a more threatening combination, and Underwood was now bowling over the wicket, aiming at the rough outside the right-hander's leg-stump. When he was 67 Chappell was beaten by one which turned sharply to miss his off-stump; he also chopped a no-ball into his stumps, but he was still punishing the slightest error of length with flawless drives or cuts. Hookes, timing the ball well, managed to keep pace, and it was a single by him which made sure that England would have to bat again. Another hour with these two together might have transformed the match, but Miller was introduced an hour after the interval and in his third over he found the perfect ball for Hookes, inviting him to drive a ball turning away from the off-stump. Brearley made no mistake with the simple catch to slip.

Within ten minutes Marsh and Bright had gone too and with them most Australian hopes. Underwood tempted Marsh to play one of the lofted on-drives he adores and for once his strength was not enough to help the ball clear of the one-saving fielders. Randall at wide and deepish mid-on was the man in the path of the stroke and he, of all people, very nearly dropped it, recovering to catch the ball at the third attempt before subsiding flat on his back with relief. Oddly enough his first catch in Test cricket, made as substitute fielder at Delhi, had been identical: a catch off Underwood to wide mid-on which he had juggled with before accepting. This time, Underwood followed up by catching a return drive by Bright in the same over. However O'Keeffe is one of the most difficult of batsmen to dig out in a situation where his side is up against it, and he duly dropped anchor whilst Chappell coolly continued to despatch anything remotely loose.

Chappell was 92 not out at tea and soon afterwards a hook and a straight drive off two no-balls from Willis took him to his fourteenth Test hundred. Of the six he had scored against England I had seen five, and if all were memorable displays this, played as it was with scant support from anyone else and against Underwood on a wicket starting to turn enough for most mortals, was arguably the best. His sheer technical excellence, his marvellous decisiveness whenever an attacking opportunity presented itself, and his self-absorbed dedication were the features one most admired.

Underwood got his man in the end. Chappell had just hit him away off the back foot through extra-cover for four, but in attempting to repeat the shot to a ball which turned a little and kept low as well he dragged the ball onto his stumps and departed with the bat tucked underneath his arm to a hero's reception from a warmly appreciative crowd. Underwood and his team-mates leapt for joy. The rare prize of a Test victory over Australia was now definitely in their grip and it did not take long for Underwood to finish the job. Walker was caught by Greig at point, off bat and pad, and Thomson, after a quiet request from Brearley to Randall to move a little deeper, obligingly hit the next ball straight into his hands.

Underwood has rarely bowled better than he did after lunch, drawing on his vast experience of dry, easy-paced wickets, and varying his pace and trajectory with the skill of one of the greatest of all slow bowlers. It made his fascinating duel with Chappell all the more piquant and precious to know that this in all probability was to be one of the last Tests that either of them would play in.

England were left with only 79 runs to win and before the fourth day was over Brearley and Amiss had made eight of them, Brearley bearing the brunt of two very fast overs from Thomson.

It took England an hour and a half on the cloudy Tuesday morning to complete what was only their eighth home victory over Australia since the war. It was also only the second England win in the last fourteen Tests against Australia since the defeat of Illingworth's side by Ian Chappell in 1972 in the final Test at the Oval, the game which levelled that series after Derek Underwood had made sure of retaining the Ashes by bowling Australia out on the notorious 'fusereum' pitch in the previous match at Headingley.

No one had done more, except perhaps Lillee, to undermine England in the intervening years than Jeff Thomson, and he did not let them forget now that there was some way to go before any long-term issues were settled. He bowled very fast and Amiss looked less than happy against him, but Brearley stood up resolutely and sensibly, leaving anything he did not have to play and dealing firmly with anything he did. Amiss battled through with gradually increasing conviction and looked much safer against Thomson in his second spell, as well as playing O'Keeffe with admirable skill. The leg-spinner was getting turn and bounce now and must have wished that he had been granted even a hundred more runs to play with to make England sweat. He did get Brearley, driving without getting to the pitch, but by then only four more runs were needed. Brearley was duly confirmed as England captain for the three remaining matches of the series.

My own last memory of the Test is the sight of a white blob appearing with startling suddenness in the mirror of my car as I rattled south down the motorway. The blob soon transformed itself into Tony Greig's Jaguar and there was a fleeting glimpse of Greig in the driving seat and Brearley in the passenger's next to him, engaged in earnest conversation. Captain and vice-captain had always got on well but they had never been closer in the eight months of their successful association than now, when they knew they were bound to be split.

Chapter Six
TRENT BRIDGE – BOYCOTT'S RETURN

The England victory at Old Trafford lifted the shadow which the Packer affair continued to cast over the summer, and the criticism which the Australian team received made the tourists all the more determined to prove their detractors wrong. No one was keener to do so than Chappell himself, who yet again dwarfed all about him in making 161 not out (six runs less than half his side's total) against Northamptonshire. The Australians twice declared in this game but Northants were strong enough to draw the match comfortably on the last day. Warwickshire, however, were not so resistant in the next match and went down by 130 runs, despite a fine century by John Whitehouse in the first innings and a good 80 by Alvin Kallicharran, soon to have second thoughts about his Packer contract, in the second.

The match at Edgbaston was significant for other reasons too. Dennis Amiss failed twice, being caught off Pascoe for 14 in the first innings and off Thomson for 11 in the second. Whilst this probably decided the England selectors to discard Amiss and recall Boycott, two fine innings for the Australians by Richie Robinson (who scored 207 runs in the game without being dismissed) made it hard for the Australian selectors to ignore his claims for the Trent Bridge Test.

The other significant happening took place off the field. It had been the team's custom to have two men available every match to look after the duties of twelfth man and to let the four remaining players who were not involved in the game do as they wished. At Edgbaston, where birthday celebrations for Geoff Dymock coincided with a benefit party for Rohan Kanhai, the unfortunate position was reached where only ten men were fit and available to field for the touring team. Accordingly Chappell called a team meeting at which he ordered that in future *all* the party of seventeen must be on parade for all matches. Some frank words were bandied about as the problems of the tour in general were discussed by the players and their manager, Len Maddocks, who had become, for various reasons, increasingly separated from his team. Someone suggested that the manager was not doing all he should. He, in turn, said he felt the captain was not always pulling his weight either. Rodney Marsh jumped in at this point and offered characteristically belligerent support for his captain. In other words there were what industrialists and trade unionists might describe as 'frank and meaningful discussions'.

Unfortunately the story was misreported in one national newspaper, which wrongly claimed that Max Walker had threatened to 'lay one' on the manager – hardly likely behaviour from so genial a character. It was all rather unsavoury, and indicative of the growing pressures of the Packer affair and of being one-down in the series.

Leicestershire produced a drawn game, with rain intervening on the last day; the main features were a distinguished bowling performance by Walker and a timely 59 not out by McCosker. Now all attentions turned to the ICC meeting at Lord's, where the bans on the Packer men were finally decided upon, and then to Trent Bridge, where advance sales of tickets had broken all records as the knowledgeable Nottinghamshire public sensed that form and morale were ripe for another English victory.

The Australian selectors had a difficult decision to make over their team for Trent Bridge. There was never much doubt that Pascoe would return for Bright, but, apart from the captain, there was still little to choose between the batsmen. Chappell, Marsh and Walters eventually decided that Robinson could not be left out after his fine performance against Warwickshire, and they decided to omit Serjeant to make way for him. After his fine début at Lord's, where Robinson failed, and McCosker's nightmare of a match at Old Trafford, one could only feel that Serjeant was extremely unlucky not to have been selected, and one had to accept on faith that it was coincidental that Serjeant was the one man in the touring party known to have turned down an offer from Packer's organisation. The other non-Packer men in the party – Cosier, Hughes and Dymock – were again relegated to the 'substitute's bench'. However the decision by Jeff Thomson to pull out of his contract with Packer was announced the night before the game began, and as the capacity crowd made its way to Trent Bridge on the sunny morning of 28 July they did so in the hope that the game would once again prove itself bigger than the players.

Trent Bridge, sadly devoid of Parr's tree but looking pleasantly modern on the Hound Road side with the smart electrically-operated scoreboard dwarfed by an exceptionally well-designed new office block and an impressive temporary stand alongside, generally provided a splendid setting for a crucial match. The stand was packed tight with people, many of them protected by bright lime-green sun-hats which provided a mass of colour as Chappell again called correctly and without hesitation chose to bat first on a straw-coloured pitch, which looked as though it would be the batsman's paradise which Trent Bridge has traditionally provided over the years.

England left Graham Roope out of their twelve – he had come in for Barlow, the twelfth man at Old Trafford – but their side showed three changes, an unusually high number for a team which had just won a Test against Australia by as wide a margin as nine wickets. Old, because of a shoulder injury, had not been considered, so this change at least was enforced. His replacement as the late-order all-rounder was Ian Botham, who at 21 became the youngest England cricketer since Alan Knott to earn a Test cap. This move strengthened the batting but weakened the bowling. The attack was further changed by the dropping of Lever and the introduction of Hendrick, which for all Hendrick's excellent form was a brave decision and a hard one on Lever who had done so well in all his eight successive Tests. The last change had been expected: the faithful Amiss was dropped – his poor record against Australia, who had reduced him to a batting average of fifteen, made this almost inevitable – and his double failure in the county match against the tourists cooked his goose. His omission allowed Boycott to return. On batting form there was no question but that he deserved to do so, and his decision not to sign for the Packer circus had helped remove the moral objections of those who believed him to be a deserter. His crime was certainly no worse than that of the men whose own desertion was about to begin.

The early moments of the match soon confirmed the benign appearance of the pitch. McCosker hooked a four in the first over from Willis, a confident start, but both Willis and Hendrick extracted what life they could in the next few overs and there were one or two lucky escapes, though no chances went to hand. England's fielding was sharp, as it needed to be on an outfield that was exceptionally fast. Botham replaced Willis after five overs and might have had McCosker caught with his second ball if there had been a third slip, but McCosker was soon turning two successive leg-stump half-volleys for four to mid-wicket and at the other end Davis hooked Hendrick effortlessly for six to the packed Hound Road stand. Otherwise Hendrick bowled excellently, but without luck, his first six overs conceding only four runs. The 50 was posted after an hour's batting and Australia's first reverse didn't occur until twenty minutes before lunch, when Davis, beaten in the air by Underwood, drove too soon and was joyfully caught by Botham at mid-on.

This was only the beginning for the young Somerset all-rounder. Chappell started impressively before the interval with a cultured offside four off Underwood, and McCosker reached a well-merited fifty, warmly applauded by a crowd which recognised that this marked the end of a miserable run for a batsman everyone respected. 51 not out at lunch, McCosker could not add to his score afterwards; in Hendrick's third over of the afternoon he shuffled across to a ball which nicked the outside edge of his bat and carried low to Brearley at first slip. From the other end Willis bowled much better in his early afternoon spell than he had at the start, but it was the replacement of Hendrick by Botham at the Pavilion End which really started the Australian rot. With his first ball, delivered at three-quarters pace, he got the wicket England always wanted most. Chappell was quickly in position to force a shortish ball through the covers but succeeded only in dragging it back onto his stumps.

Hookes had come in in his new position at number four and although he might have been unsettled by one vicious bouncer from Willis – a no-ball – which caused him to fall over as he took late evasive action, he played well and sensibly. He and Chappell had added 30 cautious runs when Botham got his lucky break, but Hookes soon followed his captain to the pavilion, the victim of a superb diving slip catch by Hendrick, held at full stretch to his left in one hand.

England were on top now for the first time and soon they were kicking themselves in disbelief as four Australian wickets went down for two runs in an exciting flurry of bad shots and fine catches. Walters fell obligingly and characteristically to a catch in the gully, pushing out in that wasteful way of his without moving his feet, and at the other end Robinson chased a wide delivery from Greig and saw Brearley clutch onto a high chance with both hands. Botham followed up by having Marsh l.b.w. as he shuffled across his stumps and played a crooked shot to a straight ball, and then managed to persuade Walker into the improbable achievement of getting an outside edge to a ball which actually came back in from off to leg. The art of swing and cut which Botham had learned from watching Tom Cartwright was being put to excellent use now as he followed in the recent footsteps of John Lever and Phil Edmonds in taking five wickets in an innings on his Test début. In his purple patch Botham had taken three for one in 14 balls.

With the score at 155 for eight, however, England's almost irresistible progress at last came up against an immovable object in the person of the admirable O'Keeffe. Attempting nothing which was not beyond his limitations, but hitting anything loose with authority, he never looked in trouble either in defence or attack, and it was noticeable that when England's bowlers tested him with short deliveries on the basis that they considered him a poor hooker, he had time to play the shot with confidence. In other words he emphasised again the slowness of the pitch and the dismal performance by the middle-order batsmen.

Nor was O'Keeffe alone in his resistance. Thomson, coming in shortly before tea to an affectionate welcome which clearly showed how much the crowd appreciated his efforts to pull out of the Packer circus, survived an early carve outside his off-stump against Botham and afterwards kept pace with O'Keeffe, hitting anything pitched up with powerful, cross-batted drives. England, who had gone into tea hardly able to believe their good fortune, now had to work much harder for the last two wickets.

Her Majesty the Queen, in the course of her Jubilee tour of the Midlands, had been due to meet the teams during the tea interval but huge crowds had delayed her arrival. A green helicopter hovering low over the ground with the Royal Ensign flying beneath it announced her arrival along with the hoisting of the Royal Standard from the pavilion. She was in time to see Botham take his fifth wicket as Thomson slashed at an outswinger, but Pascoe was in an equally obdurate mood and neither he nor his partner had any intention of hurrying the end of the innings to allow Her Majesty to continue with her itinerary.

Pascoe had become one of the characters of the tour, and jokes were starting to circulate about him as they did about Randall in the England camp. Pascoe was said, for instance, to have signed his autograph on the back of a bat upside down (or at least in the opposite way to everyone else). When this was pointed out to him he asked: 'How did you know it was me who signed the wrong way?' On another occasion when discussing his bowling action he is reputed to have observed that a 'tiger can't change its spots'.

On this occasion, he played with the determination of any tiger and his stand with O'Keeffe was eventually interrupted at half-past five when the two teams lined up in front of the pavilion and were presented to the Queen and the Duke of Edinburgh. Did any of the Australians, or any of the three Englishmen concerned, re-gret, one wondered, that they would probably never again have the honour of shaking hands with their Sovereign? Surely Tony Greig must have felt one tiny pang of remorse as the Queen smil-ingly greeted him like an old friend. It was now Mike Brearley, not his friend and predecessor, who introduced the team and who, in an absent-minded moment, put his arm about the shoulder of the Queen in a charmingly paternal manner.

The last-wicket stand reached 47 after this happy eight-minute interruption and the frailty of the middle-order batting had been underlined by O'Keeffe's typically gutsy innings and by the very fact that the last two wickets had added 88 and the first two 94. Brearley and Boycott were left with just under fifteen minutes' batting against Thomson and Pascoe, and although Boycott calmly turned his first ball in Test cricket for three years for a con-fident single to square-leg, it was the captain who bore the brunt, Boycott not having to face a single ball from Thomson. At the close England were 9 for no wicket – 234 runs behind Australia's first-innings score.

The traffic jams stretched way back over the Trent Bridge and some 5,000 spectators were believed to have been locked out when the gates were closed before the first ball of the second day had been bowled. The building developments on the eastern side of the ground which had been necessary to keep the famous club in exist-ence had severely cut the ground's capacity from around 30,000 to a mere 20,000. Although spaces were left on the grass outside the boundary board to ensure the crowd did not become un-controllable, locals with memories believed they had not seen the historic ground so crammed since 1948 when Bradman's all-conquering team attracted vast numbers of spectators who had been starved of cricket during the war years.

At first the cricket was strictly for the connoisseur. Only 21 runs came off fourteen overs in the first hour. Walker bowled from the Pavilion End, with Thomson and Pascoe firing away alternately downwind from the Radcliffe Road direction. Both Brearley and Boycott looked generally safe, though Boycott was beaten early on by a Walker away-swinger and took exactly half an hour to score his first run. At one point five maidens in succession were bowled by Thomson and Walker. Brearley looked for runs with marginally more industry, his only unhappy moment coming when Pascoe got one fast, short delivery to leap back over his stumps as the batsman wisely drew back out of harm's way.

The first semblance of a chance came after a break for drinks when Chappell replaced Walker and Boycott cut him perilously close to O'Keeffe, diving in the gully. In the very next over Brearley shaped to force past cover a ball from Pascoe which was wide of the off-stump and far enough up to the bat to demand a forward rather than a backward movement. Brearley got a thick edge and Hookes flew to his left in the gully to fasten on to a fine catch. Three balls later Woolmer followed his captain to the pavilion, l.b.w. on the back foot to a ball from Pascoe which cut back and beat his defensive stroke.

Enter Randall, the first Nottinghamshire man to play in a Test at Trent Bridge for more than twenty years (Reg Simpson in 1954 being the last), to a rapturous reception. He got off the mark with a four off his gloves and the top of his bat which passed just over Marsh's head. This was fine, hostile bowling by Pascoe. But Randall was casual, carefree and classy as ever. He had made 13 quicker than anyone else when, shortly before lunch, Boycott pushed a ball from Thomson down the pitch, no more than two feet to the onside of the stumps. Boycott set off, head down, on an extremely risky single. Randall had turned, after backing up, to make his ground, the instinctive reaction of any batsman when the ball is played straight down the pitch by the striker: many a backer-up has been run out by an unfortunate deflection off the bowler's hand. Randall looked up in horror to see Boycott still coming at full pelt down the pitch with no intention of sacrificing himself. He had virtually made his ground when Thomson athletically picked the ball up as Randall began a belated and hopeless sprint towards the other end. Marsh collected Thomson's deft, back-handed return and with an almost bullying relish swept off the bails. Randall, a sad Chaplinesque figure, departed to the pavilion whilst Boycott put his head in his hands and tried to shut out the boos of an angry crowd. Poor man, he could hardly have done anything worse than to run out the local hero on his own ground.

Before lunch Greig had time to hit two defiant offside fours off Walker, one off the back foot, the other off the front, but at the interval England's sorry score was 61 for three and Boycott's reward for two hours' struggle was 13 runs. Unlucky 13 for Randall, and unlucky 13 for the man who had cast away the crowd's affection in one fatal moment of misjudgment. It was not, of course, the first run-out incident in which Boycott had been involved, although his record in this respect had recently been much better. But the morning belonged to Australia and especially to Pascoe, who at lunch had taken two for 15 from nine overs.

The match was alive again now and a peerless atmosphere of Anglo-Australian cut-and-thrust developed during the warm, overcast afternoon. Australia knew that Boycott was the man they most needed to get out. Boycott knew that after the sad demise of Randall England expected him even more to get the traditional hundred which would mark a fairy-tale recall.

Thomson was given the first spell down wind after lunch and he very soon drew blood. The West Indies had shown in the previous summer how to deal with Greig. He will murder most balls pitched wide of his stumps, but if you bowl straight and fast at him you will fell timber soon enough. In fact the ball with which Thomson removed his middle stump on this occasion would have missed the leg stump, so far did it come back. Greig made a late stab and the ball brushed off his pads and onto the wicket.

Soon after this, Boycott square-cut for his first four off the 115th delivery he faced. Miller hit a beautifully timed four off his legs off Walker, then snicked another through the slips off Pascoe. In the same over he was out much as he had been at Old Trafford, caught in two minds by a short rising delivery and managing only to fend the ball off his face with his gloves. The only difference now was that Robinson at short-leg took the catch instead of Marsh, and that Pascoe, not Thomson, delivered the fatal ball. Miller looked to have ample time against anything well pitched up but he clearly had a temporary problem against the short lifter, and it was one the Australians had every intention of exploiting.

The crucial moment of the day, perhaps of the entire series, came just after England's nadir of 82 for five. Boycott had made

20 when he pushed forward to Pascoe and edged to second slip where McCosker grounded a straightforward chance. Alan Knott was just embarking at this point on an innings of great brilliance and it was of more than just symbolic importance that the time when he threw off the shackles with three savage square-cut fours off short offside deliveries from Walker was also the time when the sun broke through the clouds. The ball swung less as a result and batting once again looked fun. Boycott soon caught the mood of gaiety. Some would say it was about time too, but he had carefully laid the base and having had his one great slice of luck he deserved to cash in on it. He played his best shot, a glorious cover-drive off Walker, and was now confident enough to aim a hook at Pascoe's next short delivery. In fact it was not an entirely convincing stroke because the feet were moved only the minimum distance towards the off and the ball was skied just in front of the ubiquitous Walker, running in from deep fine-leg. But Boycott was gradually winning his duel with Pascoe, a point he emphasised when he turned him off his legs for four off successive balls. His fifty came after 234 minutes with his fifth four, a square-cut off O'Keeffe, and the fifty partnership was appropriately arrived at by means of a beautifully timed four off his legs by Knott off Thomson.

Pascoe was still fiery enough to bowl three bouncers in an over to Knott, and when he produced another to Boycott umpire Bird warned him for excessive use of the short-pitched delivery. Pascoe's ability to bowl at such speed off so short a run was most impressive.

Tea came with the sixth-wicket pair still together, Boycott 63 not out and Knott 34 not out. Things went still better for them afterwards. There was a flurry of runs, mainly from the flashing bat of Knott, who several times cut O'Keeffe, once in the air past Chappell at slip. Boycott joined in with two more incisive cover-drives off the same bowler, and the 100 partnership soon followed Knott's 50, reached in only 110 minutes off 92 balls with six fours. Knott had his moments of luck. A slightly wayward throw from McCosker gave him a bonus four and he aimed a cut off Thomson which resulted in an inside edge past the wicket-keeper for another boundary. But there were many an authentic cut and drive too, and only the athleticism and determination of young Hookes in the covers prevented him from reaching his hundred by the time of the premature close for bad light, half an hour before the due time of six-thirty. He had had one further moment of luck when he chipped the ball neatly over Walker's head, perfectly bisecting mid-off and mid-on, who vainly converged on the descending ball.

With fortune clearly on their side, well-deserved in the event since Boycott (88 not out) had played with marvellous concentration and composure after being visibly upset by the run-out, and Knott (87 not out) had transformed the game with his unique genius, some people might have expected the batsmen to continue when the umpires gave them the choice of coming off for poor light. But the new ball was due and Boycott was tired. He had once again displayed the peerless solidity of his technique and the inflexible strength of his character. In the moment when he ran Randall out, the Nottingham folk would happily have delivered him up to the sherriff; now he had thoroughly earned their forgiveness.

So England ended the second day on 242 for five – just one run behind Australia.

Saturday began as a perfect English summer day: sunny, balmy, warm but not hot. Boycott stroked the second ball of the day from Pascoe for four backward of cover and the new ball was taken immediately afterwards. Thomson, bowling from the Pavilion End for the first time, was exceptionally fast. He bowled successive wides, one down either side of the wicket, both producing glorious diving takes from Marsh. Then Knott edged the ball so fast through the slips that barely a fielder had moved by the time the ball hit the boundary board at third man with a loud clunk. In his next over Thomson beat Boycott for pace; the ball flew off the edge at shoulder height between second and third slip, and both Robinson and Hookes dived without being able to hold on to a very difficult chance.

There was a palm-tingling excitement in the air as Knott and Boycott moved step by step through the nineties; then, after one vain swish, Knott cut Thomson firmly to third-man and the crowd of 20,000 rose to applaud a marvellous innings. He had reached 100 in seven minutes under three and a half hours, hitting twelve fours and a five, and once again he emphasised how much England would miss him. This was his sixty-fourth successive match for England and there would, in all likelihood, be only two more.

Boycott followed Knott to a very different but equally well-merited century six balls later with a square-cut off Thomson. Walters very nearly ran him out from third-man as he hared back for the second run which got him to his 98th first-class hundred, his thirteenth in Tests and his fourth against Australia. It was a moment to be savoured by all Boycott – and England – supporters.

The next milestone was the 200 partnership, which duly came with a carve over the slips by Knott off Pascoe. Then, with a two to extra-cover, Boycott took the partnership to 215, equalling England's sixth-wicket record against Australia set by Hutton and Hardstaff at the Oval in 1938. But the reference books will in future have to devote two lines to the sixth-wicket record, because as Boycott endeavoured to steer a ball from Thomson towards third-man he edged in the air for the third and final time. McCosker, who might have caught him for 20, did so now when Boycott had scored 107.

Thomson's relief may be imagined, especially since he had bowled erratically with a new ball which was swinging a good deal. However, he now bowled a superb over to young Botham, who soon realised that not all things come easily in Test cricket. He was dropped off an outswinger before he had scored by, of all people, Chappell, and he did no more than survive before lunch, twice being rapped on the gloves and once on the groin by Thomson and Walker. But Knott restored the English ascendancy by means of a series of dashing strokes. Three fours came in one over off Thomson, and against Pascoe he took outrageous chances when he stepped away to leg to give himself room to hit the ball away through the offside.

At lunch Knott was 135 not out. Thomson's first ball afterwards was wide outside the off-stump and Knott sliced it to square third-man where Davis took a fine catch which bore comparison with the one made by O'Keeffe off a similar stroke in Knott's previous Test innings. It was quite an achievement to be caught at third-man in successive innings, and it might be argued that the final stages of Knott's magnificent innings had bordered on the foolhardy; yet there is a thin line between carefree and careless and the fact was that Knott had played his highest Test innings and given his side a fine chance of winning the game. Botham might possibly have been caught off the next ball, a full toss, but he stayed to play some good shots before dragging a ball

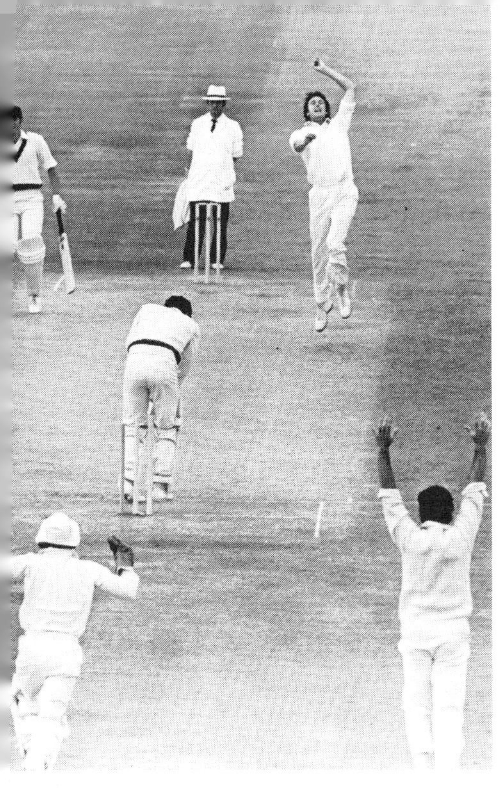

The third Test. *Above* Chappell is beaten by a superb break-back from Hendrick; and Australia show the virtues of bowling straight at Tony Greig: Thomson bowls him for 11 in the first innings. *Below* Walker bowls him for nought in the second.

Above Two of England's matchwinning bowlers in action at Trent Bridge: Willis (left), awkward in action, but even more awkward to play; and Botham, with his more classical sideways action. *Below* Greig dives to catch Marsh brilliantly in front of a delighted Brearley.

Above McCosker hooks Willis for six to reach his hundred at Trent Bridge, and a typical punched cover-drive by Boycott off Thomson heralds his triumphant return to Test cricket. *Below* Alan Knott, the puckish genius, on the way to his unforgettable 135, and England's captain – skull-cap visible – opens his shoulders against O'Keeffe.

Above The worst and best moments of Geoff Boycott's return: Randall is on the point of being run-out by Marsh after a Boycott misjudgment; all is forgiven, though, as the returned prodigal acknowledges the cheers for his 100. *Below* Victory champagne for Brearley, Greig, Randall and Hendrick.

onto his stumps, which hastened the end. Underwood was yorked, Hendrick was bowled by an inswinger, and England's lead in the end was 121.

Australia's attempt to bat long enough to force a draw began in the middle of Saturday afternoon. The innings started well enough, too, with McCosker and Davis getting into line sensibly against Willis and Hendrick and meeting the ball with the middle of the bat. There was a momentary diversion when Nottinghamshire's female physiotherapist came onto the field to put a plaster on Derek Randall's grazed elbow and he could not resist entertaining the crowd by literally sweeping her off her feet. Later 'Arkle' was as sparkling as ever in the field, although his eyes were watering all the time from hay fever, from which he suffers whenever the pollen count is high.

Davis hit two pleasing and controlled strokes through mid-off at the expense of Willis, but in his third over the big man got a couple of breakbacks past the bat and in his fourth Davis did not get far enough across and edged into the sure hands of Greig.

Chappell's first runs had a slightly feverish air about them: an uppish drive through extra-cover played with the weight on the back foot, which brought a super-human airborne dive from Randall that almost turned four runs into a catch, and then a savage cut past gully which again was not wholly along the ground. But the captain soon overtook McCosker, who had settled down to play the innings which was needed. At tea he was 13 not out and Australia, 49 for one, had reason to hope for the best.

Their optimism was dashed, however, by Hendrick, whose virtuous adherence to the ageless principles of bowling to an accurate line and length was rewarded at last. First Chappell edged an outswinger in front of gully; then he was castled by a virtually unplayable ball which came back and kept low. Hendrick beamed with pleasure as his colleagues circled him to offer their congratulations. The crucial wicket had been taken.

But England were to make no more inroads that Saturday evening. Hookes batted in a way which showed his fast-increasing maturity, opening with two smooth strokes through mid-off off Botham. At the other end McCosker was not only sound as a bell but had the confidence to hook Hendrick solidly for four when for once Hendrick pitched short. As the shadows began to lengthen, Brearley turned to Underwood, who bowled over the wicket to Hookes, aiming at the rough, a faint brown scar on the otherwise flawless-looking pitch. But Hookes, hemmed in by close fielders, emerged well from this severe test, showing his innate skill with two deft, wristy strokes, played with the spin through mid-wicket. A potentially great batsman of the future was learning his trade against a master bowler. McCosker could also be satisfied with the job he had done when at the end of the day and the score 112 for two he accompanied Hookes back to the sanctuary of the pavilion, although he must have been lucky to get the benefit of the umpire's doubt when he played no stroke to a late inswinger from Botham. The latter also came close to achieving a run-out with a quick and aggressive pick-up and throw from gully. England were, in short, looking a most formidable side, confident enough now to expect victory rather than merely hope for it.

Monday was another sunny day and brought another full house. At first for home supporters there was little to cheer but much to admire in the resolution of the Australian third-wicket pair. Hendrick, a model of accuracy, beat the bat occasionally, and Willis once found the edge of McCosker's bat only for the ball to drop just short of the slips. However McCosker soon reached a well-merited fifty with a firm hook off Willis and demonstrated his determination to get the other half of his century by hitting his pads repeatedly with his bat, rather like Jimmy Connors bracing himself for renewed efforts after achieving a service break.

Miller came on after fifty minutes for his first and, as it transpired, only bowl of the match. He delivered five tidy overs, once getting Hookes to chop a ball close to his stumps, but it was his Derbyshire colleague who achieved the breakthrough when Hookes played across a ball which straightened.

Walters as ever was a mixture of very good and very bad. His first full-blooded shot was a glorious drive off his toes off Willis, whom he then cut at knee height between the two gully fielders placed for his special benefit. The same pattern continued after lunch, when he and McCosker were starting to build another partnership which seriously threatened England's chances. He hit one magnificent drive for four past cover off Greig, tried to repeat the stroke and struck the ball straight at Randall's lap. The ball had been a widish half-volley and if Greig had bowled it on purpose it was another case of Walters grabbing at the bait and finding himself hooked.

The ball was swinging considerably for both Greig and Botham in the heavy heat of the afternoon and Brearley delayed the taking of the new ball. McCosker, hitting anything near his leg-stump with the broadest of bats, played manfully on, but Robinson looked vulnerable from the start, though as usual the runs he scored came quickly. In the first over with the new ball McCosker reached his hundred with a bold hook off Willis which flew with a satisfying crack from the middle of the bat over the square-leg boundary. But in the third over of a spell which was finally to turn the game England's way McCosker cut at Willis; he was deceived by the fractional extra bounce of the new ball, and Brearley at first slip clung onto a catch which flew hard and fast at his midriff.

In his next over Willis also rid England of the dangerous Marsh, who pushed out at a good-length ball and edged it between Greig and Brearley. Both men dived but it was Greig, falling in front of his captain, who seized the ball at the end of a telescopic right arm. One has simply lost count of the dazzling slip catches this extraordinary cricketer has held.

Robinson's precarious tenure of the crease might have ended first ball after tea when he edged Underwood past Brearley's left hand at slip or a ball later when he played through the hands of Greig at point. In fact, it ended in the next over from Underwood as the arm ball hurried past an intended forcing shot and hit Robinson's back pad before going off the bat into the covers.

With seven wickets down, Australia were only 149 runs on. The last two wickets in the first innings had added 88, however, so there was work to do yet for the bowlers. O'Keeffe again looked thoroughly sound and Walker was in a suitably defiant mood, but Willis soldiered nobly on in the heat and after a fifty-minute stand between Walker and O'Keeffe he again took two wickets in two overs, first slanting a ball around Walker's intended drive and then producing another inswinger to pierce the gap between Thomson's bat and pad. Underwood smartly completed the job as Pascoe played across a ball which turned just a little and Hendrick once again made no mistake with the chance at second slip.

So England were left 189 to make to go two up in the series with two to play, a position they had last achieved on home soil in, believe it or not, 1905. In the intervening years they had often failed to get the 200 or so needed to win in the fourth innings. Now the lasting qualities of the Trent Bridge pitch and the psychological initiative were in their favour. Brearley and Boycott, much more confident and assertive than in the first innings, played seven sharp overs from Thomson and Pascoe with admirable conviction and when stumps were drawn the target had been reduced to 172.

England may have been hoping to go two up after three games against Australia – for the first time in any rubber since 1928–29 – but even with such glories in prospect it could not have been expected that Trent Bridge would be as full on the fifth day as it had been on the first four. All the same, a crowd of 8,000, very much bigger than normally watches the final day of a Test, gave the ground a suitable atmosphere of excitement and occasion as Thomson strained every nerve to earn Australia the early break-through they had to make. He bowled six excellent overs, off which Boycott and Brearley scored only two runs. The weather was again uncomfortably muggy, and it often seemed as though a thunderstorm was looming up around the floodlights of the Nottingham Forest and Notts County football clubs, which peer over like naughty schoolboys at grandfather Trent Bridge. But the threat never materialised and Boycott and Brearley were not going to be hurried by the weather forecasters. They scored seven, all behind the wicket, off the first over of the day bowled by Pascoe, but in the next hour only 14 more runs were squeezed out and in the hour after that only 29.

O'Keeffe's appearance after ten overs of the morning did not greatly increase the rate of scoring, although Brearley swept and square-cut him confidently enough for fours, and Boycott once cover-drove him with a meticulously moulded stroke. No one hits boundaries with more deliberate intent or more certainty of success than Boycott. One can almost see the instantaneous decision that *this* is the ball to hit, the body being positioned exactly for the perfect execution of the relevant stroke. With other great players batting is often a matter of instinct; with Boycott it is a carefully prepared process of manufacture.

Boycott looked virtually infallible in making 45 of England's 92 without loss at lunch. Brearley had some luck. He edged Thomson at catching height wide of second slip in the course of an over in which he might also have been given out l.b.w. to a ball which kept low. But at lunch he too was 45 not out and England were halfway there.

After the interval Brearley became the more adventurous, hitting the occasional loose ball with growing confidence and authority. The main danger seemed to lie in a certain lack of communication between openers unused to running between the wickets together. But they had added 154 – the best opening stand since one of 157 by Dennis Amiss and David Lloyd against India in 1974 – when Brearley, now anxious to finish the job quickly, played onto his wicket off the inside edge as he drove at Walker.

Word had come to the captain that there was rain only twenty miles from Trent Bridge. He called in Knott to try to get the runs quickly. Instead he was brilliantly caught by O'Keeffe, diving to his left in the gully. Then Walker, moving the ball considerably in the clammy atmosphere, got an inswinger past Greig's drive to reduce England to 158 for three. In six balls Walker had taken three for two.

Randall, whom the crowd were longing to see and who had per-haps been a little tactlessly held back, now came in to restore some sanity, but he too might have been out – caught and bowled by O'Keeffe – before, with a straight drive for three soon after tea, he gave England their second successive victory over Australia. Not since 1956, and before that 1890, had England beaten the old enemy twice running on home soil. No wonder Boycott, with 80 not out on top of his first-innings 107, returned with arms aloft through a sea of rejoicing Englishmen. The folk of Nottingham had given wonderful support and seen a marvellous Test match. The total crowd attendance was 87,000 and would have been much greater if space had allowed. The final receipts were a record outside Lord's: in excess of £152,000.

Australia were a troubled team: not so seriously outplayed as England had been when they had lost the Ashes in Australia in 1974–75, but almost so. Then the Lillee/Thomson combination seemed an insurmountable problem for Mike Denness's team. Now it was still possible for Greg Chappell to drive his side towards a recovery. As he said, England were not so superior as successive victories by nine and seven wickets would suggest. If Boycott had been caught in the first innings when he was 20, making England 87 for six, the end might have been less melan-choly for a struggling team. But without Lillee, with the sombre shadow of Mr Packer overhanging them, with an inconsistent and inexperienced batting team and an unbalanced bowling attack devoid of a spinner of the highest class, Australia were down and almost out.

England, like most winning sides, were a good deal happier than their opponents. Brearley had proved his batting worth to any remaining doubters; Boycott had returned triumphantly and achieved the improbable feat of batting on all five days of the game; Knott had played perhaps his greatest Test innings; Botham and Hendrick had thoroughly justified their selection. Above all, England had held all their catches, Australia had not.

The only sad reflection one had on England's victory at the time was that a well-balanced team with a nice mix of youth and experience would soon have to be broken up by the departure of Greig, Knott and Underwood, three of the most important cogs in an efficient machine.

Even as the curtain dropped on the happy scene at Nottingham, with the England team waving from the balcony to a crowd bursting with local pride and national patriotism, Kerry Packer was preparing for the press conference in London at which he was to announce his High Court actions against the cricket authorities. Yet he must have known that nothing he would stage could compare with the Test which had just finished. For behind all the tensions and excitements, the successes and sufferings of the players, and the demonstration of their skills before large crowds, was the century-old tradition of England versus Australia. That could never be bought.

Chapter Seven
JUBILEE ASHES, AND A HERO COMES HOME

It is one thing for a captain to seem cheerful and patient when his team is winning; it is quite another to be so when things are going badly, even disastrously, as they were now for the Australian team. Yet Greg Chappell had so far come through all the disappointments and frustrations of a long tour which had taken so many wrong turnings with the calm fortitude of a strong man. His self-discipline and determination were impressive. Unfortunately his team-mates could not follow his lofty, sometimes apparently detached style of leadership. Nevertheless, despite their inadequacies on the field, the rather slovenly impression they often gave off it, and the feeling that their pride was less injured by their defeats than it ought to have been if they were men true to their cricket traditions, the 1977 Australians were not as bad as all that, and they were not quite beaten yet.

In fact, in the game following the third Test they suffered one of their most humiliating defeats, at least on paper, though manager Len Maddocks put the first-ever victory by a Minor Counties team against an Australian touring side into truer perspective when he said: 'This was not so much a win for the Minor Counties as a win for cricket. We came here to give cricket in the North-East a boost and that's what we did.'

It could not have been done, of course, without the Minor Counties team, who thoroughly deserved their famous victory, getting the winning run with one over to spare from a leg-bye after they had been set to score 207 in 100 minutes plus twenty overs by the acting captain Kerry O'Keeffe. It was indeed a boost for minor county morale, but it was certainly not a measure of the strength of the touring team, and the result was more on a par with previous 'sensational' defeats by minor teams, such as a win by Holland over a previous Australian team and the famous victory by Ireland over the West Indies side of 1966, who were bowled out for 25.

The Australians rebounded from this little setback by returning to Old Trafford and beating Lancashire with a much-improved performance. Thomson, Dymock and Malone all did well to bowl Lancashire out cheaply, although it would have been even cheaper but for some tailend heroics, and a substantial first-innings lead was acquired mainly through a very good 89 by Kim Hughes. Bright, with 5 for 67, set up a possible win after a certain amount of time had been lost to bad weather, and then Chappell, with an assured 70 not out, and Cosier, playing the sort of innings he revels in, hit the ball hard to achieve a thoroughly worthy win against the clock by seven wickets.

It might have been thought that Hughes had earned himself a Test chance at last, but Robinson did just enough, with another useful fifty, to convince the tour selectors that he should be retained in the Test side which now crossed the Pennines knowing that their last chance to salvage a sad tour had come. In the words of the song, it was now or never.

It had so far been a summer during which cricket and cricketers had been obsessed with the subject of money, and as the Headingley Test approached this obsession amounted almost to mania. In a further attempt to dissuade any more English cricketers from signing away part or all of their Test careers, the London office-cleaning boss David Evans got together three small businessmen whose companies each put forward £3,000 as a direct gift to the England team at Leeds. The three Father Christmases made it known that the money was intended for the players who had not signed for Mr Packer's organisation, but since they had no wish to disrupt the unity of the England team they left it to the captain to decide what to do with the £9,000 cheque which was handed to him, and Brearley decided to split the money evenly. With this bonus, their normal match fee of £210, and the possibility of a share of the £2,500 given by the TCCB to the winners of the match, the English players stood to make a record sum of £1,250 each. Anyone contesting their right to such a sum was soon confronted with the figure of £85,000 received in advance ticket sales by Yorkshire before the fourth Test began.

As if convinced that they would see the historic achievement of Geoffrey Boycott reaching his 100th first-class hundred on his home ground against Australia – the perfect Boycott dream come true – people began queuing at 5.30 a.m. on Thursday 11 August. They waited patiently outside the high brick wall which divides Headingley from the uniform family houses which climb up the slope on all four sides. Inside the small island of green in this sea of red brick, George Cawthray was putting the finishing touches to the Test pitch which had seen such excitement in recent years and which was about to become the stage for further historic achievements. Here Bradman and Morris had led Australia to their famous win in 1948, when 404 runs were scored to win on a crumbling pitch on the last day. Here, more recently, England spinners had bowled out Australia cheaply – Laker and Lock in 1956 and Underwood to win back the Ashes in 1972 when the 'fusereum' grass disease infected the pitch; and here in 1975 an evenly poised match ended when oil was poured on the wicket and knives and forks were used to dig it up to draw attention to the protests of innocence from a man found guilty of crime in the East End of London.

Now a crowd of 22,000 were packing into the ground on a glorious sunny morning. The gates were closed forty minutes before play began, and the spectators were to witness a great batsman enjoying his finest hour. Geoff Boycott believes, as Winston Churchill believed, that he has a destiny to fulfil. From the moment that Brearley won the toss on a good batting wicket it seemed that nothing would prevent the course of that destiny, and so it was to prove. Since his century and his 80 not out at Trent Bridge he had scored another century for Yorkshire, the 99th of his career, and those who saw it felt it was almost as if he were deliberately setting up the much greater triumph which was to follow.

Brearley, choosing without hesitation to bat, took first strike as Thomson began by bowling up the slope from the Grandstand End. His third ball was a wide outswinger which the batsman played at. The Australians went up in instant appeal for a catch behind the wicket; Brearley looked indignantly at the slips and turned belatedly to see umpire Budd's finger raised. Brearley apparently thought that his bat had hit the ground and not the ball, but the overwhelming consensus of opinion was that he had got an outside edge.

Boycott's first runs were cheered as if he had already reached his hundred. As he later said, the crowd were much more certain that he would eventually achieve his goal than he was. Indeed many had backed him to do so at four-to-one against. It was destined to be an expensive day for Ladbroke's, cricket's bookmakers.

Brearley's early demise did not alter his good fortune at winning the toss. It was a perfect morning for batting, the light ideal, the temperature warm but not steamy, the outfield lightning fast, sloping down on all sides, as John Woodcock aptly wrote, like a crown bowling green, and the pitch itself true and easy-paced. There were, however, small veins of lush green growth on it, and the seam bowlers were to move the ball enough to worry batsmen and give themselves hope throughout the day.

Woolmer began his scoring with a most elegant stroke off his toes for four off Thomson, a stroke which had the knowledgeable Yorkshire crowd murmuring 'shot!' in unison even as the ball sped off the face of the bat towards the new pavilion at square-leg. Walker, rather than Pascoe, shared the new ball with Thomson, who was replaced by Pascoe after a testing five-over spell. Thomson, in fact, bowled courageously all day, suffering silently but painfully from haemorrhoids.

For Thomson and all the other Australian bowlers, however, it was to be a largely frustrating day. Boycott might have been out twice in the twenties. At 22 he edged a rising leg-cutter from Walker off the shoulder of the bat and Marsh, changing direction, was a fraction too late to take the low, wide, extremely difficult chance in his right glove. At 26 the last of three bouncers in a very hostile over from Pascoe, a ball which from the angle I was watching looked suspiciously like that occasional 'chuck' which Ted Dexter had accused Pascoe of producing from time to time, brushed Boycott low on the arm as with a brilliant late adjustment he played a stroke at the ball in front of his face. The Australians appealed confidently, but umpire Budd agreed with Boycott that the ball had struck not the glove but the forearm. In the over after this Woolmer was beaten by a lifting outswinger from Thomson, and there was no doubt that both batsmen were struggling to survive.

Woolmer, in fact, was the more fluent, interspersing vain prods outside his off-stump with the occasionally flowing stroke; Boycott was the more sound, eliminating all risk, despatching the rare bad ball with calculated precision, as often as not through the covers, and counteracting the moving ball with a broad defensive bat. At lunch England were 76 for one, Boycott 34, Woolmer 33. At lunch the previous year West Indies had been 147 for no wicket!

Woolmer was out fifteen minutes into the afternoon, pushing

out at Thomson and edging low to Chappell at first slip. The sticky batting was now all too briefly transformed by an ebullient little innings from the great entertainer himself, Derek Randall. He twice chopped down on fast rising deliveries from Thomson, his natural good timing sending the ball skimming to the third-man boundary. A full-toss from Pascoe was faultlessly driven through the offside for four, but after he had made 20 out of 23 in 26 minutes the carefree atmosphere was abruptly halted as Randall played slightly across a fine ball from Pascoe which nipped back in sharply and hit his right leg in front of the stumps.

Randall's innings, like a sudden breeze on a hot day, was the only time when Boycott's personal battle did not seem the focal point of attention. A sterner atmosphere returned to the proceedings now, but the arrival of Greig appeared to prompt the Yorkshire captain to sudden action. He reached 50 with a cover-drive off Walker, the eighth of his fours which included one that resulted from a wild overthrow. He lifted an arm to salute the crowd, who rose to give him an ovation which would normally be accorded to a century.

Greig was out of touch at first, while busily looking for runs. He swivelled to pull a short ball from Chappell just over Pascoe's head on the long-leg boundary for six. Chappell looked increasingly frustrated, several times appealing in vain as he struck Greig on the front pad. Boycott drove him straight for four to raise the fifty partnership and soon afterwards Chappell called up Ray Bright, preferred to O'Keeffe as the spinner in the side, to bowl the most significant over of the day just after four o'clock. Boycott drove him for four, cut him past slip for four more two balls later to reach 75 and then, off the last ball of the over, shaped to glance a ball pitched just wide of the leg stump. Marsh took it, and he and the bowler went up in instant appeal for a catch. Umpire Bill Alley said 'not out' and Bright reacted furiously, seizing his sun-hat from Alley and hopping about in uncontrolled anger. Alley, not a man to tangle with, waggled an admonishing finger, and Chappell hurried across and put both hands on Bright's shoulders as he told him to cool down, then apologised to Alley. Bright did so too, an over later, and the incident was officially overlooked, although it was not forgotten, of course, in the Australian dressing-room. Nothing now was to stop the inexorable progress towards the apparently predestined moment of Boycott's triumph.

At tea Boycott was 79 and England, who were indeed being well served by him but whose team cause seemed on this particular occasion to be secondary to the individual's, were 185 for three. Greig was out twenty minutes into the last session, having played another mixed but valuable innings, driving just inside the line of a good delivery from Thomson which came back to hit his off-stump. It was Walker, however, who now produced the outstanding spell of the day, one which on a luckier day might have earned him three or four wickets. He actually beat Roope outside his off-stump four times in one over as the raw-boned Surrey right-hander made his usual fidgety start. Walker even beat Boycott – something which was becoming rarer than a brick wall on a Yorkshire moor.

More often one marvelled at Boycott's ability to adjust his stroke late enough to cover any late movement off the seam, and with cloud now occasionally covering the sun there was more of this than ever. But Roope gradually settled in, Walker came off to a warm reception after seven overs for nine runs, and with a cover-drive, a square-cut, an isolated hook and endless pushes into the mid-wicket gap, Boycott reached 96.

Chappell was bowling from the Grandstand End when, at 5.49 p.m., Boycott with total conviction seized on a half-volley on his off-stump and smacked it crisply through the mid-on gap for four. Headingley erupted in joyous acclamation; Boycott lifted both arms high and was lost, a lonely, balding, strained but happy-looking figure, in a sea of congratulating Yorkshire invaders. It was eight minutes before the cricket could resume, Boycott having received his cap back from a spectator who had pinched it and then thought better of it. Boycott took his time, sorted himself out, made sure everything was in place and together with Roope calmly played through the last half-hour as if there had been no interruption. But when the day was over and he took his place on the balcony to wave to the hoards of cheering Yorkshiremen, he must have felt like a Roman Emperor returned from exile to win a battle on home soil.

The new ball had been in use for only two overs when play began with England's score on 252 for four, and there was much more cloud about than there had been the previous day; yet the ball seemed to move rather less in the early overs as Roope launched the day before another full house with some handsome strokes. Two half-volleys from Walker were unerringly hit through mid-off for four and Boycott soon settled in again with the same concentration, assurance and painstaking attention to detail. Minute care was taken not only in his actual batting but even in the way he adjusted his pads, wiped his brow and scratched at his crease with his bat, like a badger cleaning out its set.

Soon after noon Thomson beat Roope outside the off-stump and next ball had him caught, driving, at third slip by Walters. Thomson followed up by actually beating Boycott with the last two balls of one over and the first one of the next. He was replaced by Pascoe, who was noticeably faster and who found the edge of Boycott's bat with his first ball which scudded through at catching height where third slip would have been. He continued to bowl short and fast at Boycott, but all danger was calmly avoided.

Knott made a circumspect start, playing nothing he was not forced to play, but when Bright relieved Walker after a nine-over spell from the Grandstand End, Knott at once greeted him with a sweep for four to bring up England's 300. He tried some less successful sweeps, changed tactics and a few overs later danced down the pitch and hit Bright deftly off his toes through mid-wicket.

Once again, as so often happens in cricket, what luck there was went against the underdogs. Boycott, for instance, did not time a drive towards extra-cover, Davis swooped on the ball from cover, threw down the stumps at the bowler's end just after Boycott had made his ground and for his pains saw Boycott amble a second run from the overthrow. This is one of cricket's unfairest laws: it should be changed so that, if a throw hits the stumps, the ball becomes dead and no further runs are permitted. As it stands at present, good cricket is penalised.

The next, similar, half-volley which Boycott received from Thomson was firmly driven through extra-cover for four, and in the same over he leg-glanced for four more. Knott joined in, hitting Bright through mid-wicket again, then dabbing him past slip for another four. 22 runs came from these two overs. At lunch England were 339 for 5; 87 had been added in the two hours of the morning and Boycott was one short of his 150.

He reached the next milestone with a controlled edge for two to third-man and the applause this time was noticeably more muted. Strangely enough this was only the second time in official Tests that Boycott had exceeded 150, the first being the notorious occasion when on the same ground he made 246 not out against India and was dropped from the next match, officially because he disobeyed his captain's orders to get a move on. This was now the highest score at Headingley by an English batsman against Australia. But any hope that Boycott would cut loose was a vain one. He was in his own limited top gear, and he had no overdrive. The progress after lunch was slow and miserable, Australia being partially responsible as they fired away well wide of the off-stump, inviting impatience but not getting it. The ninth hour of the innings produced only 34 runs from 16 overs, above the average of a generally slow over-rate. A full-toss from the tired Walker enabled Boycott to raise the 100 partnership with a firm straight drive. Knott reached his fifty and Boycott was then handed a bonus four from a wild overthrow by Hookes. A message had come from the dressing-room by way of the twelfth man Miller to accelerate, but Knott, who might with luck have torn the attack apart, perished in the attempt. He moved down the pitch and hit Bright over the top of extra-cover but was given out l.b.w. next ball as he aimed to sweep a straight ball and was hit on the front pad.

Ian Botham came in at 398 for six, hoping to thrash a tired attack. He played forward to Bright's first ball and hit his second beautifully off the back foot but straight to extra-cover. 'I don't think he's going to hang around long,' I said sagely in the commentary-box. He didn't, because he tried to cut the next ball and lost his off-stump: a clear case of running before he could walk or, in other words, of inexperience, but it hardly mattered in the circumstances.

Underwood *did* hang around for a while but was missed by Chappell at slip off Bright before slicing Pascoe wide of Bright, who dived to his right in the gully and held a brilliant one-handed catch. Boycott looked on at all this with lofty calm. At tea he had batted four hours of the second day for 69 and ten hours in all for 179. The sympathies of the crowd were not lost but they were starting, unlike Boycott himself, to lose patience. As for the Australian side, they seemed to have become resigned to his inevitable presence. The only questions to be answered now were whether or not Boycott would carry his bat through the innings, and whether or not he would reach 200. In the event he did neither. Hendrick was out soon after tea, caught at short-leg off Pascoe who was bowling with admirable fire and venom and who had his just reward now when Boycott, still hopeful of a double hundred with Willis looking secure at the other end, drove and edged to Chappell at first slip. Boycott had batted every minute of the ten and a half hours of England's innings.

Australia were left with an hour and twenty-five minutes' batting in good light. They were tired and dispirited but they cannot have been prepared for the rout which was about to begin. McCosker, in fact, hit the first ball of the innings for a confident four to square-leg, but off the second ball of the second over Davis was trapped l.b.w. by a ball which nipped back at him. Hendrick was from the start a formidable proposition, swinging the ball very late with his lovely high action and able to pitch the ball up with the confidence born of success. England, with 436 behind them, could attack without fear, and Hendrick knew that he was bowling to an array of brilliant fielders in the slips. He claimed the prize of Chappell's wicket with an outswinger edged high to Brearley at first slip and Australia were 26 for two. They had this many only because of an aggressive start by McCosker, who hit Willis for three fours and a six (a hook over long-leg's head) in three overs. Willis, in all, was hit for 35 in five overs. The ball was swinging much less for him; McCosker played well and Hookes attacked anything pitched up with inappropriate levity. Both were much less certain against the dangerous Hendrick but McCosker was actually out to a piece of magic conjured out of thin air by Randall. Hookes played a ball quietly towards mid-off; Randall moved like quicksilver from extra-cover, scooped the ball in underarm and hit the wicket at the bowler's end from which McCosker had backed up no further than the normal amount. He was possibly as much as a yard short and for Australia to lose a wicket like this from nowhere must have seemed the last straw.

It was not, however, the end of their afflictions. Willis was replaced by Botham, whose ability to swing the ball was just what was needed. Hookes had played one really fine shot worthy of the memory, a hook off a ball from Willis which was barely short of a length, but when he pushed half-forward to Botham and was struck on the front pad umpire Alley had not a second's hesitation in sending him on his way.

Walters did his best to try to buckle down and see the day out, but before long Botham produced the outswinger required and Hendrick bent to his left and took a good catch at knee-height at third slip. The wheel of fortune had now turned its full circle. England had known this sort of despair when they were on the receiving end against Lillee and Thomson in 1974/75. Now they were going to regain the Ashes as overwhelmingly as they had lost them then. Australia needed 170 to save the follow-on when the dizzy final session of the day finished with their score 67 for five.

There was no longer any getting away from it: Australia were a divided, downhearted and disintegrating team. With some players staying in one hotel, some with their wives in another, the cricketers went off in ones and twos to try to forget their troubles. Poor Rick McCosker, who had been batting so well before he was run out, sat by himself unable to raise a smile, a graphic picture of glumness.

If there was to be any escape from their present predicament on the field, the Australians must have hoped for a sunny Saturday. But the weather in Leeds was as grey as the local stone. Another capacity crowd mingled in cheerful anticipation of another England victory, yet secretly hoping, surely, that the Australians would not go down without a fight.

The three Yorkshiremen who had scored 100 hundreds – Herbert Sutcliffe, Sir Leonard Hutton and Geoffrey Boycott – were photographed together in the middle before play began, with Botham and Hendrick renewing the attack against the two wicket-keepers. Robinson had got many more runs than Marsh on this tour, and he started the day with some positive strokes which were at once brave and rash. Marsh was able to avoid the ignominy of four successive noughts by pushing Botham into the cover gap for two but he was then superbly caught in Knott's right hand off a leg-glance.

Robinson, it seems, can play cricket only one way. Sooner or later Hendrick would get him out. Robinson drove at an outswinger on the up and carved it past the leaping Roope in the gully; he repeated the stroke a few balls later and this time the ball flew off the outside shoulder of his bat and was caught by Greig at the second attempt at second slip.

Bright and Walker at least ensured that their side would reach 100, but there was no longer the slightest doubt that Australia would be forced to follow on for the first time against England since the second Test at Lord's in 1968. Walker perished to a wild swing, Thomson to a 'pearler' which pitched on middle-and-leg and knocked back the off-stump and Pascoe to an off-cutter which found its way without difficulty through an open door between his bat and pads.

It was almost no contest. Australia had been bowled out for 103 in two hours and eleven minutes and 31.3 overs. Botham had taken three wickets for 12 runs in the morning and five wickets in an innings for the second Test in succession.

The follow-on was enforced without hesitation by Brearley but Australia's second innings began rather more promisingly. Davis took his time before avoiding a 'pair' with a fine stroke through the covers off Hendrick, who was replaced by Greig at the Grandstand End. Davis three times hit the new bowler crisply through the offside off the back foot, and had just on-driven Willis for three when he shaped to leg-glance a relatively harmless ball from Greig and was given out caught behind off bat and pad.

Soon after this possibly fortuitous dismissal, the ball went out of shape and was replaced by another which, from the outset, swung far more. The score was 31 for one when the ball was changed (after five balls of the twelfth over) and Greig looked a different bowler at once. In the last over before lunch he beat McCosker with an outswinger and the batsman survived an appeal for a catch behind the wicket. A few balls later he was not so lucky, as Knott dived again to take a fine low catch in his right hand and Australia lunched at 35 for two.

The talk around Headingley now was mainly concerned with whether Australia could extend the match into Monday. Chappell, looking like a man angry at facing impossible odds, gritted his teeth and concentrated as he had not done in the first innings, and Hookes took his cue from his captain, although his scoring rate was twice as fast. Chappell simply refused, with one exception when he tried to drive Hendrick and missed, to play anything he did not have to and survived the balls he did need to play with astute defence. Hookes did his best without suggesting that he would ever settle in with any permanence and was l.b.w. for 21 to Hendrick, once again playing a straight ball with a crooked bat. On his native Adelaide Oval pitch this was all very well. In the very difficult conditions facing batsmen that afternoon it was not.

No one knew the differences in English and Australian conditions better than Doug Walters, who now used his experience sensibly as he continued the struggle in company with Chappell against an unrelenting attack of swing bowling, mainly from Greig and Botham. Greig was eventually rested after a spell of 14 overs broken only by lunch, in which he had consistently made the ball swing like a banana. He was replaced by Woolmer, who was able to swing it just as much but who needed what seemed to be a generous piece of umpiring to get the fourth wicket. Walters had just played one of the few memorable strokes of an afternoon of gritty struggle – a quick-footed hook off a rare short ball – when he went forward to an outswinger and was sent on his way (l.b.w.) by umpire Alley. This certainly looked a questionable decision but Walters accepted it without demur. Australia at tea were 114 for four, and three balls from Hendrick after the interval the umpires conferred about poor light; they offered the batsmen the opportunity to come off and no one was surprised when they did so. The crowd drifted away in droves as bad light turned to rain, but soon after six o'clock the skies lightened again and just before half-past six play resumed, with the possibility of it continuing until half-past seven. The ruling, introduced in 1974 to give spectators a chance of more cricket when rain spoils their fun, states that if play has resumed by half-past six and more than an hour's play has been lost during the day it may continue until half-past seven so long as the players are on the field at six-thirty. In the event play did resume, but only for eleven balls, because, rather than give Underwood a chance on a wet wicket, Brearley unleashed Willis, and some thoroughly understandable acting by Chappell convinced the umpires that the light had deteriorated again.

So the Australians returned to their hotels once more to try to forget their worries. The gap in class between Chappell and the other batsmen had been less apparent this time, but the fact remained that he was the only Australian (apart from Bright) whose wicket had not fallen to the English bowlers during Saturday's play.

After divers cricket matches around Leeds on the Sunday – a Lord's Taverners game at York, a Silver Jubilee match at Barnsley in which I got some badly needed fresh air and much enjoyment, and a press contest between the respective corps of Australia and England in which Australia, with the aid of 'guest artists' Ian Chappell and Kerry Packer (eager as ever to promote the right image) emerged victorious – we all assembled at Headingley on Monday for the serious business to begin again. It was delayed however by rain, which happily stopped soon after eleven and did not reappear until the evening, when the battle was lost and won.

The hurly-burly, in fact, commenced again at two o'clock, so (apart from eleven balls) four hours' play had been lost since teatime on Saturday: not that anyone seriously doubted England's ability to finish the job with time to spare. The remarkably large Monday crowd who had been patiently waiting were to be rewarded by a thoroughly entertaining two hours and forty minutes' cricket, at the end of which they could go home to tell all their friends that they had run onto the turf of Headingley on the afternoon that England regained the Ashes on home soil for only the third time this century, 1926 and 1953 being the other notable dates.

Willis and Hendrick began the attack. Chappell crisply hit the second ball from Willis towards the cover boundary off the back foot. Earlier in the match it would have been a certain four; now because of the damp outfield the batsmen had to be content with three. Willis pitched a little short to start with but the pitch was lively and circumstances were once again in favour of England. Chappell was beaten by a superb ball from Hendrick which swung away and then bit back off the pitch inside his pads. Australia's captain looked as though he was already resigned to inevitable defeat. At the other end against Willis he seemed more intent on trying to persuade the umpires that the light was not good enough than on concentrating on playing the ball. Consequently, when Willis got a ball just where he wanted it at last, after twenty-five minutes' cricket, Chappell's drive seemed to lack conviction. In any case it resulted in a comfortable catch to Greig at second slip. He had batted three hours for his 36 and set a good example, but any hopes of a draw went with him.

However, where the captain had been tentative and lacking in conviction, the vice-captain was full of rugged defiance. Marsh began to wipe away the memory of his recent failures with some savage driving. When he was 16 he was dropped by Roope, of all people, at fourth slip off Hendrick. It was the first chance England had failed to accept since the Lord's Test. Marsh celebrated with some ferocious square-cuts which brought him four fours in two overs from Willis. In between, Willis had his moral victories and one never felt that the initiative would change hands. It was just a matter of time, and time was on England's side.

Robinson as usual played some good shots and some wild ones. There was a certain irony, indeed, that this man, who finds it so hard to resist playing a shot at everything, should have fallen playing no shot to a snorter from Hendrick which leapt back at him as he turned his back to defend his stumps and which glanced down off his arm onto the stumps. Hendrick followed up by having Bright caught by Greig at second slip as he drove at a widish outswinger. He was helped here by a typically astute field change by Brearley who had called up a silly mid-off the previous ball. Bright was keen to force him back with a meaty four through the covers, hence his downfall. This is the beauty of cricket: a piece of subtle foresight by the captain, a bait laid for an inexperienced player, and another fish neatly hooked.

Happily for everyone, Australia did not fold as quickly as they had in the first innings. Marsh continued to hit hard and judiciously, and Walker, starting with a reputable boundary square on the offside, settled in to play with equal spirit. Marsh reached a fine fifty off only 57 balls with nine fours. Underwood was introduced but for once could not break the partnership. Walker drove him handsomely over the top of mid-on and before long he and Marsh had put on 50 together. Marsh was given a second unexpected life when he miscued a drive at Greig, bowling his medium pace in order to give Hendrick a rest after a well-sustained spell of eleven overs in which he had taken two for 24. Greig, uncharacteristically and much to his annoyance, missed the catch off his own bowling after an agonised juggle. Woolmer was then given a bowl in Greig's stead with the ball which had swung so prodigiously for so long from the time it had been swapped for the original new ball before lunch on Saturday. Botham, incidentally, had again made it swing most of all but had sustained an injury to tendons in the top of his foot, and had gone off.

Eventually, ten minutes before tea, Brearley decided to delay no further the taking of the new ball and for once its effects were immediate and decisive. Willis, eager to get into the act after a relatively unsuccessful match, burst through Walker's defences with the sheer speed of his third delivery. Walker's middle stump was uprooted. Willis's first ball to Thomson was a rapid no-ball outside the off-stump. The next one knocked the off-stump out of its ground. Pascoe survived another no-ball and the last two balls of a very fast over, but Marsh decided that it was now to be death or glory. He stretched to drive an outswinger from Hendrick and sent it high towards extra-cover off a thick outside edge. Randall circled underneath the ball, caught it safely to his chest, hurled it in the air, turned a cartwheel symbolic of a nation's joy, and England had won the Ashes on home soil in Jubilee Year for the first time since Coronation Year, 1953.

The scenes at Headingley were emotionally reminiscent of those at the Oval then after Denis Compton had swept Arthur Morris for the winning runs. The Yorkshire crowd swept onto the outfield like an incoming tide and formed in a cheering mass in front of the pavilion to salute first Willis and Hendrick, who had finished the job so well; then Brearley, who had masterminded this historic hat-trick of wins, the first on home soil against Australia since 1886; and finally and above all Boycott, whose batting had laid the immovable foundation-stone of a great victory.

In the dressing-room behind the balcony the two teams mingled happily and shared the champagne. England's dominance, everyone knew, would not last for ever. Brearley, who two years before had not dreamt he would even play for England, let alone captain them to success against Australia, had been lucky in his timing, as he well knew. So too, though more by judgment, had Boycott. For Woolmer, Randall and Botham an exciting if uncertain future lay ahead. For Roope there was pleasure in playing a part in a famous match. But for the other five members of the team – Greig, Knott, Underwood, Hendrick and Willis – the sweetest thought was that they had got their revenge. They had suffered the misery of heavy defeat in Australia just two and a half years before, and they knew now what it felt like to be an Australian in that dressing-room at Headingley.

Chapter Eight
ANTI-CLIMAX AT THE OVAL

Beaten and bowed, the Australian team must have wished there was a direct flight home from Leeds. Nothing had gone right for them, the tour had been too long by at least a month, and now, as if to mock them in their misery, the rain which had washed out most of their cricket at the start of the tour returned to plague them anew. By some miracle play was considered possible at Arundel where, two days after the end of the Test at Headingley, a one-day contest was scheduled in aid of the Queen's Silver Jubilee Fund. It was entitled 'Australia versus the Rest of the World', a billing which might have been reconsidered if the organisers had originally known of the plans of the Packer organisation. However, as an advertisement for similar games to be played in Australia later in the year this was a non-starter.

The match was played in miserably grey weather and in sodden conditions. Even Arundel's peerless natural beauty could not dispel the gloom, and after Bob Willis had exploded through the early Australian batting with three wickets in four balls (which must have made Mr Packer himself wonder, if he had not already done so, how his advisers could have overlooked England's bushy-haired terror) the game settled into a painful struggle by batsmen on both sides. Hookes and Chappell put on 46 for the sixth Australian wicket to ensure some sort of contest, and then the world eleven struggled to get the required runs with only a few overs to spare. Pakistan's Sadiq and Imran, one patient and the other belligerent, scored the most runs.

Lord's itself was the venue for the final county match of the tour, against the reigning county champions Middlesex, who had just spent three days watching the rain and wondering when they were ever going to play their Gillette Cup semi-final against Somerset. Any cricket was better than none, the players of both sides must have felt, but the brew was mild after the heady stuff at

Headingley. Brearley played a typically studious knock, taking a good long look at Malone in case this bowler should take the place of the injured Pascoe at the Oval. Featherstone was the only other Middlesex man to make a score of any substance, and he played freely and attractively as usual. Thomson and Malone both bowled well for three wickets a piece and Dymock was unlucky not to take more. The touring team had their chance on Sunday afternoon but they found the formidable Wayne Daniel too hot to handle and a score of 34 by David Hookes was the best any of them could muster. It rained on Monday, so now they could only wait for the final Test and the last chance to salvage some respect from the tour.

Many a one-sided series has taken an unexpected twist towards the underdogs in the last match, and Australia had the example of Denness's side in 1975, which won the final Test by an innings after losing four of the first five, to encourage them. England over the years had had much the better of the matches on this famous but dilapidated ground, which has staged more Tests than any other venue in England. Of 26 games at the Oval against Australia they had won twelve to Australia's five, starting with the first Test in England in 1880 when 'W.G.' scored 152. There followed such memorable encounters as the 1902 match, when Gilbert Jessop scored his amazing 104 in 75 minutes on the final day, the one in 1930 when the Don scored 232 and Ponsford 110 as Australia amassed 695, the still greater glut four years later when Bradman scored another double hundred and England were murdered by 562 runs, and the almost indecent revenge exacted by England the year before the war when Hutton got his 364 and England won by the cruel margin of an innings and 562 runs.

England had good reason to be confident of another win this time. They made only one enforced change to their twelve, John Lever returning to replace Ian Botham, who had fractured a bone in his left foot – though he bowled with the injury for a short while at Headingley – and who therefore missed a golden chance to become the first man since Fred Titmus in 1967 to achieve the double of 1000 runs and 100 wickets in an English season.

Australia initially named thirteen from whom their team would be picked shortly before play began. They at last brought in Craig Serjeant and Kim Hughes, the two West Australians around whom their future batting order would have to be built, and it was not just because the two batsmen they replaced, Davis and Robinson, had signed for Mr Packer that one felt that these two players had a more promising future. (Davis might come again in easier batting conditions but Robinson had never looked a player of Test class.) Mick Malone also had a chance of a first Test cap, since Len Pascoe's hamstring was considered unlikely to stand a five-day match. At any rate he was named in Australia's thirteen, as were both spinners, Bright and O'Keeffe.

But the announcement of the final XI's of both sides was postponed because, much to everyone's chagrin, the umpires decided at half-past two on the first day that no play would be possible. It was a day of wind and sun, ideal for drying out wet grounds, but so heavy had been the rain in the previous ten days that it was considered that the muddy patches at either end of the wicket would not dry out in time to allow any cricket. As usual one felt sorriest for the spectators who had long planned their day out at the Oval and who had contributed towards the £84,000 taken in advance for reserved seats. All the reserved tickets, in fact, had been sold for the first three days.

Those who had booked for the Friday's play were more fortunate. It was bright and sunny, with billowing clouds blowing up over the Oval from a Constable sky. Play began on time, Australia winning the toss and Chappell putting England in in the hope of moisture in the pitch and movement through the air. His final XI included three West Australians who had not played in the previous Test, with Malone winning his first and possibly only Test cap in place of Pascoe, who, as expected, was not considered fit. England again left out the unfortunate Miller.

Thomson and Malone shared the new ball and although Boycott edged Malone just short of slip it was soon evident that there were no terrors in the pitch. A square drive by Boycott off Thomson in the seventh over signalled that he and Brearley were confident that Chappell had erred in asking England to bat first with rain forecast. A lovely stroke off his toes through midwicket off Malone took Brearley to double figures, but it was noticeable that though the stroke was well-timed it earned only two runs on the sluggish green outfield.

Walker relieved Thomson after five innocuous overs, and it was clear to discerning eyes, though not to the umpires, who were unsighted, that he was using face cream to impart shine to the ball, an uncomfortable echo of the vaseline gauzes which caused such a furore at Madras on the MCC tour of India. Now, as then, the original application of cream was probably innocent but the television camera clearly showed Walker dabbing his fingers first on the cream and then onto the ball, a blatant, if unconscious, breaching of Law 46. Brearley quietly drew umpire Constant's attention to the illegality, but for some unknown reason he chose to leave Walker unreprimanded. It was noticeable, however, that after lunch Walker was content to apply only perspiration to the ball.

Australia should have broken through at 42 when Brearley pulled his bat away too late from a lifting offside ball from Malone and was missed at second slip by McCosker from a straightforward chance. Thomson came back in Walker's place for a burst before lunch but a drive by Boycott and a push past gully by Brearley brought the fifty, and eight runs came off the over. An intent crowd basked in the sun and counted their blessings. To them the pattern of England's domination must have seemed as clear as the immaculate stripes etched out by the mowers, broad ones on the outfield, narrow ones on the square. The Palace of Westminster stood out clearly on the skyline behind the rusty green gas-holders. The Ashes were safe at Lord's, present there now by right as well as by tradition, the Queen was on the throne and all was right with the world. Brearley must have felt doubly sure of this when he went into lunch 29 not out, the same score as his partner, because he was greeted by the news that his county, Middlesex, had defeated Somerset in the Gillette Cup semi-final across London at Lord's.

However, whether because of any artificial interference or not, the ball appeared to swing much more after lunch, especially for the two medium-fast men, and both Malone and Walker had reward for beating the bat quite frequently with late movement through the air. Boycott went first, almost inevitably in slightly controversial circumstances, as he played forward to an inswinger from Walker and in the umpire's opinion, although obviously not in Boycott's, he edged onto his pad and then on to McCosker at second slip. Woolmer had barely had a look at his surroundings before Brearley too was out, edging an outswinger from Malone to give the strapping West Australian his first Test wicket. It turned out to be the first of many as, keeping the ball well up to the bat and swinging it both late and far, he worked on remorselessly through the bright afternoon, comparing favourably with Walker and making one wonder again whether he should not have been given his chance earlier in the tour. Malone generally swung the ball later, kept the ball further up to the bat and attacked the stumps more accurately. The red patch on his chest, like tomato ketchup on a film cowboy about to bite the dust, aroused further suspicions that the prodigious swing he was achieving had been artificially induced. But whether it was this or a subtle change in the atmosphere, the fact is that the ball did swing and Malone continued to bowl superbly. Randall played an innings of uncharacteristic pawkiness and suspicion before attempting a half-hearted cut and top-edging a catch to Marsh.

Woolmer played with his usual poise but he followed Randall to the pavilion almost at once, beaten for pace by a straight ball from Thomson and clearly l.b.w. as he pushed only half-forward. Greig, anxious no doubt to make an impact in his final Test, was out of luck, driving optimistically at Malone and edging to Bright in the gully. Some delightful, flowing strokes by Roope enabled England to go into tea in rather better heart than they might have done, but they had lost five wickets for 68 runs in a dismal afternoon session and Malone had bowled right through it for overall figures of three for 38 from 29 overs.

Malone continued to plug away from the Vauxhall End to the close of play. Apart from two overs from Bright just before lunch he therefore delivered every over bowled from that end all day, and not a boundary was hit off him, although he shared the wickets in the last session with Thomson, who, as usual, put his faith in straightness and the occasional really fast ball. Malone dismissed Knott, who must have been reminded of Massie's performance at Lord's in 1972, and Lever; and Thomson, with the new ball, eventually hit the stumps of both Roope and Underwood. A spirited stand between these two, however, kept the bowlers at bay for some time. Roope played exceptionally well, mixing a few elegant drives with some authoritative cutting, and Underwood combated the swinging ball with skill in one of his best Test innings for some time.

However, the day ended with England's last pair, Willis and Hendrick, together and with the six-foot two-inch, fourteen-stone figure of Malone sprinting towards the pavilion ahead of his colleagues. His bowling, more than Chappell's decision to ask England to bat first, had made this Australia's happiest day in their unhappy series. His remarkable figures at the end of the day read: 43-20-53-5. After 20 overs he had taken nought for 21, but in his next 14 overs his figures were five for nine. For stamina and control it was a piece of bowling to rank with the best in Test cricket. England's grafting, groping performance against him had taken them to a close of play score of 181 for nine.

Nothing so raises the morale of one side and deflates that of the other as a last-wicket stand. With a new ball in their possession on Saturday morning, the Australian fast bowlers would have expected to get rid of Hendrick or Willis, two genuine tailenders, straightaway. In fact these two batted for 55 minutes, and their stand of 40 was the second largest of the innings. Willis had equalled his highest Test score of 24 not out and Hendrick surpassed his when he was bowled by Thomson for 15. He hit one magnificent cover-drive off a half-volley from Malone, who finished with 5 for 63, but it was Willis, with a variety of shots including some perfectly timed leg-glances, who caused most trouble to the increasingly frustrated Australians. By taking the final wicket Thomson achieved four wickets in an innings for the fourth time in the series.

Bad light and a shower delayed the start of the Australian reply, which began 25 minutes before lunch. It began disastrously, too. Serjeant, rather than McCosker, took the first over from Willis and after nervously keeping out the first five balls missed the last one, which was straight and fast, and was leg-before-wicket.

Chappell, coming in to the all-too-familiar atmosphere of crisis, got a wonderful reception from the Oval crowd and the England team, who warmly applauded him all the way to the middle. Memories of the great Bradman's failure after just such a reception in 1948 may have been in Chappell's mind but he and McCosker safely negotiated the remaining five overs before lunch The light was murky but the ball was swinging only a very little.

Alas, this was almost the end of the entertainment for the day. It grew darker still during lunch, and although the inevitable rain was a long time coming the umpires rightly ruled that the light was too poor for batting in. They came out frequently to the middle to check on the position, which was sensible public relations. They may have been jeered a little louder each time they shook their heads and returned to the pavilion, but at least they showed the crowd that they were trying to get play started as soon as possible. Too often the understandable resentment of paying spectators is simply ignored. A couple of likely lads tried to swing the issue on this occasion by stripping off their shirts and lying down in the outfield as if sunbathing. Not long afterwards play did resume, but sadly for one over only before another umpire's conference resulted in the usual offer to the batsmen to come off and the equally customary acceptance by the latter. The over did include, by way of consolation, a crisp on-drive by Chappell off Willis and a brilliant stop by Randall.

Eventually, just before four o'clock, the rain arrived and fell heavily enough for play to be abandoned for the day and for Underwood to lick his lips. However, mercifully for the Australians, who were overdue some luck, Sunday was sunny and the pitch seemed virtually to have dried out by the time that Monday's play began before a large Bank Holiday crowd. As if determined to make up for lost time the cricket at first was full of urgency. Lever was given the first over from the Pavilion End, and a good one it was too. Chappell got up onto his toes to hit the first ball of the day away on the offside for two, but he was beaten by a perfect late outswinger before edging another one through the slips for three fortunate runs. McCosker almost lost his leg-stump to the last ball, so Lever was distinctly unlucky to be taken off after only one over and to be replaced by Hendrick. Perhaps it was a psychological move by Brearley because, in the second over, Hendrick had missed a straightforward chance at third slip offered by McCosker off Willis. McCosker had made only two.

These early incidents over, the cricket settled down into a more sedate tussle between the accurate Willis and Hendrick and two generally cautious batsmen, although Chappell picked up any runs that were going. A woolly black dog, a Kerry Blue terrier, made an appearance by way of diversion and Randall created another when he cut his hand stopping a ball just in front of the fence and so allowing the Surrey captain Robin Jackman to make a brief appearance on his home ground. But generally the cricket was stern and slow, punctuated only by the occasional elegant drive or cut by Chappell.

A double change in the bowling, introducing Lever and Underwood in place of Willis and Hendrick, almost brought the scoring to a complete halt. Eventually on the stroke of one o'clock Underwood got a ball to turn and off the next delivery Chappell, desperate to get the scoreboard moving, was neatly caught in the spider's trap as he drove a low return catch.

Kim Hughes came in to face an attacking field in an atmosphere of tension. After surviving an l.b.w. appeal he defended resolutely and safely but by appearing to be totally uninterested in run-scoring he surrendered the initiative at once. McCosker was no more enterprising and by lunch Australia, in friendly batting conditions, had added only 49 runs in two hours.

Happily there was altogether better entertainment to come. Willis and Hendrick started the bowling after lunch and both were formidably accurate. McCosker manufactured the occasional leg-side run but absolutely nothing was given away. Hughes had been in for 48 minutes when he pushed Hendrick square on the offside for his first run. Hardly had the ironic cheers died, however, than all his patience was wasted. He edged a lifting ball from the remorseless Hendrick to third slip, where Willis fell forward to hold a sharp low chance. In immediate contrast to Hughes's stern innings Hookes settled in cheerfully, taking two off his first ball to square-leg and then hitting a lovely square-cut for four off Underwood.

But Willis restored England's control when he claimed McCosker l.b.w. for 32. McCosker was possibly beaten for pace as he played across the ball, shaping to play one of his favourite onside strokes to a straight ball.

As usual the arrival of Walters was the signal for frenetic activity. Willis greeted him with a bouncer which flew straight at his head like a guided missile. Walters ducked just in time, but he was already softened up. He slashed at his second ball, hard enough for Hendrick to drop another hot chance.

Hookes had his luck as well, but a cover-drive for four off Willis brought up the hundred. Moments later Walters played a tentative forward stroke down the line of his middle stump to a ball from Willis which moved in a little through the air and then straightened to knock back the off-stump.

At 104 for five Australia were facing another ignominious collapse, but happily for them Marsh had by this stage of the tour recovered his touch and confidence and from the moment that he arrived batting looked an altogether easier business. So, indeed, it should have done because any moisture that had still been in the pitch early in the morning had long since dried out; the sun was burning down from a cloudless sky and batting conditions were well-nigh perfect.

It was on an afternoon like this that Hookes had first made his mark on Test cricket five months before in Melbourne. Now, with

the same heavily-bound red-handled bat in his hands, he looked
for the first time in the present series like the player who had
roused such high expectations during that inspired performance.
An effortless four square on the offside off Lever made him the
highest scorer of the match, but he slashed the next ball between
the wicket-keeper and first slip. Knott came across in front of
Brearley but the catch did not carry as far as he had judged. This
was typical of Hookes's innings: a mixture of gems and blemishes.
A good many of his fours came off Underwood, now bowling over
the wicket from the Pavilion End into the bowlers' rough. He followed one gorgeous off-drive by moving down the pitch to hit
another boundary over mid-wicket.

With the two left-handers batting together and enough rough to
make the occasional ball turn around the off-stump, England
could have done at this point with the services of the absent
Miller. Instead it was the ever-useful Greig who finally broke the
enterprising sixth-wicket partnership when Hookes drove firm-
footed at a widish offside ball and departed 15 runs short of a first
Test century which, perhaps, he had not really deserved. Most of
his 12 fours were glorious, perfectly timed strokes but he had
always looked likely to get an edge sooner or later and, as with
Walters, one wondered if he would ever come to terms with
English conditions.

The stage was now left to Marsh, who celebrated by jumping
down the pitch to bludgeon Underwood over long-on for six. He
square-cut a four in the same over and it was hardly surprising
that Brearley should have called for the new ball at the first opportunity. Willis demanded respect from Marsh with another hostile
spell of bowling but Brearley erred for once in preferring a weary-
looking Hendrick to the unfortunate Lever, who had been kicking
his heels in the outfield for too long. Shortly before the close
Marsh reached a thoroughly worthy 50 with a resounding hook
off Willis, and Australia, 12 runs ahead, could for once be satisfied with their batting.

Now that they were in front, Australia had every intention of
making the most of their position. The final day began in cloudy
weather before a sparse crowd, with the series apparently doomed
to a quiet end. To win, Australia needed to build a substantial lead
quickly and then turn to their bowlers to produce a miracle in conditions perfectly suited to batting. England's best hopes on the last

day were to acquire some useful batting practice. They would certainly have expected to wrap up the Australian innings smartly with the new ball. But on this docile pitch they needed to latch on to their chances, and for the first time in the series the slip catches had been going down.

Willis and Hendrick began the attack and for a while all went smoothly for them. Hendrick had Marsh l.b.w. for 53 as he pushed forward around the off-stump, and Bright, after a useful knock, went the same way when he missed a straight half-volley from Willis. But a succession of fielding lapses now allowed Walker and Malone to put together a record Australian ninth-wicket stand at the Oval. Walker began by giving Lever an extremely difficult, low, wide chance to his right hand in the gully, but before he had scored Malone was dropped by Greig at second slip off Hendrick and fifteen minutes later Walker, then 19, edged another straightforward catch to Brearley at first slip. This too was put to grass and from that moment the two husky Australian Rules football experts prospered. Both drove heartily at anything pitched up, and on the most benign of pitches none of the bowlers troubled them. Hendrick beat the bat more than most but Underwood's figures came in for further damage when he took over at the Vauxhall End and Lever could not find any venom when his turn rather belatedly came. Walker reached his first Test fifty, simultaneously taking the lead to 110, and before long the partnership had gone past a hundred at a run a minute. It was fine, spirited, sensible batting, the one thing which could have kept alive any interest in the game. England, who knew that on such a pitch they were not likely to be in much danger of losing, nevertheless lost their normal image of clinical expertise in the field, and one or two of the fielders began to look a little lacklustre.

Both batsmen had reached their highest first-class scores in the slightly end-of-term atmosphere which prevailed when, hoping to reach his fifty before lunch, Malone tried to turn a well-pitched ball from Lever to the legside and was bowled. It was not until 25 minutes after the interval that Willis finally put an end to his side's embarrassment by yorking Thomson after he had stayed long enough and played well enough to give Walker dreams of a century in what for him, as for eleven other cricketers in the match, threatened to be his final Test match.

One or two dreams of an Australian victory were aroused too, though not amongst the realists, when Thomson removed

Brearley with a lifting ball which England's captain, newly appointed to lead the team on the forthcoming winter tour, could only fend to short-leg. Woolmer played a couple of pretty strokes off his legs, then fell, as he does too often, stroking amiably at a ball leaving his off-stump. This completed a triumphant first Test for Malone, but Boycott, though he once hooked him only just over square-leg's head and once also played him off the inside edge close to his leg-stump, played generally with his usual massive assurance to extend his average for the series to 147. He also passed 5,000 runs in Test cricket, a target he would long ago have reached if he had not exiled himself. However, the new Boycott was presenting a figure of greater maturity in every sense, and whatever his wider obligations may have been there was now little doubt that he had absented himself in his own best interests and was now better able to lend the full and formidable weight of his batting ability to his country.

Happily, too, Derek Randall was not out at the end. He had not had the luckiest of summers after his great triumph at Melbourne and his form for Nottinghamshire had been poor, but this cheerful and exciting cricketer symbolised better than anyone or anything the new spirit abroad in English cricket.

The Oval Test often ends in an atmosphere of sadness, the more so on this occasion when the match itself had never, because of the weather, really got off the ground. The game ended shortly before five o'clock when the umpires decided that the light was too poor for further cricket. So the old order passed with barely even a whimper. The English cricketers left the murky Oval to return to their counties for the last few games of the season; the Australians returned to the Waldorf Hotel to pack for the long journey home. Between them the two teams had attracted nearly 400,000 spectators who had brought in total receipts of £736,000. The regular England players had earned £4,000 each from fees, prize money and sponsorship.

An era in cricket history had ended. The age of player power had grown closer, but the players' brave new world would founder unless they remained true to the basic virtues of cricket. If they did so there was no reason to fear that the uncertain future would not turn out happily in the end.

England's fielding was at its most brilliant in the Headingley Test. Knott sparkled as usual: *Above* McCosker is brilliantly caught off Greig in the second innings. *Below* Marsh sees an authentic leg-glance gobbled up in the first innings.

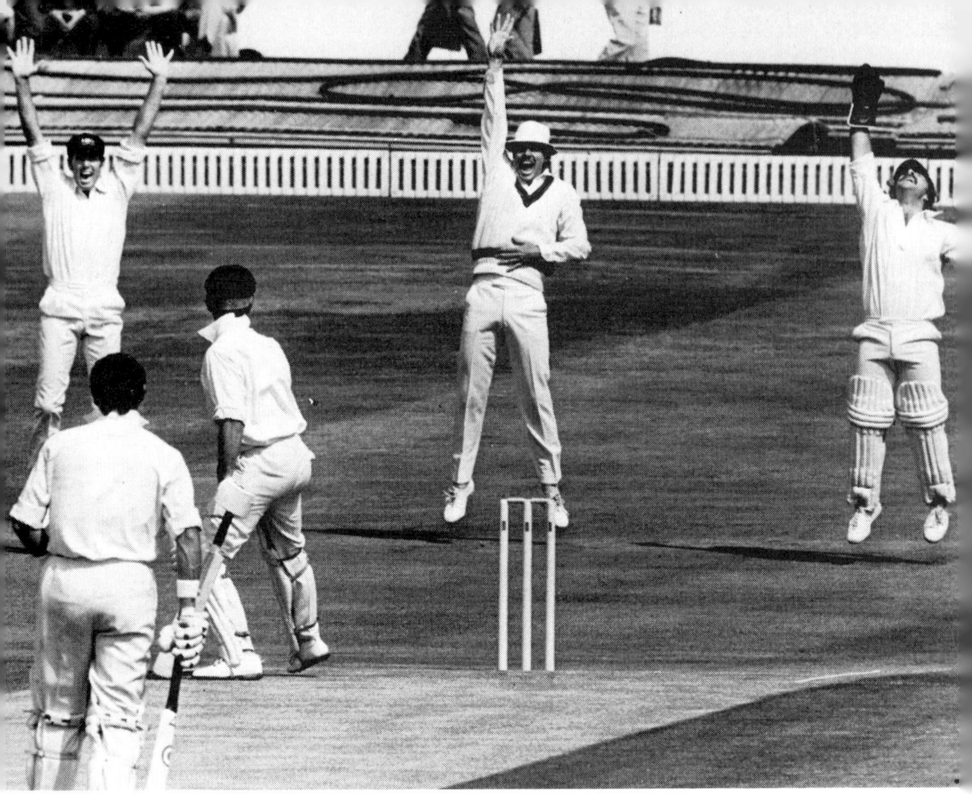

Captains caught out. *Above* Brearley c Marsh b Thomson in the first over of the match.
Below Chappell is snapped up by his opposite number off Hendrick.

Above A rare moment in cricket. Geoffrey Boycott becomes the 19th man to score 100 hundreds, with this decisively struck four off Chappell; he was the first man to reach this milestone in a Test match. *Below* He poses with the two other great Yorkshire openers who scored 100 hundreds – Herbert Sutcliffe (seated) and Sir Leonard Hutton.

Above Scenes reminiscent of 1953 – England have regained the Ashes at home for the first time since then. *Below* Two Australians in action in the final rain-affected match at the Oval – Mick Malone and David Hookes.

Chapter Nine
A SUMMER SUMMARY

Sometimes everyone can agree a verdict on a season's cricket. There are rare occasions – and the Centenary Test in Melbourne was one of them – when spectators and players on both sides can go home equally satisfied. But there was no room for a blurred view of the English summer of 1977. If you followed England it was a triumphant year; if you followed Australia it was a disastrous one.

There were many reasons for Australia's failure and not the least of them was the excellence of England's cricket. After Lord's the general prediction that it would be a close series between two equal sides was apparently confirmed. The feeling was that neither side's batting was reliable but that both were full of talent in bowling and fielding. Sure enough, apart from numbers ten and eleven, only Randall and Woolmer got into double figures in England's first innings in the first Test. At one point Australia were 22 runs ahead with only three first-innings wickets down but this was almost the last moment in the series when they held the initiative. Bob Willis burst through with the new ball, England reached scores of 132 for one and 224 for two in their second innings and Australia finished the match battling for survival. They made the mistake of dropping Pascoe in the expectation of a spinner's pitch at Old Trafford, where Woolmer, Randall and Greig led the way to a big England score. Undermined by indifferent close fielding, the attack – which in any case lacked a top-class spinner – lost its power of penetration. A vulnerable and inexperienced batting team was therefore left exposed and England, accepting almost every opportunity in the field, swept them aside with a ruthlessness seldom equalled even by more distinguished England bowling attacks in the past.

The balance might have lasted longer had Lillee been in Chappell's side. Thomson, who performed with admirable whole-heartedness and never let his side down on the big occasions, would obviously have been a greater threat with his old hunting partner at the other end. Lillee is a magnificent bowler, possibly at his very best in English conditions. His decision to conserve his energy and fitness for the circus was one he was perfectly entitled to make, but with the benefit of hindsight one might argue that it doomed Chappell's young team to defeat from the start.

Not only was Thomson, who always had to guard against a re-currence of his shoulder injury, less effective without Lillee but so too was Max Walker. He seemed to have learned nothing from his 1975 tour of England and failed to make the most of his great ability to swing the ball either way. He several times bowled sides out in the minor matches but in the Tests tended to pitch a fraction too short – an Australian good length rather than an English one – and bowled too wide of the stumps to make the batsman play.

Len Pascoe had a very promising first tour, working up a brist-ling hostility off a short, no-nonsense run-up. He would have had a future in Test cricket if he had not thrown in his lot with the Packer group. He looked a cheerful and hardworking cricketer and no one seemed to take very seriously the suggestions made by Ted Dexter during the Lord's Test that his action was suspect when he put everything into his occasional bouncer, although there were times when, looking at him from an angle of 45 degrees, one saw why the former England captain had his doubts. But no official suspicion was aired and Pascoe may be presumed there-fore to be innocent of any charges against him.

The two other bowlers of slightly lesser pace, Mick Malone and Geoff Dymock, were, overall, both disappointing. Dymock was one of those unfortunate cricketers who through no special fault of their own become passengers on a tour. A friendly, happy-go-lucky character, he never complained because he had never expected to tour England with an official Australian team in the first place. Dymock is unlikely to play much Test cricket in the fu-ture, with plenty of younger seam bowlers waiting for their oppor-tunity, but Malone seemed sure to have a glowing Test future when he signed on with Mr Packer. Instead, until the last game of the tour, he too was an also-ran. He was unable, for reasons diffi-cult to pinpoint, to take the wickets which his fine high action suggested he should have done. But the Oval Test salvaged an otherwise disappointing tour for him, and he remains a top-class medium-fast bowler who will be a great and, one hopes, only tem-porary loss to State and Test cricket in Australia.

It is a long time since any spinner of whatever nationality

helped to win a Test series in England or even made a substantial contribution to winning a Test. Chandrasekhar, Gibbs and Benaud are three who come to mind over the last fifteen years, but neither O'Keeffe nor Bright was in the exalted class of these three at their best and although both had productive tours against the counties neither could make an impact in the Tests. O'Keeffe did have the consolation of batting more soundly than the majority of his colleagues, and when he was left out of the side at Headingley the Australian batting looked frailer than ever. O'Keeffe is a gutsy all-rounder true to the Australian tradition, but he would not have had the necessary class to get into many previous Australian teams. The same is true of Bright, an efficient, workmanlike cricketer but very definitely not in the 'super' class into which he was about to be raised.

There was indeed only one undisputed 'super-star' in the whole Australian team. Greg Chappell, though he tried hard to lead with conviction and human understanding, nevertheless gave the impression all through the tour that he was a god whose head was in the clouds and who was surrounded by mere mortals, whose attempts to emulate him he viewed with stoicism, yet also with disdain since they were dragging him down to their level when he should have been pulling them up to his. This, I repeat, was the impression he gave: one of lofty coolness. Yet he tried so hard to overcome the problems he faced: those of a team whose experienced members could find no form, whose inexperienced ones could not settle down soon enough and whose attentions were divided, after a miserably unfortunate start in abysmal May weather, between the matters in hand and the fate that awaited them when they returned home in the wake of the Packer revolution. All this, combined with the embarrassment of having a well-meaning but inevitably ineffectual manager in Len Maddocks (who was a member of the Australian Board which was so bitterly opposed to the players' coup and, in the case of some of its members, not sorry to see the tour going badly) was a recipe for disaster.

Chappell emerged as a batsman whose high reputation was enhanced and as a person of dignity and infinite patience. It probably would have needed impossible qualities of leadership to have overcome the odds against his side, but there is little doubt that an extrovert, inspirational captain would have got more out of his team than this stern, reserved figure with his aura of icy coolness.

The truth was that Chappell did not greatly enjoy his tour, and his lack of really heartfelt enthusiasm conveyed itself to the others. He yearned in his quiet moments for his wife Judy and his two young children, and his formal announcement that he was retiring from Test cricket at the end of the tour (though it was no more than a confirmation of his decision to play for Packer and to accept the consequent ban) merely underlined his disenchantment with Test cricket. After 51 Tests concentrated into seven years this was perhaps understandable, but he had the consolation of knowing that Test cricket was certainly not disenchanted with *him*. His masterly batting, all poise and effortless grace, gave great pleasure and many happy memories.

One has an equally vivid impression of the batting style of Doug Walters, who finished his career in England, as he had begun it, on a note out of chord with the merry symphony of his batting everywhere else. Just occasionally, and notably at Old Trafford, there were flashes of the dazzling brilliance which adorns his play overseas: the mercurial footwork, the wrists of steel, the savage power of his strokes. But more often the glaring inadequacies of his firm-footed technique against the seam bowlers were quickly exposed and his talent was squandered as he fell time and again to a catch at slip or gully.

The other experienced batsmen, McCosker and Marsh, were no more reliable. McCosker was undoubtedly affected by the injury to his jaw in the first half of the tour, and this was just another of his side's misfortunes. By the end he was again looking like the solid and determined opener who first forced his way into the Australian team through sheer weight of runs. Marsh, as tough a competitor as ever, had a poor tour by his own high standards, both as batsman and as wicket-keeper. Australia in the field reflected his image – often ragged and messy – just as England reflected the sparkling brilliance of Alan Knott. Though he occasionally produced a powerful performance his consistency was missing. Maybe this loyal, likeable, earthy character was more affected by the passions aroused by the Packer crisis than he realised.

No one played more worthily throughout the tour than Marsh's intensely keen understudy Richie Robinson, whose feverish activity in the field and with the bat was one of the lasting memories of the summer. He is an admirable cricketer, but not one of true Test class.

Somewhere amongst the group of young batsmen on the tour – Ian Davis, Craig Serjeant, Gary Cosier, Kim Hughes, and David Hookes – there *is* a player of class, but not one of them did enough to prove it. Davis is an attractive batsman with a square-on technique which was soon exposed by good English seam bowlers. Cosier never really settled. He is a sound enough batsman when he concentrates but nothing much went right for him and, instead of buckling down when he lost his Test place, he also seemed to lose his sense of responsibility. He will come again in Test cricket.

Kim Hughes and Craig Serjeant will also be heavily relied on in the next few years and it may be no bad thing in the long run that they escaped the worst of the humiliations heaped on their colleagues by England's bowlers. Hughes had little chance to realise his undoubted promise, but his time will surely come. Serjeant conducted himself admirably throughout the tour. I have seldom seen a more dedicated cricketer than this strapping West Australian who was often to be seen jogging around cricket grounds by himself long after play had finished. Despite this, his fielding was moderate but his first Test innings showed what he can and will do in top-class cricket and his failure to measure up to that form later was hardly surprising in the light of his inexperience.

So finally to David Hookes, the enigma of the tour. It seemed in the artificial glow of that unforgettable Centenary Test that cricket had discovered a new batting genius. It transpired that in fact Hookes was as yet only a very raw colt, possessed of a wonderful gift of timing but not yet of the mature temperament to make the most of it. The flaws in his technique were soon exposed by England's seamers – notably a lack of footwork against them and a tendency to play across the line – and the stormy atmosphere of the tour was simply not the right one for him to settle down quietly and work out what was going wrong. The loss to Test cricket of this brash but amusing and talented young character is the saddest of all amongst the Australians.

England, of course, could say goodbye to their 'defectors' with equal sadness but much less cause for anxiety. None was indispensable, though all would be hard to replace. Greig's successor, Ian Botham, has already shown his worth, though he will have to play very well in the years ahead to equal the contribution made by Greig in his extraordinary career. At once the most adored and hated cricketer of his time, Greig has been England's best all-rounder since the war, the first true successor to Trevor

Bailey whom he gradually superseded as batsman and fielder, although Bailey remained a better bowler. Greig enlivened cricket with his exuberance, his occasional big hitting, so popular especially overseas, his versatile and often inspired bowling and his superb fielding in the slips, where he held some of the best catches ever seen in Test cricket. One does not often remember catches after a period of time, but several of Greig's come instantly to mind, amongst them a left-handed catch at full stretch to dismiss Gary Sobers for a duck in a Test in Barbados, an extraordinary leap on the very boundary's edge at Lord's to catch Wasim Raja of Pakistan, and the right-handed effort to dismiss Rodney Marsh at Trent Bridge in the Jubilee series itself. Greig made many errors, both off the field and on it, which tarnished his golden image, but this should blind no one to his overall contribution to the English team which after the 1974–75 Australian tour needed his injection of courage and confidence.

The two great Kent cricketers will be no less easy to replace. Knott is one of cricket's few geniuses, a phenomenon of a man whose innate skill was used to the full year after year because of his admirable pluck, dedication, concentration and fitness. I believe, as I said earlier, that his desire to take his wife and child away with him in the winter rather than leave them behind as he would have done if he had gone to Pakistan had more to do with his decision to join the circus than any desire for more money. The same may well be true of Underwood, who, with 265 Test wickets in the bag, felt the wrench more than most. If he had gone on playing he would have become the highest wicket-taker in Test cricket. He left the first-class game a much more versatile bowler than he had entered it, as a teenager with Kent, for whom he took a hundred wickets in his first season and continued to perform prolifically year after year. Several overseas tours had made him increasingly adaptable to different types of pitch, and though he still loathed anyone scoring a run off him he was more prepared to vary his flight and better able to operate over the wicket if conditions demanded it. He had been a godsend to every captain for whom he played. No bowler has been so reliable at keeping down the runs if required or so sure to bowl a side out if he got the drying wicket on which he was usually unplayable.

Underwood's obvious replacement was Phil Edmonds, who had already made a brief mark in Test cricket and whose main rivals for a spinning place were Geoff Miller and John Emburey, both off-spinners, and three left-arm spinners in Ray East, David Graveney and Bob Arrowsmith. The wicket-keeping problem was easily solved in the short term, since Bob Taylor, so long established as Knott's understudy, was still as good as any 'keeper in the world, though his batting was not in the same class. In the long term the choice seemed to lie between three very young and very promising wicket-keepers – Paul Downton of Kent, Bruce French of Notts and Jack Richards of Surrey – and a number of good batsmen-wicket-keepers in Andy Stovold, Geoff Humpage, David Bairstow, Derek Taylor and Roger Tolchard. The cupboard, at any rate, was far from bare, and Downton especially seemed to have everything required to follow the footsteps of Ames, Evans and Knott.

The future for England, indeed, looked better than it had for many years. Only the lack of a really fast bowler as reserve for Bob Willis caused anxiety. With scant resources in this department, so crucial in modern Test cricket, England still did not possess the right equipment to retaliate against an attack of sustained, ferocious pace such as the West Indies bowlers had subjected them to the year before. It was questionable too how reliable the batting was, although the return of Boycott made for a much greater feeling of stability, Woolmer made great strides forward in the first two Tests and Randall was the middle-order player of flair and quality for whom the selectors had long been searching. Moreover there were far more good young batsmen making their mark in county cricket than there had been since the prosperous days of May, Cowdrey, Dexter, Graveney and Barrington.

At last, after the jittery years of the early 1970s when an England collapse became almost an accepted feature of any Test against a reasonable bowling attack, the team led by Mike Brearley had scored enough runs to make winning a possibility. In the field they completed the job with an efficiency equalled by very few teams of the past. Willis had a triumphant summer, maintaining his speed, his control and above all his fitness in an admirable way. Only two other bowlers, Jim Laker and Alec Bedser (like Willis, both former Surrey cricketers) have taken more than his 27 wickets in a home series against Australia. To the tender lambs in the Australian batting order he must have loomed like some outsized wolf, remorselessly hungry for their flesh. Willis is, and always has been, a cricketer of immense heart and it was good to see him enjoying such success after miserable luck with illnesses and injuries in the past.

The latter may be said equally of Mike Hendrick, who had to fight to wrestle back his place from John Lever and who this time bowled for England as he has done so many times for Derbyshire. 'Hendo', a humorous and friendly man off the field, has long been a feared competitor on it, and with his brilliant close catching such a bonus he should be an automatic selection for years now if he can only keep fit. Chris Old lost his place only because of his injury, but with himself and Lever, who temporarily lost his place but not his reputation, plus the help of all-rounders like Botham, England is rich in seam bowling strength at present.

What assured these men of their success against Australia was the superb close catching. Anyone who saw the 1974–75 series in Australia will find it hard to believe that the work of the Chappells, Mallett, Redpath, Walters and others could ever be bettered, but it is quite impossible to overestimate the importance of England's fielding, which more than any other factor won back the Ashes. This was almost certainly the best England fielding side of all time. Fielding, both on the ground and in the air, crucially affects the whole morale of a side. No wonder English spirits were so high, with Randall darting about like quicksilver in the covers and men like Greig and Brearley clinging on to everything in the slips. Randall's influence on the team had been enormous since he was first selected for MCC's tour of India, and the speed, confidence and aggression of Graham Barlow had an equally good effect on his team-mates. It is sad that the Middlesex man's form fell away so badly in the second half of the season that he was struggling to hold his place even in his county side, but any assessment of his brief Test career should not overlook his contribution in the field (often as twelfth man) and the moral influence he had. This for me personally was the happiest aspect of the sudden turn in England's cricketing fortunes. For too long the England image had been a dull one – safety-first cricket played by efficient professionals with survival rather than victory the primary objective in any match. Suddenly England had a side bursting with vitality and confidence. A boring team had become an exciting one and a new enterprise was added to the old efficiency

The man who rightly took much of the credit for all this was the grey-haired captain with the abundance of grey matter, Mike Brearley, the right man in the right place at the right time. No one has come to the highest playing position in English cricket by a stranger path than Brearley, yet paradoxically, when he was captaining Cambridge University well over a decade ago and building up the highest tally of runs ever made by a Cambridge batsman, many people would have expected him to lead his country in the natural order of things. He won a First in Classics at Cambridge and then a first-class Second in Moral Sciences, the Cambridge title for Philosophy. When he came down he followed up by coming joint first in the highly competitive Civil Service examinations. But this quietly spoken, liberally minded son of a Yorkshire schoolmaster, though London-born and bred himself, had no intention of burying himself in Whitehall. He went to an American university, which enables him, when other cricketers from England mutter how impressed they are by their first sight of a place like Sydney, to say in a matter of fact way; 'Yes, but it's not as *charming* a place as San Francisco.' Brearley then lectured at a university in northern England before deciding to accept an offer to go back to cricket full time as captain of Middlesex. He took over Middlesex at a time when a team with many talented players – men like Fred Titmus, John Murray, John Price, and Peter Parfitt – were in a mess because no one could get them to play with any harmony. It is a measure of Brearley's character that he should have returned in 1971 and soon begun to show the old pros who was boss.

In the Middlesex side then, as in the England one later, he had to prove that he was worth his place as a batsman, and in this respect the turning-point came when he decided to move up the order and open the innings. It took him a long time to find the consistency he had achieved as an undergraduate but in 1975 and 1976 he began to look again like the prolific player who had gone on tour with MCC to South Africa in 1964–65 and who had amassed 312 not out for the MCC Under-25 team against North Zone of Pakistan two years later.

Literally only two years before his 1977 triumphs, however, it seemed doubtful whether Brearley would ever play for his country, let alone captain it. Eventually he more or less demanded his own selection by sheer weight of scoring, and although he was dropped after only two Test matches against West Indies in 1976 he looked as sound as anyone against the exceptionally fast battery which England faced. He has courage, he lifts the bat high as the bowler advances, plays rigidly straight and never resorts to the brutish. The method served him well enough against Australia.

He is prone to periods of strokelessness and reminds one of Colin Cowdrey at times when he goes through periods of introspection. But on his day he can be a handsome and dominating player.

As captain he worked assiduously to maintain the spirit built up on tour under Tony Greig, whose performance in India had won from Brearley an intense loyalty which showed itself publicly throughout the summer when many others lost faith in Greig's character. It did not take much intellect, of course, to know that team spirit was the most priceless asset which he inherited from Greig, and as Brearley cheerfully admitted this was only the beginning of his good fortune. He had a better side too, but he missed hardly a trick in emphasising the point, manipulating his bowlers and fielders shrewdly and always keeping the pressure on his opponents. He is altogether a more complete captain than Greig, and if one good thing came out of Greig's dismissal it was that England retained his all-round brilliance whilst gaining a leader even better at getting the most out of his players and at exploiting favourable situations for his side.

Brearley overcame his main difficulties, keeping together a side divided in theory between the Packer men and the rest and establishing a right to a batting place by some timely personal performances. Though he was appointed in Greig's place when the latter offended the establishment, he is himself anything but an establishment man. He was prominent in the movement to stop the 1970 South African tour of England, and he is so adamant that players should make all they can out of cricket that one gets the feeling that he would not himself have rejected Mr Packer if an offer had come. He himself was a very much wealthier man at the end of 1977 than at the start of it, with an expensive new car awarded to him by a London businessman on top of the increased Test fees and the various sources of income which came his way with sudden fame. No one could say any more, as a BBC sports executive had said to me when I proposed a feature on the Middlesex captain early in 1976, 'who's heard of Mike Brearley?'

Much, indeed, had changed in cricket since then, and the changing fortunes of the England Test team paled by comparison with the Packer revolution. Throughout the Jubilee Year the outcome of that revolution had been the burning sporting topic. *The Times* referred to Mr Packer himself as 'our new national obsession'. Cricket professionals, club cricketers, cricket spectators and people who weren't really interested in cricket at all talked about the matter constantly. Kerry Packer was on more people's lips than Jim Callaghan was. Many of us who wanted the cricketers to be paid what they were worth but who feared a cheapening of the game we had grown up with were fearful of the future. I find it hard to rationalise why I found so chilling, for instance, some of the predictions made in an article by Tony Lewis in the *Sunday Telegraph*:

'By 1984 it may be the boyhood dream of every young cricketer in the world to receive the golden invitation to report to the Australian headquarters of the world's top circuit, as indeed our top golfers now strain for their American tournament ticket . . . Cricket in the evening under the sodium lights, which make the yellow ball look red, will offer cricket for those who can only view at that time of day. From now on the TCCB must expect its best senior players to seek out contracts through their agents. The two-year ban from English cricket means nothing at the end of a career . . . The best youngsters could go too. At the age of 16 the call may come to join the Junior Superstars. Off to the Packer nursery they will fly and develop their single-minded talent. Should they not make the ultimate Grand Prix squad, they can go back to English cricket and play for a county after a two-year ban . . . The Packer scheme has few limits. A tour of England will be demanded by the people here. The Superstars of television, who are mere video spectacles, will draw crowds for live appearances . . . when they come they will play three Tests against England and a second circuit of Zonal games. They will coach, show their super films and speak with silver tongues. They will jet in and out and on to the next country. Then, once a year, there will be a Grand Prix competition . . . The cricket world will widen and Kerry Packer might ultimately offer the control of it to the ICC . . . K.P. can take over the world.'

One could take issue with much of this. Is the boyhood dream of so many previous generations – to play for one's country – no longer enough? Can one really compare golf with cricket, and anyway, are not the golf tournaments with history behind them, like the Open Championship, still the most interesting and important? Is not Wimbledon still worth a dozen sponsored superstar tennis tournaments? Will the hard core of cricket followers in England really welcome the brash, commercialised gift-wrapped cricket they are apparently going to be offered? Will old county and national loyalties really disappear so fast?

We shall simply have to wait and see. I believe it is sad if cricket is going to be governed in future only by monetary considerations. On the other hand, because anything other than Test cricket has not for many years been able to pay for itself, cricket has long been a vulnerable sport.

Or will this vision of 1984 be no more than a nightmare, and instead will the traditional structure of cricket survive with the Packer Circus being seen, in the end, not as the new form of cricket at the top but as the experiment which had the happy effect of giving the best players even better rewards for their skills than they were getting already? In England, at least, the threat of further defections from traditional Test cricket seemed to have been averted by the announcement, on the Saturday of the Oval Test, that the Cornhill Insurance Company would be putting a million pounds into cricket in Britain over the next five years for the right to sponsor Tests in England. The players were now guaranteed a continuation of the £1000 fee per Test, and those who played a full season for England, picking up prize money in addition to their county salaries and a winter tour, could now expect around £15,000 a year from their cricket earnings. On top of this there was a potentially substantial income from advertising, endorsements of sporting goods, and possibly also from books, articles or television work. With additional perks such as free cars, travel and hotel accommodation, plus the tax-free benefit towards the end of a career, English Test players were, if they even had been, nobody's poor relations any longer. Despite all this, Bob Woolmer decided to turn his back on county and Test cricket and to join the rebels. Woolmer had the world at his feet when he took his fateful decision. If things had gone his way he might have become captain of Kent and even of England. His decision brought into question not just his loyalty but also his good sense. It suggested that there was more to the revolution than just a battle for more pay. The firm of English cricket was offering its top workers a directorship, a rich pension, expenses and a 400 percent pay rise. The employee was turning up his nose at this and joining a brand new company overseas. To hell with many of his friends and clients: something newer, bigger and more exciting was luring him away. Was it enterprise or greed? Would the new company soon swallow up the old or collapse like the South Sea Bubble and leave its employees to go home with their tails between their legs, hoping for their old jobs back?

Some of the Cornhill money was to be ploughed back into the grass roots of the game, to insure against the less prosperous times which seemed likely for British cricket in the 1978 and 1979 seasons when less attractive Test visitors meant that smaller profits were likely to be made and therefore less money would be available to bale out the counties. The voice of Tony Greig, silent for a while as far as the public was concerned, although he had continued to be active as a recruiting agent for Packer, helping to dismantle the very team he was playing for and had himself done much to create, began to be heard aloud again. He claimed that the Cornhill cash was a justification of his original assertion that the circus would help the run-of-the-mill county cricketer. However, the county players, in a well-attended Extraordinary General Meeting of the Professional Cricketers Association at the end of the season at Edgbaston, voted in favour of the two-year TCCB ban on 23 of their fellow professionals. The voting in favour of the ban was 91 to 77, although Hampshire, who were the only county not represented, had been 16 to one in favour of it in a dressing-room vote which was not taken into account at Edgbaston. The PCA meeting also called for full membership of the TCCB and a minimum wage for county cricketers. They were concerned now to raise the earnings of the county player. The battle for the Test star had been won.

Of course the TCCB had been seeking a Test sponsor for some time. They had also been searching for a way to raise the salaries of the Test players, having minuted after one meeting two years before, when they were restricted by the Government's pay freeze, that Test cricketers were underpaid. Undoubtedly, however, the Packer circus had both hastened the sponsorship of Tests and given the players a much bigger rise than they would otherwise have got.

The circus itself, whatever its incidental and beneficial effects, remained a threat to Test cricket, the life-blood of the game in every Test-playing country of the world. The Packer games were to be called 'Super-Tests', so by this very name they were setting themselves up to be something better than what for a hundred years had always been considered the best.

The year which had begun with a magnificent match to celebrate that great Anglo-Australian Centenary was ending with a bitterly ironic threat to the future of Test cricket. It had happened partly because players had not been given a fair share of the rewards from the recent boom in the game, and partly because a stubborn business tycoon had been refused a television contract by stubborn cricket administrators. The county professionals voted by a large majority to ask the ICC and the TCCB to reopen negotiations with Mr Packer on condition that he should change the dates of his matches to avoid a clash with the Australia v. India series. But they seemed to forget the Pakistan v. England series which would suffer come what may. It seemed too late for the war to be averted, but a spirit of compromise was in the air, and it was possible to hope for some sort of reconciliation by the time that Australia and England next met on a cricket field, in December 1978. One does not have to be a blind reactionary to believe that much of the charm of cricket lies in its history and its tradtion, and that nothing will ever replace true Test matches, in which controlled personal and national pride mean more than money.

The Jubilee Tests 1977

A statistical survey compiled by Patrick Allen

1 THE TEAMS

The Australian touring team to England

Players	State	Date of Birth
CHAPPELL, Gregory Stephen (Captain)	Queensland	7 August 1948
MARSH, Rodney William (Vice-Captain)	Western Australia	11 November 1947
BRIGHT, Raymond James	Victoria	13 July 1954
COSIER, Gary John	South Australia	25 April 1953
DAVIS, Ian Charles	New South Wales	25 August 1953
DYMOCK, Geoffrey	Queensland	21 July 1945
HOOKES, David William	South Australia	3 May 1955
HUGHES, Kimberley John	Western Australia	26 January 1954
McCOSKER, Richard Bede	New South Wales	11 December 1946
MALONE, Michael Francis	Western Australia	9 October 1950
O'KEEFFE, Kerry James	New South Wales	25 November 1949
PASCOE, Leonard Stephen	New South Wales	13 February 1950
ROBINSON, Richard Darrel	Victoria	9 July 1946
SERJEANT, Craig Stanton	Western Australia	1 November 1951
THOMSON, Jeffrey Robert	Queensland	10 August 1950
WALKER, Maxwell Henry Norman	Victoria	12 September 1948
WALTERS, Kevin Douglas	New South Wales	21 December 1945
Manager		
MADDOCKS, Leonard Victor	Ex-Victoria and Tasmania	24 May 1926

Their England Opponents

Players	County	Date of Birth
BREARLEY, John Michael (Captain)	Middlesex	28 April 1942
AMISS, Dennis Leslie	Warwickshire	7 April 1943
BARLOW, Graham Derek	Middlesex	20 March 1950
BOTHAM, Ian Terrence	Somerset	24 November 1955
BOYCOTT, Geoffrey	Yorkshire	21 November 1940
GREIG, Anthony William	Sussex	6 October 1946
HENDRICK, Michael	Derbyshire	8 September 1952
KNOTT, Alan Philip Eric	Kent	9 April 1946
LEVER, John Kenneth	Essex	24 February 1949
MILLER, Geoffrey	Derbyshire	8 September 1952
OLD, Christopher Middleton	Yorkshire	22 December 1948
RANDALL, Derek William	Nottinghamshire	24 February 1951
ROOPE, Graham Richard James	Surrey	12 July 1946
UNDERWOOD, Derek Leslie	Kent	8 June 1945
WILLIS, Robert George Dylan	Warwickshire	30 May 1949
WOOLMER, Robert Andrew	Kent	14 May 1948

2 THE RESULTS

Match record of official Australian teams in England

Season	Captain		First-Class Matches			
		P	*W*	*D*	*L*	*T*
1878	D. W. Gregory	15	7	4	4	—
1880	W. L. Murdoch	10	5	3	2	—
1882	W. L. Murdoch	32	17	11	4	—
1884	W. L. Murdoch	31	17	7	7	—
1886	H. J. H. Scott	37	9	21	7	—
1888	P. S. McDonnell	37	17	7	13	—
1890	W. L. Murdoch	34	10	8	16	—
1893	J. M. Blackham	31	14	7	10	—
1896	G. H. S. Trott	34	19	9	6	—
1899	J. Darling	35	16	16	3	—
1902	J. Darling	38	22	14	2	—
1905	J. Darling	35	15	17	3	—
1909	M. A. Noble	37	11	22	4	—
1912	S. E. Gregory	36	9	19	8	—
1921	W. W. Armstrong	34	21	11	2	—
1926	H. L. Collins	33	9	23	1	—
1930	W. M. Woodfull	31	11	18	1	1
1934	W. M. Woodfull	30	13	16	1	—
1938	D. G. Bradman	29	15	12	2	—
1948	D. G. Bradman	31	23	8	—	—
1953	A. L. Hassett	33	16	16	1	—
1956	I. W. Johnson	31	9	19	3	—
1961	R. Benaud	32	13	18	1	—
1964	R. B. Simpson	30	11	16	3	—
1968	W. M. Lawry	25	8	14	3	—
1972	I. M. Chappell	26	11	10	5	—
1975	I. M. Chappell	15	8	5	2	—
1977	G. S. Chappell	22	5	13	4	—
TOTALS		844	361	364	118	1

Matches abandoned without a ball being bowled are excluded.

England v Australia in England

	England	Australia	Drawn	Total
1880	1	0	0	1
1882	0	1	0	1
1884	1	0	2	3
1886	3	0	0	3
1888	2	1	0	3
1890*	2	0	0	2
1893	1	0	2	3
1896	2	1	0	3
1899	0	1	4	5
1902	1	2	2	5
1905	2	0	3	5
1909	1	2	2	5
1912	1	0	2	3
1921	0	3	2	5
1926	1	0	4	5
1930	1	2	2	5
1934	1	2	2	5
1938*	1	1	2	4
1948	0	4	1	5
1953	1	0	4	5
1956	2	1	2	5
1961	1	2	2	5
1964	0	1	4	5
1968	1	1	3	5
1972	2	2	1	5
1975	0	1	3	4
1977	3	0	2	5
TOTALS	31	28	51	110

*The Matches at Manchester in 1890 and 1938 were both abandoned without a ball being bowled.

3 THE AVERAGES

Test Match Averages
Australia—batting and fielding

	M	I	NO	Runs	HS	Av	100	50	Ct/St
K. J. O'Keeffe	3	6	4	125	48*	62.50	—	—	3
G. S. Chappell	5	9	0	371	112	41.22	1	1	6
D. W. Hookes	5	9	0	283	85	31.44	—	2	1
R. B. McCosker	5	9	0	255	107	28.33	1	1	5
K. D. Walters	5	9	0	223	88	24.77	—	2	5
M. H. N. Walker	5	8	1	151	78*	21.57	—	1	1
C. S. Serjeant	3	5	0	106	81	21.20	—	1	1
R. W. Marsh	5	9	1	166	63	20.75	—	2	9
I. C. Davis	3	6	0	107	34	17.83	—	—	2
R. D. Robinson	3	6	0	100	34	16.66	—	—	4
R. J. Bright	3	5	1	42	16	10.50	—	—	2
J. R. Thomson	5	8	1	59	21	8.42	—	—	—
L. S. Pascoe	3	5	2	23	20	7.66	—	—	—

Played in one Test—K. J. Hughes 1, M. F. Malone 46

Australia—bowling

	O	M	R	W	Av	5w/I	BB
M. F. Malone	57	24	77	6	12.83	1	5–63
J. R. Thomson	200.5	44	583	23	25.34	—	4–41
L. S. Pascoe	137.4	35	363	13	27.92	—	4–80
R. J. Bright	72.1	27	147	5	29.40	—	3–69
M. H. N. Walker	273.2	88	551	14	39.35	—	3–40
K. J. O'Keeffe	100.3	31	305	3	101.66	—	1–25
K. D. Walters	6	1	10	0	—	—	—
G. S. Chappell	39	5	105	0	—	—	—

England—batting and fielding

	M	I	NO	Runs	HS	Av	100	50	Ct/St
G. Boycott	3	5	2	442	191	147.33	2	1	—
R. A. Woolmer	5	8	1	394	137	56.28	2	1	2
A. P. E. Knott	5	7	0	255	135	36.42	1	1	12
G. R. J. Roope	2	2	0	72	38	36.00	—	—	—
D. W. Randall	5	8	2	207	79	34.50	—	2	4
A. W. Greig	5	7	0	226	91	32.28	—	2	9
J. M. Brearley	5	9	0	247	81	27.44	—	1	7
R. G. D. Willis	5	6	4	49	24*	24.50	—	—	2
D. L. Underwood	5	6	2	66	20	16.50	—	—	3
C. M. Old	2	3	0	46	37	15.33	—	—	2
D. L. Amiss	2	4	1	43	28*	14.33	—	—	2
M. Hendrick	3	3	0	20	15	6.66	—	—	5
J. K. Lever	3	4	0	24	10	6.00	—	—	2

Played in two Tests—G. Miller 6*, 13, I. T. Botham 25*, 0. Played in one Test—G. D. Barlow 1 & 5.

Bowling

	O	M	R	W	Av	5w/I	BB
G. Miller	24	7	47	3	15.66	—	2–18
R. G. D. Willis	166.4	36	534	27	19.77	3	7–78
I. T. Botham	73	16	202	10	20.20	2	5–21
M. Hendrick	128.4	33	290	14	20.71	—	4–41
D. L. Underwood	169.1	61	362	13	27.84	1	6–66
A. W. Greig	77	25	196	7	28.00	—	2–64
R. A. Woolmer	16	5	31	1	31.00	—	1–8
J. K. Lever	75	22	197	5	39.40	—	3–60
C. M. Old	77	14	199	5	39.80	—	2–70

Australian Tour Averages

First-Class Matches

Batting

	M	I	NO	Runs	HS	Av	100	50	Ct/St
G. S. Chappell	16	25	5	1182	161*	59.10	5	2	18
K. J. O'Keeffe	13	19	12	355	48*	50.71	—	—	5
R. D. Robinson	14	23	4	715	137*	37.63	1	4	31/3
C. S. Serjeant	15	22	2	663	159	33.15	1	6	2
D. W. Hookes	17	26	1	804	108	32.16	1	6	4
G. J. Cosier	12	20	1	587	100	30.89	1	4	7
I. C. Davis	13	20	0	608	83	30.40	—	5	5
K. J. Hughes	14	19	0	540	95	28.42	—	5	10
K. D. Walters	17	26	1	663	88	26.52	—	3	7
R. J. Bright	14	19	8	287	53*	26.09	—	1	5
R. B. McCosker	18	32	1	737	107	23.77	1	4	19
R. W. Marsh	17	24	2	477	124	21.68	1	2	30/2
M. H. N. Walker	15	17	2	250	78*	16.66	—	1	2
G. Dymock	10	6	5	16	8*	16.00	—	—	2
M. F. Malone	10	10	3	95	46	13.57	—	—	4
J. R. Thomson	16	17	1	130	25	8.12	—	—	3
L. S. Pascoe	11	9	3	44	20	7.33	—	—	—

Substitute fielders took 2 catches.

Bowling

	O	M	R	W	Av	5w/I	BB
R. J. Bright	333.5	114	794	39	20.35	2	5–67
L. S. Pascoe	323.4	79	893	41	21.78	1	6–68
M. H. N. Walker	514	154	1184	53	22.33	3	7–19
M. F. Malone	327	95	837	32	26.15	1	5–63
J. R. Thomson	383.2	84	1207	43	28.06	—	4–41
K. J. O'Keeffe	335.4	112	1035	36	28.75	—	4–21
G. Dymock	192	54	468	15	31.20	—	3–30
G. S. Chappell	106	28	304	6	50.66	—	3–45
K. D. Walters	17	5	30	0	—	—	—
G. J. Cosier	16	3	36	0	—	—	—
D. W. Hookes	4	0	18	0	—	—	—
R. W. Marsh	1	0	6	0	—	—	—
R. B. McCosker	2	1	5	0	—	—	—

Centuries For (11)

G. S. Chappell (5)	161*	v. Northamptonshire	Northampton
	113	v. Somerset	Bath
	112	v. ENGLAND (2nd Test)	Manchester
	102	v. Gloucestershire	Bristol
	100*	v. Worcestershire	Worcester
G. J. Cosier	100	v. Nottinghamshire	Trent Bridge
D. W. Hookes	108	v. Somerset	Bath
R. W. Marsh	124	v. Essex	Chelmsford
R. B. McCosker	107	v. ENGLAND (3rd Test)	Trent Bridge
R. D. Robinson	137*	v. Warwickshire	Edgbaston
C. S. Serjeant	159	v. Nottinghamshire	Trent Bridge

Centuries Against (10)

G. Boycott (3)	191	for ENGLAND (4th Test)	Headingley
	107	for ENGLAND (3rd Test)	Trent Bridge
	103	for Yorkshire	Scarborough
R. A. Woolmer (2)	137	for ENGLAND (2nd Test)	Old Trafford
	120	for ENGLAND (1st Test)	Lord's
A. P. E. Knott	135	for ENGLAND (3rd Test)	Trent Bridge
K. S. McEwan	100*	for Essex	Chelmsford
G. R. J. Roope	107*	for Surrey	The Oval
B. C. Rose	110*	for Somerset	Bath
J. Whitehouse	114	for Warwickshire	Edgbaston

Lavinia, Duchess of Norfolk's XI v Australians (not first-class)
Arundel, April 27 (45-Over Match).
Australians 186 – 5 wkts (45 Overs) (C. S. Serjeant 65, G. S. Chappell 44, R. A. Woolmer
3 – 17)
Duchess of Norfolk's XI 166 (41.3 Overs) (P. Willey 50, D. W. Randall 41, G. J. Cosier
4 – 18)
Australians won by 20 runs.

Surrey v Australians

The Oval, April 30, May 2, 3
Match drawn
Surrey   *First Innings*
*J. H. Edrich c Marsh b Walker 70
A. R. Butcher c Marsh b Pascoe 23
†L. E. Skinner c Chappell b O'Keeffe 17
Younis Ahmed c Hughes b Walker............. 40
G. R. J. Roope not out 107
D. M. Smith lbw b Walker.................... 0
Intikhab Alam b O'Keeffe 16
R. D. Jackman c Marsh b Dymock 16
G. G. Arnold b Chappell 11
R. P. Baker not out 11
P. I. Pocock....................................
Extras (b2, lb 11, w 2, nb 1) 16
                         Total (8 wkts dec)..327
Fall of Wickets
1 – 48 2 – 81 3 – 147 4 – 165 5 – 165 6 – 192 7 – 244 8 – 281

Bowling	*First Innings*			
Pascoe	27	6	75	1
Walker	25	4	70	3
Dymock	24	5	54	1
O'Keeffe	26	7	97	2
Chappell	5	0	15	1

Australians: I. C. Davis, C. S. Serjeant, G. S. Chappell, D. W. Hookes, K. D. Walters, K. J.
Hughes, R. W. Marsh, G. Dymock, K. J. O'Keeffe, M. H. N. Walker, L. S. Pascoe.

Kent v Australians

Canterbury, May 4, 5, 6 Match drawn

Australians *First Innings*

I. C. Davis b Jarvis	0	Jarvis	9	5	20	2

Australians *First Innings*

		Bowling				
I. C. Davis b Jarvis	0	Jarvis	9	5	20	2
C. S. Serjeant c Nicholls b Woolmer	55	Kemp	12	4	37	0
K. J. Hughes c Ealham b Johnson	80	Woolmer	7	3	23	1
G. J. Cosier lbw b Jarvis	0	Hills	10	2	37	0
K. D. Walters c Asif b Cowdrey	23	Cowdrey	7	0	30	1
R. D. Robinson run out	18	Rowe	14	3	48	1
*†R. W. Marsh c Hills b Rowe	23	Johnson	13	3	31	1
R. J. Bright not out	11					
M. H. N. Walker not out	16					
M. F. Malone ⎱ Did not bat						
J. R. Thomson ⎰						
Extras (b4, lb5, nb5)	14					
Total wkts dec)..240						

Fall of Wickets
1 – 0 2 – 79 3 – 79 4 – 128 5 – 169 6 – 208 7 – 208

Kent *First Innings*

		Bowling				
G. W. Johnson c Marsh b Bright	17	Thomson	3	2	7	0
R. A. Woolmer not out	12	Malone	7	2	18	1
C. J. C. Rowe c Robinson b Malone	0	Bright	5	4	4	1
†D. Nicholls not out	0					
A. G. E. Ealham, G. S. Clinton,						
*Asif Iqbal, R. W. Hills, ⎱ Did not bat						
C. S. Cowdrey, N. J. Kemp, ⎰						
K. B. S. Jarvis						
Extras (nb 4)	4					
Total (2 wkts).. 33						

Fall of Wickets
1 – 28 2 – 29

Sussex v Australians

Hove, May 7, 9, 10 Match drawn

Australians *First Innings*

		Bowling				
I. C. Davis b Snow	14	Imran Khan	8	1	21	0
C. S. Serjeant not out	55	Snow	10	1	36	1
*G. S. Chappell not out	34	Greig	5	0	19	0
D. W. Hookes, K. D. Walters,		Buss	7	3	15	0
K. J. Hughes, †R. D. Robinson, ⎱		Spencer	4	0	12	0
K. J. O'Keeffe, J. R. Thomson, ⎰ Did not bat						
L. S. Pascoe, G. Dymock						
Extras (b4, lb2, nb2)	8					
Total (1 wkt)..111						

Fall of Wicket
1 – 34

Sussex: K. C. Wessels, J. R. T. Barclay, R. D. V. Knight, Javed Miandad, P. J. Graves, A. W. Greig*, Imran Khan, M. A. Buss, J. A. Snow, A. Long†, J. Spencer.

Hampshire v Australians

Southampton, May 11, 12, 13. Match abandoned: no play.

Glamorgan v Australians

Swansea, May 14, 15, 16. Match drawn.

Glamorgan   *First Innings*

		Second Innings	
*A. Jones c Robinson b Dymock	59	c Walker b Bright	47
J. A. Hopkins b Walker	7	st Robinson b Bright	66
D. A. Francis c Cosier b Walker	0	c Walters b Bright	2
G. Richards c Robinson b Walker	11	not out	19
M. J. Llewellyn b Dymock	1	c Hughes b Bright	9
A. Lewis Jones c Robinson b Pascoe	46		
R. C. Ontong lbw b Dymock	0		
†E. W. Jones lbw b O'Keeffe	13		
M. A. Nash c Hughes b O'Keeffe	9	(6) not out	11
K. J. Lyons lbw b Pascoe	2		
A. E. Cordle not out	10		
Extras (b5, nb7, w2)	14	(lb5, w4, nb1)	10
Total	172	(4 wkts dec)	164

Fall of Wickets

1 – 32 2 – 32 3 – 60 4 – 61 5 – 96 6 – 96 7 – 128 8 – 142 9 – 158

1 – 107 2 – 119 3 – 130 4 – 148

Bowling	*First Innings*				*Second Innings*			
Pascoe	14.3	2	50	2	11	2	46	0
Walker	12	4	27	3	5	0	11	0
Dymock	13	3	30	3	7	1	22	0
Bright	6	3	22	0	12	0	53	0
O'Keeffe	9	2	29	2	8	3	22	0

Australians   *First Innings*

		Second Innings	
I. C. Davis lbw b Cordle	14	b Nash	12
†R. D. Robinson b Nash	20	lbw b Nash	0
K. J. Hughes c E. W. Jones b Nash	4	c E. W. Jones b Nash	0
G. J. Cosier c Francis b Nash	56	(5) c Llewellyn b Nash	5
*K. D. Walters lbw b Ontong	36	(6) b Nash	6
D. W. Hookes lbw b Nash	0	(4) b Cordle	11
K. J. O'Keeffe not out	10	not out	21
R. J. Bright not out	8	not out	26
M. H. N. Walker			
L. S. Pascoe	Did not bat		
G. Dymock			
Extras (lb4, nb1)	5	(w1, nb4);	5
Total (6 wkts dec)	153	Total (6 wkts)	86

Fall of Wickets

1 – 27 2 – 38 3 – 40 4 – 134 5 – 134 6 – 134

1 – 0 2 – 0 3 – 11 4 – 24 5 – 30 6 – 39

Bowling	*First Innings*				*Second Innings*			
Nash	18	2	71	4	12	4	32	5
Cordle	10	1	47	1	7	2	31	1
Richards	1	0	8	0	3	2	3	0
Ontong	7	1	22	1	5	0	15	0
Lyons					2	2	0	0

Somerset v Australians

Bath, May 18, 19, 20. Somerset won by 7 wickets.

Somerset   *First Innings*

			Second Innings	
B. C. Rose not out	110			
P. W. Denning c Marsh b Dymock	39	c Marsh b Thomson	27
I. V. A. Richards c Hookes b Malone	18	b Chappell	34
*D. B. Close c McCosker b Malone	0	c Cosier b O'Keeffe	53
I. T. Botham c McCosker b O'Keeffe	59	not out	39
P. A. Slocombe not out	55	(4) not out	8
D. Breakwell c Chappell b O'Keeffe	23		

G. I. Burgess
†D. J. S. Taylor
J. Garner } Did not bat
H. R. Moseley
K. Jennings

Extras (b4, lb7, w1, nb24)	36	(b4, lb3, w3, nb11)	21
Total (5 wkts dec)	340	Total (3 wkts)	182

Fall of Wickets
1 – 83 2 – 116 3 – 117 4 – 156 5 – 228
1 – 50 2 – 129 3 – 129

Bowling	First Innings				Second Innings			
Thomson	16	2	60	0	12	1	57	1
Dymock	17	7	48	1	5	0	25	0
Malone	22	4	70	2	9	2	18	0
O'Keeffe	35	15	114	2	5.1	0	32	1
Chappell	2	0	11	0	8	4	29	1
Walters	2	1	1	0				

Australians   *First Innings*

		Second Innings	
R. McCosker c Botham b Garner	2	run out	2
C. Serjeant st Taylor b Burgess	13	c Garner b Botham	50
*G. Chappell b Garner	113	(7) c Garner b Botham	39
G. Cosier b Garner	44	(3) c Taylor b Botham	2
D. Walters c Denning b Burgess	23	b Botham	25
D. Hookes b Botham	3	(4) b Burgess	108
†R. Marsh b Garner	3	(6) b Garner	0
K. O'Keeffe c Denning b Burgess	11	c Denning b Moseley	20
J. Thomson b Burgess	0	c Botham b Garner	0
M. Malone b Burgess	2	c Richards b Breakwell	17
C. Dymock not out	0	not out	6

L. Pascoe   Did not bat

Extras (b10, w2, nb6)	18	(b4, lb10, w1, nb5)	20
Total	232	Total	289

Fall of Wickets
1 – 2 2 – 57 3 – 177 4 – 197 5 – 200 6 – 204 7 – 223 8 – 223 9 – 231
1 – 16 2 – 18 3 – 141 4 – 172 5 – 183 6 – 214 7 – 251 8 – 252 9 – 271

Bowling	First Innings				Second Innings			
Garner	20	5	66	4	23	6	71	2
Moseley	16	5	52	0	17	6	55	1
Burgess	9.3	2	25	5	9	3	41	1
Botham	15	2	48	1	22	6	98	4
Breakwell	7	0	23	0	0.3	0	4	1

Gloucestershire v Australians

Bristol, May 21, 23. Australians won by 173 runs.

Australians *First Innings*

			Second Innings	
I. C. Davis c Brassington b Brain	11		b Procter	18
R. B. McCosker lbw b Shackleton	2		lbw b Brain	4
†G. S. Chappell c Graveney b Shackleton	11		c Shepherd b Shackleton	102
K. J. Hughes lbw b Brain	7		lbw b Shackleton	27
K. D. Walters b Brain	32		c Shackleton b Graveney	24
†R. D. Robinson b Brain	5		c Brassington b Vernon	26
R. W. Marsh b Brain	0		c & b Graveney	9
R. J. Bright not out	53		lbw b Graveney	9
M. H. N. Walker b Brain	4		b Graveney	22
M. F. Malone c Brassington b Brain	5		not out	5
L. S. Pascoe b Vernon	17		b Graveney	4
Extras (b4, lb1, w1, nb1)	7		(nb1)	1
Total	154		Total	251

Fall of Wickets

1 – 3 2 – 25 3 – 27 4 – 47 5 – 53 6 – 53 7 – 87 8 – 97 9 – 121
1 – 6 2 – 48 3 – 145 4 – 152 5 – 202 6 – 202 7 – 215 8 – 222 9 – 247

Bowling	First Innings				Second Innings			
Procter	5	3	5	0	8	3	36	1
Shackleton	20	4	70	2	10	2	40	2
Brain	19	6	51	7	11	0	57	1
Vernon	3.5	0	21	1	13	0	47	1
Graveney					16	3	70	5

Gloucestershire *First Innings*

			Second Innings	
Sadiq Mohammad c McCosker b Walker	14		c Walters b Pascoe	12
A. W. Stovold c Robinson b Malone	22		b Malone	27
Zaheer Abbas c Hughes b Walker	3		c Robinson b Walker	5
J. C. Foat c Robinson b Walker	3		b Pascoe	26
*M. J. Procter c Bright b Walker	0		c Marsh b Bright	15
D. R. Shepherd c Chappell b Malone	2		c sub b Bright	26
D. A. Graveney c Robinson b Malone	8		st Robinson b Bright	18
J. H. Shackleton lbw b Walker	4		b Pascoe	17
M. J. Vernon c Robinson b Walker	0		st Robinson b Bright	4
†A. J. Brassington lbw b Walker	10		c Walters b Pascoe	5
B. M. Brain not out	0		not out	1
Extras	0		(b4, lb4, nb5)	13
Total	63		Total	169

Fall of Wickets

1 – 36 2 – 36 3 – 36 4 – 36 5 – 41 6 – 41 7 – 49 8 – 53 9 – 61
1 – 36 2 – 47 3 – 68 4 – 83 5 – 113 6 – 133 7 – 153 8 – 157 9 – 168

Bowling	First Innings				Second Innings			
Walker	11.5	4	19	7	13	5	20	1
Malone	11	2	44	3	12	3	31	1
Pascoe					16.4	4	36	4
Bright					19	5	63	4
Marsh					1	0	6	0

Gloucestershire v Australians

Bristol, May 24 (45 Overs). Australians won by 6 wkts.
Gloucestershire: 195 (44.5 Overs) (M. J. Procter 52)
Australians: 196 – 4 wkts (38 Overs) (K. D. Walters 52*, K. J. Hughes 51, R. B. McCosker 46).

MCC v Australians

Lord's, May 25, 26, 27. Australians won by 79 runs.

Australians *First Innings*

		Second Innings	
R. B. McCosker c Botham b Jones	24	c Miller b Botham	73
C. S. Serjeant c Botham b Hendrick	3	c Lyon b Jones	22
*G. S. Chappell b Jones	21	c Athey b Edmonds	44
G. J. Cosier c Lyon b Hendrick	19	c Randall b Miller	18
K. J. Hughes b Miller	60	lbw b Botham	5
D. W. Hookes c Lyon b Hendrick	3	c Lyon b Hendrick	8
†R. W. Marsh b Miller	16	lbw b Hendrick	23
K. J. O'Keeffe lbw b Botham	8	c Botham b Hendrick	5
M. H. N. Walker lbw Miller	1	c Botham b Hendrick	17
J. R. Thomson c Athey b Hendrick	19	c Botham b Miller	12
G. Dymock not out	8	not out	0
Extras (b5, lb5, w1, nb1)	12	(b4, lb2, nb2)	8
Total	194	Total	235

Fall of Wickets
1 – 13 2 – 42 3 – 50 4 – 75 5 – 83 6 – 116 7 – 156 8 – 167 9 – 168
1 – 39 2 – 118 3 – 146 4 – 164 5 – 173 6 – 196 7 – 205 8 – 210 9 – 235

Bowling	First Innings				Second Innings			
Hendrick	17.5	4	28	4	22.5	7	32	4
Jones	15	5	50	2	15	2	62	1
Botham	16	5	31	1	15	5	46	2
Edmonds	10	1	29	0	7	2	27	1
Miller	18	5	44	3	32	13	53	2
Willey					5	1	10	0

MCC *First Innings*

		Second Innings	
C. W. J. Athey c Marsh b Walker	4	c Marsh b Thomson	1
*J. M. Brearley run out	4	c Marsh b Dymock	47
D. W. Randall lbw b Thomson	50	c Chappell b O'Keeffe	51
G. D. Barlow lbw b Dymock	21	st Marsh b O'Keeffe	54
P. Willey c McCosker b Thomson	4	(5) c Serjeant b Dymock	6
G. Miller c Marsh b O'Keeffe	5	(6) lbw b Thomson	13
I. T. Botham not out	10	(7) c Marsh b Thomson	0
P. H. Edmonds b O'Keeffe	15	(8) c Chappell b Walker	25
†J. Lyon lbw b Walker	6	b O'Keeffe	0
M. Hendrick absent hurt	0	not out	2
A. A. Jones c Thomson b O'Keeffe	0	lbw b O'Keeffe	0
Extras (lb3, nb14)	17	(b1, lb4, w1, nb9)	15
Total	136	Total	214

Fall of Wickets
1 – 8 2 – 8 3 – 54 4 – 75 5 – 110 6 – 115 7 – 120 8 – 135 9 – 136
1 – 1 2 – 101 3 – 109 4 – 119 5 – 175 6 – 176 7 – 206 8 – 209 9 – 212

Bowling	First Innings				Second Innings			
Thomson	15	3	50	2	12	1	50	3
Walker	12	5	29	2	21.3	6	49	1
Dymock	5	1	11	1	14	5	37	2
O'Keeffe	13.4	5	29	3	20	7	56	4
Chappell					1	0	7	0

Worcestershire v Australians

Worcester, May 28, 29, 30. Match drawn.

Australians *First Innings*

				Second Innings	
R. B. McCosker c Humphries b Boyns	33			c Humphries b Inchmore	0
I. C. Davis c Humphries b Inchmore	83			c Boyns b Gifford	41
†G. S. Chappell retired hurt	100			run out	21
G. J. Cosier b Patel	15			lbw b Gifford	44
D. W. Hookes c Neale b Cumbes	4			b Gifford	8
K. D. Walters st Humphries b Patel	37			c Ormrod b Boyns	23
*R. D. Robinson c Neale b Gifford	44			c Inchmore b Gifford	38
R. J. Bright b Gifford	16			not out	29
M. F. Malone run out	8			not out	2
J. R. Thomson b Gifford	7				
L. S. Pascoe not out	0				
Extras (b4, lb6, w1)	11			(lb3, nb1)	4
Total	358			Total (7 wkts dec)	210

Fall of Wickets

1 – 50 2 – 222 3 – 251 4 – 262 5 – 294 6 – 334 7 – 346 8 – 351 9 – 358

1 – 0 2 – 33 3 – 86 4 – 121 5 – 137 6 – 139 7 – 207

Bowling	First Innings				Second Innings			
Inchmore	16	3	53	1	12	3	56	1
Cumbes	23	7	58	1	7	0	42	0
Boyns	26	6	86	1	14	4	43	1
Patel	28	4	73	2				
Gifford	26.4	9	77	3	24	6	65	4

Worcestershire *First Innings*

				Second Innings	
J. A. Ormrod b Bright	73			c sub b Pascoe	57
G. M. Turner lbw b Pascoe	69			(6) not out	49
P. A. Neale c Chappell b Pascoe	8			not out	43
E. J. O. Hemsley c Robinson b Bright	17			b Pascoe	0
D. N. Patel c & b Chappell	1			b Pascoe	7
B. J. R. Jones b Bright	2			(1) b Bright	27
C. N. Boyns b Bright	18				
†D. J. Humphries not out	21				
J. D. Inchmore b Bright	16				
*N. Gifford c Robinson b Pascoe	2				
J. Cumbes b Pascoe	0				
Extras (b8, lb3, nb5)	16			(b14, lb1, wd1)	16
Total	243			Total (4 wkts)	169

Fall of Wickets

1 – 114 2 – 123 3 – 159 4 – 184 5 – 184 6 – 197 7 – 204 8 – 228 9 – 243

1 – 58 2 – 102 3 – 102 4 – 124

Bowling	First Innings				Second Innings			
Pascoe	13.5	4	40	4	16	4	37	3
Malone	15	1	61	0	18	4	57	0
Bright	35	8	91	5	10	4	25	1
Cosier	6	1	7	0	5	2	5	0
Chappell	10	3	28	1	10	4	23	0
McCosker					2	1	5	0
Hookes					1	0	1	0

Prudential Trophy One-Day Internationals

(not first-class)
Old Trafford, June 2. England won by 2 wickets. (See p. 80.)
Australia: 169 – 9 (55 Overs) (C. S. Serjeant 46, R. W. Marsh 42, Underwood 3 – 29)
England: 173 – 8 (45.2 Overs) (G. D. Barlow 42, M. H. N. Walker 3 – 20)
Man of the Match: R. W. Marsh.

Edgbaston, June 4. England won by 101 runs. (See p. 83.)
England: 171 (53.5 Overs) (G. J. Cosier 5 – 18, G. S. Chappell 5 – 20)
Australia: 70 (25.2 Overs) (J. K. Lever 4 – 29)
Man of the Match: J. K. Lever.

The Oval, June 6. Australia won by 2 wickets. (See p. 86.)
England: 242 (54.2 Overs) (D. L. Amiss 108, J. M. Brearley 78, L. S. Pascoe 3 – 43)
Australia: 246 – 8 (53.2 Overs) (G. S. Chappell 125*, R. D. Robinson 70)
Man of the Match: G. S. Chappell

Ireland v Australians
Dublin, June 9, 10. (not first-class). Match drawn.
Australians: 291 (C. S. Serjeant 63, D. W. Hookes 58, I. M. Monteith 6 – 97) and 96 – 5 dec.
Ireland: 200 – 4 dec. (J. F. Short 80*, B. A. O'Brien 51) and 104 – 3.

Essex v Australians

Chelmsford, June 11, 12, 13. Match drawn.

Australians *First Innings*

			Second Innings	
R. B. McCosker c Smith b Turner	25		b Boyce	6
†R. D. Robinson b Boyce	0		b Turner	15
C. S. Serjeant b Boyce	2		b Acfield	59
D. W. Hookes c Smith b Turner	20		(5) not out	69
K. J. Hughes lbw b Boyce	11		(4) b Acfield	20
K. D. Walters c Smith b Gooch	38		not out	29
*R. W. Marsh c Turner b Gooch	124			
R. J. Bright b Boyce	3			
K. J. O'Keeffe not out	15			
M. H. N. Walker c & b Gooch	7			
J. R. Thomson b Gooch	8			
Extras (b4, lb10, nb9)	23		(b3, lb1, nb4)	8
Total	274		Total (4 wkts dec)	206

Fall of Wickets
1 – 8 2 – 12 3 – 41 4 – 58 5 – 70 6 – 193 7 – 203 8 – 253 9 – 262
1 – 16 2 – 24 3 – 67 4 – 113

Bowling	*First Innings*				*Second Innings*			
Boyce	27	3	90	4	5	0	19	1
Turner	26	8	73	2	11	3	25	1
Gooch	19	6	60	4	1	0	11	0
Acfield	4	1	28	0	17	1	66	2
East					17	2	78	0

Essex *First Innings*

			Second Innings	
M. H. Denness lbw b Thomson	34		b O'Keeffe	9
B. R. Hardie lbw b Walker	10		c McCosker b O'Keeffe	27
K. S. McEwan not out	100			
*K. W. R. Fletcher not out	6		(6) not out	3
G. A. Gooch			(3) c & b O'Keeffe	8
†N. Smith			(4) b Bright	3
K. E. Pont			(5) not out	0
S. Turner		Did not bat		
K. D. Boyce				
R. E. East				
D. L. Acfield				
Extras (b2, lb4, nb13, w1)	20		(lb5, nb4)	9
Total (2 wkts dec)	170		Total (4 wkts)	59

Fall of Wickets
1 – 25 2 – 122
1 – 26 2 – 44 3 – 56 4 – 56

Bowling	*First Innings*				*Second Innings*			
Thomson	13	1	26	1	4	1	8	0
Walker	12	1	48	1	10	2	28	0
O'Keeffe	9	0	75	0	12	8	14	3
Bright	2	1	1	0	5	5	0	1

ENGLAND v AUSTRALIA (First Test)

England v Australia
Lord's, June 16, 17, 18, 20 & 21. Match drawn.

England *First Innings*		*Second Innings*	
D. L. Amiss b Thomson	4	b Thomson	0
*J. M. Brearley c Robinson b Thomson	9	c Robinson b O'Keeffe	49
R. A. Woolmer run out	79	c Chappell b Pascoe	120
D. W. Randall c Chappell b Walker	53	c McCosker b Thomson	0
A. W. Greig b Pascoe	5	c O'Keeffe b Pascoe	91
G. D. Barlow c McCosker b Walker	1	lbw b Pascoe	5
†A. P. E. Knott c Walters b Thomson	8	c Walters b Walker	8
C. M. Old c Marsh b Walker	9	c Walters b Walker	0
J. K. Lever b Pascoe	8	c Marsh b Thomson	3
D. L. Underwood not out	11	not out	12
R. G. D. Willis b Thomson	17	c Marsh b Thomson	0
Extras (b1, lb3, w1, nb7)	12	(b5, lb9, w1, nb2)	17
Total	216	Total	305

Fall of Wickets
1 – 12 2 – 13 3 – 111 4 – 121 5 – 134 6 – 155 7 – 171 8 – 183 9 – 189
1 – 0 2 – 132 3 – 224 4 – 263 5 – 286 6 – 286 7 – 286 8 – 286 9 – 305

Bowling	*First Innings*				*Second Innings*			
Thomson	20.5	5	41	4	24.4	3	86	4
Pascoe	23	7	53	2	26	2	96	3
Walker	30	6	66	3	35	13	56	2
O'Keeffe	10	3	32	0	15	7	26	1
Chappell	3	0	12	0	12	2	24	0

Australia *First Innings*		*Second Innings*	
R. B. McCosker b Old	23	b Willis	1
R. D. Robinson b Lever	11	c Woolmer b Old	4
*G. S. Chappell c Old b Willis	66	c Lever b Old	24
C. S. Serjeant c Knott b Willis	81	c Amiss b Underwood	3
K. D. Walters c Brearley b Willis	53	c sub b Underwood	10
D. W. Hookes c Brearley b Old	11	c & b Willis	50
†R. W. Marsh lbw b Willis	1	not out	6
K. J. O'Keeffe c sub b Willis	12	not out	8
M. H. N. Walker c Knott b Willis	4		
J. R. Thomson b Willis	6		
L. S. Pascoe not out	3		
Extras (lb7, w1, nb17)	25	(nb8)	8
Total	296	Total (6 wkts)	114

Fall of Wickets
1 – 25 2 – 51 3 – 135 4 – 238 5 – 256 6 – 264 7 – 265 8 – 284 9 – 290
1 – 5 2 – 5 3 – 48 4 – 64 5 – 71 6 – 102

Bowling	*First Innings*				*Second Innings*			
Willis	30.1	7	78	7	10	1	40	2
Lever	19	5	61	1	5	2	4	0
Underwood	25	6	42	0	10	3	16	2
Old	35	10	70	2	14	0	46	2
Woolmer	5	1	20	0				

Umpires—H. D. Bird & W. L. Budd. Toss won by England.

Combined Universities v Australians
Oxford, June 23, 24. (Not First-Class). Match drawn.
Universities: 130 (V. J. Marks 46, R. J. Bright 3 – 8, G. Dymock 3 – 32) and 240 – 8 wkts
   dec. (P. M. Roebuck 77, C. J. Tavare 60*, V. J. Marks 58)
Australians: 188 – 4 wkts dec. (D. W. Hookes 74, I. C. Davis 55*) and
   150 – 5 wkts (K. J. Hughes 54, R. Le Q. Savage 4 – 52).

Nottinghamshire v Australians
Trent Bridge, June 25, 26, 27. Australians won by an innings and 98 runs.

Nottinghamshire *First Innings*

			Second Innings	
M. J. Harris c McCosker b Thomson	12		c Malone b Thomson	0
B. Hassan b Bright	28		b Malone	40
C. E. B. Rice st Marsh b Bright	38		(3) c Hughes b Malone	59
P. D. Johnson lbw b O'Keeffe	37		(5) b Thomson	9
*M. J. Smedley c Marsh b Malone	38		(6) c Chappell b Bright	17
J. D. Birch b Malone	0		(7) c Malone b Bright	3
R. A. White not out	33		(8) c Chappell b Bright	8
P. A. Wilkinson lbw b Malone	6		(3) b Malone	18
†B. French b O'Keeffe	2		c Davis b O'Keeffe	18
P. J. Hacker c Cosier b Malone	0		not out	21
D. R. Doshi c Davis b O'Keeffe	8		b O'Keeffe	15
Extras (b1, nb6, w1)	8		(b4, lb2, nb8, w1)	15
Total	210		Total	223

Fall of Wickets
1 – 16 2 – 80 3 – 83 4 – 156 5 – 160 6 – 161 7 – 195 8 – 198 9 – 199
1 – 0 2 – 36 3 – 93 4 – 124 5 – 144 6 – 147 7 – 161 8 – 185 9 – 185

Bowling	*First Innings*				*Second Innings*			
Thomson	10	2	36	1	13	1	77	2
Malone	21	3	62	4	21	6	73	3
Cosier	3	0	9	0				
Bright	13	4	40	2	17	6	34	3
O'Keeffe	14.5	2	55	3	8.2	4	24	2

Australians *First Innings*

			Bowling				
R. B. McCosker lbw b Hacker	16		Rice	11	2	52	0
I. C. Davis c French b Hacker	72		Hacker	21	2	117	2
*G. S. Chappell b Doshi	48		Doshi	27	3	135	4
C. S. Serjeant b White	159		Wilkinson	28	3	83	0
K. J. Hughes c Hacker b White	95		White	27.5	6	77	4
G. J. Cosier b Doshi	100		Birch	7	0	55	0
†R. W. Marsh c Rice b Doshi	4						
K. J. O'Keeffe not out	17						
R. J. Bright b Doshi	8						
M. F. Malone c Birch b White	0						
J. R. Thomson c Harris b White	0						
Extras (b2, lb5, nb5)	12						
Total	531						

Fall of Wickets
1 – 28 2 – 90 3 – 234 4 – 312 5 – 493 6 – 498 7 – 511 8 – 521 9 – 526

Derbyshire v Australians

Chesterfield, June 29, 30, July 1. Match drawn.

Derbyshire *First Innings*

J. G. Wright c McCosker b Pascoe		0
A. Hill b O'Keeffe		45
G. Miller c Robinson b Pascoe		12
H. Cartwright c McCosker b O'Keeffe		15
A. J. Borrington c Robinson b O'Keeffe		23
*E. J. Barlow c Hookes b Pascoe		0
A. Morris b Pascoe		0
F. W. Swarbrook c Robinson b O'Keeffe		5
†R. W. Taylor lbw b Walker		7
C. J. Tunnicliffe b Walker		1
M. Hendrick not out		0
Extras (b4, lb10, nb4)		18
Total		126

Second Innings

c O'Keeffe b Pascoe		19
not out		59
c Hughes b Pascoe		21
b O'Keeffe		35
lbw b O'Keeffe		0
not out		1
(lb1)		1
Total (4 wkts)		136

Fall of Wickets

1 – 0 2 – 33 3 – 61 4 – 89 5 – 90 6 – 90 7 – 109 8 – 124 9 – 126

1 – 53 2 – 92 3 – 135 4 – 135

Bowling	First Innings				Second Innings			
Pascoe	15	5	23	4	13	4	32	2
Walker	20.3	4	48	2	17	3	57	0
Dymock	5	1	9	0				
Walters	3	1	7	0	6	2	12	0
O'Keeffe	16	9	21	4	14	5	34	2

Australians *First Innings*

I. C. Davis c Swarbrook b Barlow		53
R. B. McCosker c Miller b Hendrick		15
K. J. Hughes c Borrington b Barlow		92
D. W. Hookes lbw b Hendrick		19
K. D. Walters c Taylor b Barlow		13
†R. D. Robinson c Wright b Swarbrook		77
*R. W. Marsh b Tunnicliffe		47
K. J. O'Keeffe not out		39
M. H. N. Walker b Tunnicliffe		0
L. S. Pascoe c Taylor b Tunnicliffe		0
G. Dymock absent hurt		0
Extras (b12, lb6, nb7)		25
Total		380

Bowling				
Hendrick	29	9	61	2
Tunnicliffe	27.5	5	95	3
Swarbrook	28	8	83	1
Barlow	18	3	46	3
Miller	26	9	70	0

Fall of Wickets

1 – 31 2 – 87 3 – 129 4 – 146 5 – 291 6 – 291 7 – 374 8 – 378 9 – 380

Yorkshire v Australians

Scarborough, July 2, 3, 4. Match drawn.

Australians *First Innings*

		Second Innings	
R. B. McCosker c Bairstow b Old	0	c Leadbeater b Sidebottom	19
C. S. Serjeant b Robinson	12	b Stevenson	55
*G. S. Chappell lbw b Robinson	19	c Boycott b Robinson	13
D. W. Hookes c Bairstow b Stevenson	8	b Carrick	67
K. D. Walters b Stevenson	1	c Bairstow b Robinson	1
G. J. Cosier b Old	4	b Stevenson	1
†R. D. Robinson b Carrick	54	not out	33
R. J. Bright lbw b Robinson	1	lbw b Carrick	10
K. J. O'Keeffe c Bairstow b Stevenson	48	not out	6
M. H. N. Walker c Love b Old	27		
M. F. Malone not out	1		
Extras (b1, lb3, nb7)	11	(lb5, nb5)	10
Total	186	Total (7 wkts dec)	215

Fall of Wickets
1 – 0 2 – 27 3 – 38 4 – 41 5 – 46 6 – 46 7 – 63 8 – 118 9 – 176
1 – 50 2 – 71 3 – 111 4 – 112 5 – 116 6 – 180 7 – 200

Bowling	*First Innings*				*Second Innings*			
Old	27	8	25	3	13	2	61	0
Robinson	20	9	25	3	16	6	43	2
Stevenson	22	6	76	3	9	2	28	2
Sidebottom	8	3	9	0	10	4	46	1
Cope	10	3	13	0	4	2	4	0
Carrick	7	1	27	1	14	4	23	2

Yorkshire *First Innings*

		Second Innings	
G. Boycott lbw b Walker	0	lbw b Bright	103
B. Leadbeater c Robinson b Malone	14	c Robinson b Walker	7
J. D. Love c Robinson b Walker	1	b Walker	59
G. A. Cope b Walker	14		
A. Sidebottom b O'Keeffe	3	(4) c McCosker b O'Keeffe	10
K. Sharp c Robinson b Malone	6	not out	30
D. L. Bairstow lbw b Malone	0	not out	0
C. M. Old not out	8	(5) b Malone	12
P. Carrick c Robinson b Walker	11		
G. B. Stevenson c Bright b Malone	9		
A. L. Robinson b Walker	1		
Extras (lb6, w1, nb1)	8	(b9, lb3)	12
Total	75	Total (5 wkts)	233

Fall of Wickets
1 – 0 2 – 2 3 – 22 4 – 27 5 – 36 6 – 41 7 – 44 8 – 55 9 – 72
1 – 17 2 – 115 3 – 148 4 – 177 5 – 233

Bowling	*First Innings*				*Second Innings*			
Walker	20.2	10	29	5	17	7	45	2
Malone	19	4	38	4	25	9	68	1
O'Keeffe	1	1	0	1	15	3	50	1
Chappell					8	4	21	0
Bright					16	6	37	1

ENGLAND v AUSTRALIA (Second Test)

England v Australia (Second Test)
Old Trafford, July 7, 8, 9, 11, 12. England won by 9 wickets.

Australia *First Innings*

		Second Innings	
R. B. McCosker c Old b Willis	2	c Underwood b Willis	0
I. C. Davis c Knott b Old	34	c Lever b Willis	12
*G. S. Chappell c Knott b Greig	44	b Underwood	112
C. S. Serjeant lbw b Lever	14	c Woolmer b Underwood	8
K. D. Walters c Greig b Miller	88	lbw b Greig	10
D. W. Hookes c Knott b Lever	5	c Brearley b Miller	28
†R. W. Marsh c Amiss b Miller	36	c Randall b Underwood	1
K. J. O'Keeffe c Knott b Willis	12	not out	24
R. J. Bright c Greig b Lever	12	c & b Underwood	0
M. H. Walker b Underwood	9	c Greig b Underwood	6
J. R. Thomson not out	14	c Randall b Underwood	1
Extras (lb15, nb12)	27	(lb1, w1, nb14)	16
Total	297	Total	218

Fall of Wickets
1 – 4 2 – 80 3 – 96 4 – 125 5 – 140 6 – 238 7 – 246 8 – 272 9 – 272
1 – 0 2 – 30 3 – 74 4 – 92 5 – 146 6 – 147 7 – 147 8 – 202 9 – 212

Bowling	*First Innings*				*Second Innings*			
Willis	21	8	45	2	16	2	56	2
Lever	25	8	60	3	4	1	11	0
Old	20	3	57	1	8	1	26	0
Underwood	20.2	7	53	1	32.5	13	66	6
Greig	13	4	37	1	12	6	19	1
Miller	10	3	18	2	9	2	24	1

England *First Innings*

		Second Innings	
D. L. Amiss c Chappell b Walker	11	not out	28
*J. M. Brearley c Chappell b Thomson	6	c Walters b O'Keeffe	44
R. A. Woolmer c Davis b O'Keeffe	137	not out	0
D. W. Randall lbw b Bright	79		
A. W. Greig c & b Walker	76		
†A. P. E. Knott c O'Keeffe b Thomson	39		
G. Miller c Marsh b Thomson	6		
C. M. Old c Marsh b Walker	37		
J. K. Lever b Bright	10		
D. L. Underwood b Bright	10		
R. G. Willis not out	1		
Extras (b9, lb9, nb7)	25	(lb3, nb7)	10
Total	437	Total (1 wkt)	82

Fall of Wickets
1 – 19 2 – 23 3 – 165 4 – 325 5 – 348 6 – 366 7 – 377 8 – 404 9 – 435
1 – 75

Bowling	*First Innings*				*Second Innings*			
Thomson	38	11	73	3	8	2	24	0
Walker	54	15	131	3	7	0	17	0
Bright	35.1	12	69	3	5	2	6	0
O'Keeffe	36	11	114	1	9.1	4	25	1
Chappell	6	1	25	0				

Northamptonshire v Australians

Northampton, July 16, 18, 19
Match drawn

Australians *First Innings*

R. B. McCosker b Larkins		34
I. C. Davis c Mushtaq b Griffiths		28
*G. S. Chappell not out		161
K. J. Hughes c Sharp b Bedi		5
D. W. Hookes lbw b Mushtaq		53
G. J. Cosier c Larkins b Willey		20
†R. D. Robinson lbw b Mushtaq		2
R. J. Bright not out		22
M. F. Malone		
G. Dymock	Did not bat	
L. S. Pascoe		
Extras (lb 3)		3
	Total (6 wkts dec)..328	

Second Innings

st Sharp b Bedi		39
lbw b Griffiths		68
lbw b Griffiths		3
b Willey		47
(3) not out		54
not out		24
(b1, lb2)		3
	Total (4 wkts dec)..238	

Fall of Wickets
1 – 50 2 – 62 3 – 97 4 – 204 5 – 251 6 – 260
1 – 73 2 – 115 3 – 127 4 – 193

Bowling	First Innings				Second Innings			
Hodgson	14	4	39	0	10	0	62	0
Griffiths	19	5	53	1	19	7	49	2
Larkins	13	4	51	1	2	0	7	0
Bedi	19	4	72	1	27	7	46	1
Mushtaq	16	1	67	2	4	2	7	0
Willey	9	0	24	1	17	5	54	1
Steele	2	0	19	0	3	0	10	0

Northamptonshire *First Innings*

R. T. Virgin c Chappell b Pascoe		30
G. Cook lbw b Malone		24
D. S. Steele b Pascoe		0
*Mushtaq Mohammad c Robinson b Pascoe		37
W. Larkins c Chappell b Pascoe		5
P. Willey lbw b Pascoe		20
R. G. Williams c Robinson b Pascoe		1
†G. Sharp b Bright		34
A. Hodgson c Hughes b Bright		35
B. S. Bedi c McCosker b Hookes		27
B. J. Griffiths not out		2
Extras (b2, lb3, nb16)		21
	Total............236	

Second Innings

not out		66
not out		27
(2) c Cosier b Bright		11
(b6, lb1, nb4)		11
	Total (1 wkt)..115	

Fall of Wickets
1 – 51 2 – 51 3 – 67 4 – 86 5 – 130 6 – 131 7 – 136 8 – 179 9 – 225
1 – 25

Bowling	First Innings				Second Innings			
Pascoe	25	6	68	6	10	5	13	0
Malone	21	8	47	1	11	3	24	0
Bright	18.3	5	60	2	17	7	34	1
Dymock	13	3	23	0	9	2	16	0
Chappell					6	3	17	0

Warwickshire v Australians

Edgbaston, July 20 ,21, 22. Australians won by 130 runs.

Australians *First Innings*		Second Innings	
R. B. McCosker b Bourne	77	lbw b Bourne	21
C. S. Serjeant lbw b Bourne	0	c Humpage b Willis	3
G. J. Cosier b Bourne	16	c Whitehouse b Willis	56
K. J. Hughes lbw b Savage	25	c Hemmings b Savage	7
R. D. Robinson not out	70	not out	137
K. D. Walters c Humpage b Savage	47	c Amiss b Savage	53
*†R. W. Marsh c Hemmings b Savage	3	b Perryman	10
K. J. O'Keeffe not out	14	not out	16
M. H. N. Walker			
J. R. Thomson } Did not bat			
L. S. Pascoe			
Extras (lb5, nb3)	8	(lb12, nb5)	17
Total (6 wkts dec)..260		Total (6 wkts dec)..320	

Fall of Wickets
1 – 0 2 – 22 3 – 83 4 – 146 5 – 230 6 – 236
1 – 11 2 – 40 3 – 55 4 – 133 5 – 231 6 – 260

Bowling	First Innings				Second Innings			
Willis	14	5	35	0	11	1	51	2
Bourne	15	2	61	3	11	1	44	1
Savage	18	5	47	3	21	5	64	2
Perryman	20	5	59	0	11	1	43	1
Hemmings	19	5	50	0	21	5	83	0
Whitehouse					1.3	0	18	0

Warwickshire *First Innings*		Second Innings	
*D. L. Amiss c Robinson b Pascoe	14	c Hughes b Thomson	11
R. W. Abberley run out	72	c Thomson b Pascoe	35
J. Whitehouse c Hughes b Walker	114	lbw b Walker	5
A. I. Kallicharran c Robinson b O'Keeffe	1	c Marsh b Walker	80
K. D. Smith not out	31	lbw b Walker	0
†G. W. Humpage c Cosier b O'Keeffe	5	b Thomson	4
E. E. Hemmings		c McCosker b Thomson	0
W. A. Bourne		b O'Keeffe	16
R. G. D. Willis } Did not bat		b Walker	15
S. P. Perryman		b Thomson	13
R. Le Q. Savage		not out	2
Extras (b5, lb8, w4, nb6)	23	(b3, w4, nb2)	9
Total (5 wkts dec)..260		Total..190	

Fall of Wickets
1 – 20 2 – 154 3 – 159 4 – 233 5 – 260
1 – 27 2 – 48 3 – 54 4 – 57 5 – 66 6 – 72 7 – 111 8 – 162 9 – 184

Bowling	First Innings				Second Innings			
Thomson	14	3	46	0	11.4	3	61	4
Pascoe	15	2	54	1	9	0	56	1
Walker	14	2	72	1	14	4	36	4
O'Keeffe	20.1	7	50	2	8	3	28	1
Cosier	2	0	15	0				

Leicestershire v Australians

Leicester, July 23, 24, 25. Match drawn.

Australians *First Innings*

R. B. McCosker b Taylor		11
I. C. Davis c Davison b Shuttleworth		22
*G. S. Chappell c Steele b Booth		0
C. S. Serjeant c Steele b Booth		11
D. W. Hookes c Shuttleworth b Taylor		59
G. J. Cosier c & b Birkenshaw		32
†R. W. Marsh c Davison b Birkenshaw		4
R. J. Bright not out		43
M. H. N. Walker b Birkenshaw		5
J. R. Thomson c Tolchard b Booth		25
G. Dymock c Birkenshaw b Booth		0
Extras (b5, lb4, w2, nb5)		17
Total		229

Second Innings

not out		59
c Davison b Illingworth		65
not out		15
(b4, lb3, nb2)		9
Total (1 wkt)		148

Fall of Wickets

1 – 17 2 – 18 3 – 43 4 – 54 5 – 149 6 – 153 7 – 153 8 – 164 9 – 229
1 – 120

Bowling	First Innings				Second Innings			
Booth	13.4	4	42	4	6	0	15	0
Taylor	19	8	39	2	11	2	28	0
Shuttleworth	19	1	76	1	8	0	39	0
Birkenshaw	19	6	38	3	14	3	35	0
Balderstone	6	0	17	0	4	2	4	0
Illingworth					6	0	18	1

Leicestershire *First Innings*

N. E. Briers c Marsh b Dymock	18
J. F. Steele c Marsh b Walker	22
J. C. Balderstone c McCosker b Walker	17
B. F. Davison b Dymock	44
D. I. Gower c Marsh b Walker	4
†J. G. Tolchard c McCosker b Walker	7
*R. Illingworth c Bright b Walker	21
J. Birkenshaw c Davis b Bright	18
P. Booth c Chappell b Walker	19
K. Shuttleworth c McCosker b Walker	0
L. Taylor not out	1
Extras (lb3, nb3, w1);	7
Total	178

Bowling

Thomson	14	3	31	0
Walker	15.3	5	45	7
Dymock	24	7	67	2
Bright	13	5	28	1

Fall of Wickets

1 – 39 2 – 48 3 – 96 4 – 108 5 – 118 6 – 118 7 – 151 8 – 177 9 – 177

ENGLAND v AUSTRALIA (Third Test)

England v Australia (Third Test Match)
Trent Bridge, July 28, 29, 30, August 1, 2. England won by 7 wickets.
Australia   *First Innings*

		Second Innings	
R. B. McCosker c Brearley b Hendrick	51	c Brearley b Willis	107
I. C. Davis c Botham b Underwood	33	c Greig b Willis	9
*G. S. Chappell b Botham	19	b Hendrick	27
D. W. Hookes c Hendrick b Willis	17	lbw b Hendrick	42
K. D. Walters c Hendrick b Botham	11	c Randall b Greig	28
R. D. Robinson c Brearley b Greig	11	lbw b Underwood	34
†R. W. Marsh lbw b Botham	0	c Greig b Willis	0
K. J. O'Keeffe not out	48	not out	21
M. H. N. Walker c Hendrick b Botham	0	b Willis	17
J. R. Thomson c Knott b Botham	21	b Willis	0
L. S. Pascoe c Greig b Hendrick	20	c Hendrick b Underwood	0
Extras (b4, lb2, nb6)	12	(b1, lb5, w1, nb17)	24
Total	243	Total	309

Fall of Wickets
1 – 79 2 – 101 3 – 131 4 – 133 5 – 153 6 – 153 7 – 153 8 – 155 9 – 196
1 – 18 2 – 60 3 – 154 4 – 204 5 – 240 6 – 240 7 – 270 8 – 307 9 – 308

Bowling	First Innings				Second Innings			
Willis	15	0	58	1	26	6	88	5
Hendrick	21.2	6	46	2	32	14	56	2
Botham	20	5	74	5	25	5	60	0
Greig	15	4	35	1	9	2	24	1
Underwood	11	5	18	1	27	15	49	2
Miller					5	2	5	0
Woolmer					3	0	3	0

England   *First Innings*

		Second Innings	
*J. M. Brearley c Hookes b Pascoe	15	b Walker	81
G. Boycott c McCosker b Thomson	107	not out	80
R. A. Woolmer lbw b Pascoe	0		
D. W. Randall run out	13	not out	19
A. W. Greig b Thomson	11	b Walker	0
G. Miller c Robinson b Pascoe	13		
†A. P. E. Knott c Davis b Thomson	135	c O'Keeffe b Walker	2
I. T. Botham b Walker	25		
D. L. Underwood b Pascoe	7		
M. Hendrick b Walker	1		
R. G. D. Willis not out	2		
Extras (b9, lb7, w3, nb16)	35	(b2, lb2, w1, nb2)	7
Total	364	Total (3 wkts)	189

Fall of Wickets
1 – 34 2 – 34 3 – 52 4 – 64 5 – 82 6 – 297 7 – 326 8 – 357 9 – 359
1 – 154 2 – 156 3 – 158

Bowling	First Innings				Second Innings			
Thomson	31	6	103	3	16	6	34	0
Pascoe	32	10	80	4	22	6	43	0
Walker	39.2	12	79	2	24	8	40	3
Chappell	8	0	19	0				
O'Keeffe	11	4	43	0	19.2	2	65	0
Walters	3	0	5	0				

Umpires: H. D. Bird and D. Constant.

Lancashire v Australians

Old Trafford, August 6, 7, 8. Australians won by 7 wickets.

Lancashire *First Innings*		*Second Innings*	
B. Wood c Robinson b Malone	22	c Malone b Bright	80
*D. Lloyd lbw b Malone	24	absent hurt	—
H. Pilling lbw b Dymock	31	b Bright	27
F. C. Hayes c Robinson b Dymock	0	c Thomson b Chappell	4
J. Abrahams c Hughes b Dymock	0	(2) c Robinson b Dymock	30
D. P. Hughes b Thomson	5	(5) c Malone b Bright	2
J. Simmons b Thomson	0	(6) c Robinson b Chappell	35
†J. Lyon c Robinson b Malone	34	(7) c Marsh b Bright	0
C. Croft c Dymock b Bright	30	(8) c Dymock b Chappell	30
R. Arrowsmith not out	30	(9) c Cosier b Bright	1
P. G. Lee c Marsh b Thomson	25	(10) not out	0
Extras (b8, lb5, nb1)	14	(b14, lb8)	22
Total	215	Total	202

Fall of Wickets
1 – 46 2 – 47 3 – 48 4 – 62 5 – 77 6 – 77 7 – 106 8 – 147 9 – 157
1 – 67 2 – 126 3 – 154 4 – 154 5 – 159 6 – 175 7 – 182 8 – 202 9 – 202

Bowling	*First Innings*				*Second Innings*			
Thomson	15.4	6	37	3	13	5	28	0
Malone	24	7	60	3	10	6	21	0
Dymock	22	7	58	3	12	5	19	1
Bright	22	6	43	1	29.1	9	67	5
Chappell	2	0	3	0	15	5	45	3

Australians *First Innings*		*Second Innings*	
R. B. McCosker hit wicket b Croft	11	lbw b Croft	9
G. J. Cosier c Simmons b Lee	23	c Simmons b Arrowsmith	66
K. T. Hughes c Pilling b Arrowsmith	89	(4) c Pilling b Simmons	8
C. S. Serjeant c Lyon b Wood	32	(5) not out	7
†R. D. Robinson b Arrowsmith	50		
R. W. Marsh not out	23		
*G. S. Chappell		(3) not out	70
R. J. Bright			
M. F. Malone	Did not bat		
J. R. Thomson			
G. Dymock			
Extras (b6, lb6, w1, nb8)	21	(b1, lb1, nb5)	7
Total (5 wkts dec)	251	Total (3 wkts)	167

Fall of Wickets
1 – 38 2 – 43 3 – 122 4 – 126 5 – 251
1 – 16 2 – 122 3 – 145

Bowling	*First Innings*				*Second Innings*			
Croft	7	0	32	1	5	0	22	1
Lee	12	3	45	1	3	1	13	0
Wood	11	4	28	1				
Hughes	9	0	26	0	5	0	32	0
Simmons	18	5	52	0	15.2	2	55	1
Arrowsmith	14.2	2	47	2	13	3	38	1

ENGLAND v AUSTRALIA (Fourth Test)

England v Australia (Fourth Test Match)
Headingley, 11, 12, 13, 15 August. England won by an innings and 85 runs.

England *First Innings*

*J. M. Brearley c Marsh b Thomson	0		
G. Boycott c Chappell b Pascoe	191		
R. A. Woolmer c Chappell b Thomson	37		
D. W. Randall lbw b Pascoe	20		
A. W. Greig b Thomson	43		
G. R. J. Roope c Walters b Thomson	34		
†A. P. E. Knott lbw b Bright	57		
I. T. Botham b Bright	0		
D. L. Underwood c Bright b Pascoe	6		
M. Hendrick c Robinson b Pascoe	4		
R. G. D. Willis not out	5		
Extras (b5, lb9, w3, nb22)	39		
Total	436		

Bowling

Thomson	34	7	113	4
Walker	48	21	97	0
Pascoe	34.4	10	91	4
Walters	3	1	5	0
Bright	26	9	66	2
Chappell	10	2	25	0

Fall of Wickets
1 – 0 2 – 82 3 – 105 4 – 201 5 – 275 6 – 398 7 – 398 8 – 412 9 – 422

Australia *First Innings*

		Second Innings	
R. B. McCosker run out	27	c Knott b Greig	12
I. C. Davis lbw b Hendrick	0	c Knott b Greig	19
*G. S. Chappell c Brearley b Hendrick	20	c Greig b Willis	36
D. W. Hookes lbw b Botham	24	lbw b Hendrick	21
K. D. Walters c Hendrick b Botham	4	lbw b Woolmer	15
R. D. Robinson c Greig b Hendrick	20	b Hendrick	20
†R. W. Marsh c Knott b Botham	2	c Randall b Hendrick	63
R. J. Bright not out	9	c Greig b Hendrick	5
M. H. N. Walker c Knott b Botham	7	b Willis	30
J. R. Thomson b Botham	0	b Willis	0
L. S. Pascoe b Hendrick	0	not out	0
Extras (lb3, w1, nb2)	6	(b1, lb4, w4, nb18)	27
Total	103	Total	248

Fall of Wickets
1 – 8 2 – 26 3 – 52 4 – 57 5 – 66 6 – 77 7 – 89 8 – 100 9 – 100
1 – 31 2 – 35 3 – 63 4 – 97 5 – 130 6 – 167 7 – 179 8 – 244 9 – 245

Bowling	*First Innings*				*Second Innings*			
Willis	5	0	35	0	14	7	32	3
Hendrick	15.3	2	41	4	22.5	6	54	4
Botham	11	3	21	5	17	3	47	0
Greig					20	7	64	2
Woolmer					8	4	8	1
Underwood					8	3	16	0

Umpires: W. L. Budd and W. E. Alley

Middlesex v Australians

Lord's, August 20, 21, 22. Match drawn.

Middlesex   *First Innings*

			Second Innings	
*J. M. Brearley b Bright	46		not out	10
M. J. Smith c Marsh b Dymock	11		not out	6
C. T. Radley lbw b Malone	19			
M. W. Gatting run out	0			
G. D. Barlow c Marsh b Malone	3			
N. G. Featherstone b Thomson	41			
P. H. Edmonds c Hookes b Thomson	30			
†I. J. Gould c Cosier b Bright	3			
J. E. Emburey b Malone	1			
M. W. W. Selvey not out	41			
W. W. Daniel b Thomson	1			
Extras (b6, lb5)	11		(lb1, w1)	2
Total	207		Total (no wkt)	18

Fall of Wickets
1 – 17 2 – 61 3 – 61 4 – 72 5 – 113 6 – 128 7 – 135 8 – 138 9 – 205

Bowling	*First Innings*				*Second Innings*			
Dymock	20	6	47	1	2	1	2	0
Malone	21	5	63	3	4	2	5	0
Thomson	13.1	3	41	3	5	3	9	0
Bright	22	9	45	2				

Australians   *First Innings*

R. B. McCosker c Selvey b Daniel	0
G. J. Cosier b Emburey	12
K. J. Hughes lbw b Daniel	1
D. W. Hookes b Emburey	34
C. S. Serjeant c Gould b Edmonds	21
K. D. Walters b Daniel	29
*†R. W. Marsh c Edmonds b Daniel	22
R. J. Bright c Gould b Emburey	6
M. F. Malone b Edmonds	9
J. R. Thomson c & b Edmonds	0
G. Dymock not out	2
Extras (b6, lb5, nb2)	13
Total	149

Bowling				
Daniel	10	1	27	4
Selvey	4	1	20	0
Emburey	19.4	6	44	3
Edmonds	16	7	29	3
Featherstone	3	0	16	0

Fall of Wickets
1 – 0 2 – 9 3 – 30 4 – 54 5 – 100 6 – 129 7 – 130 8 – 145 9 – 145

ENGLAND v AUSTRALIA (Fifth Test)

England v Australia (Fifth Test)
The Oval, August 25, 26, 27, 29, 30. Match drawn.

England   *First Innings*

			Second Innings	
*J. M. Brearley c Marsh b Malone	39	c Serjeant b Thomson	4
G. Boycott c McCosker b Walker	39	not out	25
R. A. Woolmer lbw b Thomson	15	c Marsh b Malone	6
D. W. Randall, c Marsh b Malone	3	not out	20
A. E. Greig c Bright b Malone	0		
G. R. J. Roope b Thomson	38		
†A. P. E. Knott c McCosker b Malone	6		
J. K. Lever lbw b Malone	3		
D. L. Underwood b Thomson	20		
M. Hendrick b Thomson	15		
R. G. D. Willis not out	24		
Extras (lb6, w1, nb5)	12	(w2)	2
Total	214	Total (2 wkts)	57

Fall of Wickets
1 – 86 2 – 88 3 – 104 4 – 104 5 – 106 6 – 122 7 – 130 8 – 169 9 – 174
1 – 5 2 – 16

Bowling	*First Innings*				*Second Innings*			
Thomson	23.2	3	87	4	5	1	22	1
Malone	47	20	63	5	10	4	14	1
Walker	28	11	51	1	8	2	14	0
Bright	3	2	1	0	3	2	5	0

Australia   *First Innings*

		Bowling				
C. S. Serjeant lbw b Willis	0	Willis	29.3	5	102	5
R. B. McCosker lbw b Willis	32	Hendrick	37	5	93	2
*G. S. Chappell c & b Underwood	39	Lever	22	6	61	1
K. J. Hughes c Willis b Hendrick	1	Underwood	35	9	102	1
D. W. Hookes c Knott b Greig	85	Greig	8	2	17	1
K. D. Walters b Willis	4					
†R. W. Marsh lbw b Hendrick	57					
R. J. Bright lbw b Willis	16					
M. H. N. Walker not out	78					
M. F. Malone b Lever	46					
J. R. Thomson b Willis	17					
Extras (b1, lb6, nb3)	10					
Total	385					

Fall of Wickets
1 – 0 2 – 54 3 – 67 4 – 84 5 – 104 6 – 184 7 – 236 8 – 252 9 – 352
Umpires: D. J. Constant aud T. W. Spencer.

5 STATISTICAL NOTES

Somerset—Bath
G. S. Chappell's 113 was the 50th century of his career. He made 99 before lunch on the opening day.
In beating the Australians by 7 wickets, Somerset achieved their first victory against them in 23 meetings. Worcestershire and Middlesex are the only two counties never to have beaten the Australians.

Prudential Trophy
Edgbaston—The Australian total of 70 is the lowest total ever recorded in the history of the competition.
The Oval—D. L. Amiss (108) and J. M. Brearley (78) by their first-wicket partnership of 161 established a record for any wicket in the competition.
G. S. Chappell by scoring 125* beat I.V.A. Richards' individual record score of 119* at Scarborough in 1976.
G. S. Chappell and D. L. Amiss were made their teams' respective Man of the Series.

Essex—Chelmsford
R. W. Marsh in scoring 124 recorded his first century in three tours of England.

First Test—Jubilee Test—Lord's
R. G. D. Willis in taking 7 – 78 become only the third England bowler to take seven wickets or more in an innings v Australia at Lord's. The others were G. Ulyett (7 – 36 in 1884) and Hedley Verity (7 – 61 and 8 – 43 in 1934).
C. M. Old reached 100 wickets in Test matches in his 32nd Test when he dismissed R. D. Robinson in Australia's second innings.
R. W. Marsh broke A. T. W. Grout's record of 69 catches by an Australian wicket-keeper in Test matches v England.

Nottinghamshire—Trent Bridge
C. S. Serjeant recorded the highest score of his career — 159.

Second Test—Old Trafford
R. A. Woolmer's 137 was his third Test century in four successive innings v Australia and his second in successive innings. The last English batsman to score centuries in successive innings against Australia was K. F. Barrington in 1965–66, and the last to do it in England was M. Leyland in 1934, who scored three centuries in five innings.
G. S. Chappell's 112 was his 14th Test century and his 6th v England. Only D. G. Bradman (19), A. R. Morris (8) and W. M. Lawry (7) have scored more hundreds for Australia v England and only R. N. Harvey, V. T. Trumper and W. M. Woodfull have scored as many.
England's win was their first v Australia since the 6th Test at Melbourne in the 1974–75 series and their first home win since the 4th Test at Headingley in 1972. It was their first victory at home v Australia in 14 Tests—a record period of 'drought', and only their second win against Australia, home and away, in the last 14 Tests between the two countries. It was England's 8th victory over Australia in 41 Tests in England since the war.

Third Test—Trent Bridge
G. S. Chappell, when 9 in the second innings, completed 4,000 runs in Test cricket in his 49th Test.
England beat Australia at Trent Bridge for only the third time ever, the last occasion being 1930 and the only previous occasion being in 1905. Not since 1956 had England beaten Australia in consecutive Tests in a series.
A. P. E. Knott, when 25 during his innings of 135, completed 4,000 runs in Test cricket in his 87th Test. His century was the highest of his five in Tests and his second against Australia, a record for an English wicket-keeper. The only other wicket-keeper to have scored a hundred was L. E. G. Ames (120 at Lord's in 1934).
The centuries scored by G. Boycott and A. P. E. Knott were the first scored at Trent Bridge for England v Australia since D. C. S. Compton's 184 in 1948.
G. Boycott on his return to Test cricket after a three-year absence scored the 98th hundred of his career and his 5th against Australia. He batted on all five days of the Test match for his 13th Test hundred and was on the field for all but 1¾ hours.
G. Boycott and A. P. E. Knott's partnership of 215 for the 6th wicket equalled the England v Australia record made by L. Hutton and J. Hardstaff at the Oval in 1938.
R. B. McCosker reached his fourth Test century with a six off R. G. D. Willis.
R. W. Marsh in his 50th Test match was dismissed for a pair.
I. T. Botham on his Test début took 5 – 74.

Fourth Test—Headingley
G. Boycott's 191 was his 100th century in his first-class cricket career and came in his 645th first-class innings. It was the highest of his six centuries v Australia and his 14th Test match hundred. In addition it is the highest individual score ever registered for England v Australia in a Headingley Test, eclipsing the 144* of the Hon. F. S. Jackson in 1905.
R. G. D. Willis took his 100th Test wicket in 28 Tests when he bowled J. R. Thomson in Australia's second innings.
A. P. E. Knott, in dismissing I. C. Davis in Australia's second innings, made his 250th dismissal in Test cricket.
Australia, in scoring 103, made their lowest-ever total in a Headingley Test, the previous lowest score being 120 in 1961.

The Ashes were regained for the first time in England since 1953, and England had beaten Australia three times in a home rubber for the first time since 1886. The last time England had won three successive Tests v Australia was in 1954–55 under the captaincy of L. Hutton. It was also the first time since 'Laker's Match', the Old Trafford Test of 1956, that England had beaten Australia in this country by an innings.

Fifth Test—The Oval
M. F. Malone, bowling unchanged from 11.35 a.m. to 6.30 p.m. on the first day of play, had the remarkable figures on his Test debut of 43 – 20 – 53 – 5, and finished with 5 – 63.
J. R. Thomson dismissed his 100th victim in Test cricket in his 22nd Test when bowling G. R. J. Roope.
M. H. N. Walker (78*) and M. F. Malone (46) both recorded their highest scores in first-class cricket whilst adding 100 for the 9th wicket.
G. Boycott, when 4 in the second innings, became the 14th batsman to score 5,000 runs in Test cricket.
R. G. D. Willis, with 27 wickets in the series, has only been bettered in a home Test series for England v Australia by J. C. Laker, who took 46 wickets in 1956, and A. V. Bedser (39 in 1953).
Test Match receipts for the series totalled £727,000.